Migrating to Azure

Transforming Legacy Applications into Scalable Cloud-First Solutions

Josh Garverick

Migrating to Azure

Josh Garverick
AKRON, New York, USA

ISBN-13 (pbk): 978-1-4842-3584-3   ISBN-13 (electronic): 978-1-4842-3585-0
https://doi.org/10.1007/978-1-4842-3585-0

Library of Congress Control Number: 2018960822

Managing Director, Apress Media LLC: Welmoed Spahr
Acquisitions Editor: Joan Murray
Development Editor: Laura Berendson
Coordinating Editor: Jill Balzano

Cover designed by eStudioCalamar

Cover image designed by Freepik (www.freepik.com)

Distributed to the book trade worldwide by Springer Science+Business Media New York, 233 Spring Street, 6th Floor, New York, NY 10013. Phone 1-800-SPRINGER, fax (201) 348-4505, e-mail orders-ny@springer-sbm.com, or visit www.springeronline.com. Apress Media, LLC is a California LLC and the sole member (owner) is Springer Science + Business Media Finance Inc (SSBM Finance Inc). SSBM Finance Inc is a **Delaware** corporation.

For information on translations, please e-mail rights@apress.com, or visit www.apress.com/rights-permissions.

Apress titles may be purchased in bulk for academic, corporate, or promotional use. eBook versions and licenses are also available for most titles. For more information, reference our Print and eBook Bulk Sales web page at www.apress.com/bulk-sales.

Any source code or other supplementary material referenced by the author in this book is available to readers on GitHub via the book's product page, located at www.apress.com/9781484235843. For more detailed information, please visit www.apress.com/source-code.

Printed on acid-free paper

This work is dedicated to my wife Melissa, and my daughter Audrey, for allowing me to chase my lofty goal of getting published.

Table of Contents

About the Author

Josh Garverick is a Microsoft MVP and a seasoned IT professional with more than 15 years of enterprise experience working in several large industries (finance, healthcare, transportation, and logistics). He specializes in Application Lifecycle Management and is currently involved with DevOps and architecture projects, focusing specifically on software architecture and enterprise needs. Josh is a Visual Studio ALM Ranger, providing guidance, practical experience, and solutions to the developer community. When not geeking out over technology and architecture frameworks, he enjoys spending time with his wife and daughter.

About the Technical Reviewer

Willy-Peter Schaub is an Agile, DevOps, Bits & Bytes Software Engineer. Since the mid-'80s, he's been striving for simplicity and maintainability in software engineering. As a software engineer, he analyses, designs, develops, tests, and supports software solutions. He is passionate about continuous innovation and sharing learnings from the digital transformation by Microsoft and the ALM | DevOps Rangers, to a DevOps culture to adapt people, process, and products to continuously deliver value to our end users. Follow him on Twitter and LinkedIn.

Acknowledgments

First and foremost, I'd like to thank Willy-Peter Schaub for his tireless encouragement of me since my first days in the ALM Rangers program, for giving me the chance of a lifetime to jump feet first into NDA territory, and for agreeing to tech review this madness. I'd like to recognize many more people for contributing to my personal and professional growth, but the truth is I couldn't possibly list everyone here. Please know that even if you are not listed, you're in my heart somewhere.

Donovan Brown: for inspiring me to devops my face off at every opportunity. Your enthusiasm and depth of knowledge are always invigorating.

Steven Borg: for being my mentor when I first started this crazy journey with the ALM Rangers and eventually the Microsoft MVP program. Thanks for being my sounding board for countless ideas—and for helping me video-bomb Seth Juarez during a webcast while we looked for a quiet room for me to call my family from at my first Summit.

Brian Harry: for incredible leadership and attention to detail. You gave me confidence in talking to senior leadership levels due to your approachability. If I could be even a quarter of the leader you are, I will have accomplished something very magical.

Wouter de Kort: for pushing me to be better, even if you didn't know you were pushing me. You taught me that it's important to recognize when to take a break and enjoy life. You're also the first person I've ever internationally shipped anything to. I still have that empty canister of Stroopwafels.

Damian Brady: the only Aussie I know who moved to Toronto and saw me less often than when he lived in Australia. You are a great friend, my unofficial Tim Tam dealer, and an amazing talent.

Greg Duncan: the best podcast producer ever. Being able to participate in RadioTFS has been and will continue to be something I'm proud of, so thank you for giving me the opportunity.

Jessie Frazelle: for being the Keyser Sose of containers and writing a ton of cool containerized stuff so I didn't have to, and helping me understand more of the mechanics of Docker. Thank you for all that you have done and continue to do for the tech community.

ACKNOWLEDGMENTS

David Wood: for being incredibly supportive and helping me learn enterprise architecture frameworks and principles when I was really just a software goon. The analytic and problem-solving skills I obtained during your tenure have helped move me into the next major era of my career.

Introduction

This book is a result of two intertwined and sometimes equally frustrating streams in my life. One is that of looking through countless examples that scratch the surface of a topic but don't necessarily cover what happens when keeping it real goes wrong. The other is the reality that many of us face as full-time employees—corporate hierarchy, deadline-driven development, having to analyze and modernize parts of a platform at the expense of others, drifting priorities, taking shortcuts due to intentional or unintentional) ignorance, and buzzword bureaucracy.

The context of this book is based somewhat on my experiences in planning for, designing, and leading a cloud transformation for a large platform. In my case, that is a benefits administration system that tends to see its largest usage in the last two and a half months of every calendar year. The US phenomenon that is open enrollment drives our revenue, keeps our consumers happy, and at times, exacerbates problems in our platform's architecture. Oftentimes, you don't know what you don't know, and knowing where to find information can impact your decisions. Knowing what questions to ask is equally as powerful. As a developer, and having worked with many developers, I can say with a certain degree of confidence that we love to solve technical problems, sometimes in spite of the underlying business need for the functionality we're working on. I won't say that it's willful ignorance; in fact, it's generally the opposite—the eagerness to fix something that hasn't yet been fixed. That eagerness carries an amazing energy and can propel you far into your career. Knowing what questions to ask and how to explain technical work to nontechnical people will propel you into early retirement.

The first chapter is a bit of an initiation, perhaps even a hazing. Your position is that of a new solution architect at a larger corporation that is assigned to a migration project dealing with a smaller acquired company's platform. The acquired company enjoys doing things their way, using any mixture of processes and tools that get things done. Not everyone is keen on making changes, but there is at least enough interest in looking at options to give you hope that the migiration will not be a war of wills. On the surface the platform seems innocent enough, and as you traverse through the different architectural layers, you notice more and more things that have the potential for risk.

As you go through the discovery phase and gather the current state, you are also met with demands for the target state, including dependencies on other projects that you weren't involved in but have the ability to derail your efforts.

The story of "you" in this narrative carries through something I took for granted in many positions I've worked in: the current state of affairs. Yes, typically when working on an application, you will understand the world that each component lives in, what talks to it, who it talks to, and so on. But how does that component work in the grand scheme of things? What else is in the application? What are the reasons behind all of the workfows the application carries out? Is the application a part of a larger suite of applications (platform), meant to carry out many independent but related workstreams? What happens if the location the platform is hosted in gets flooded and all of the servers are destroyed? What is the expectation from the business if downtime is experienced? It can get exhausting, for sure. Getting answers to these questions, though, will save you time and probably a lot of grief as you move toward modernizing your application or platform. Understanding the reasons behind technical processes—the business process—will get you closer to developing stronger relationships with your nontechnical colleagues. It will help foster comfort and encourage trust through maturing communication.

Not everyone is cut from that cloth, and that's okay. My guess is that if you're reading this, you have the desire to solve problems from different angles and improve your ability to understand how business needs become technological solutions. My hope is that the lessons I've learned, along with the information and sources I've compiled, will serve you well and keep you from experiencing some of the pain I experienced.

- You will make mistakes—own them and learn from them.

- You will not ever know all there is to know about every cloud offering.

- More often than not, by the time you design a solution, new products will have been released for general availability and questions will come up about why you didn't choose that product instead, despite the fact that it was just released.

- Resist the urge to move fast for the sake of moving fast. Transformative efforts take months and sometimes years—not a weekend.

You will notice that some of the examples are not quite as detailed as others. The intention behind that is to allow you to explore the solution space, dig into the details as you see fit, and put together designs that make sense given the information you have. There are plenty of designs and samples in the downloadable content to review along the way. Keep in mind that while the samples illustrate one way to solve the problems, they are not the only way. You may find a better way to manage an integration point or a data transformation. Please contribute that back to the public repository—perhaps the code you contribute will help someone else who is new to this type of work. Most of all, make the most of your journey into legacy platform migration and cloud transformation!

PART I

Assessing the Legacy

CHAPTER 1

The Baseline

Congratulations! You are the newly appointed solution architect for the Andromeda Games integration. Andromeda Games is a regional storefront-based business dealing in tabletop games, trading card games, and sports memorabilia. It has also recently been acquired by a national retailer, who happens to be your current employer, GameCorp. Over the years, Andromeda Games has established a strong online presence with grassroots support from regular customers and avid gamers. Andromeda Games's flagship customer application is named Cardstock, a web app that allows fans of different trading card games to keep track of their own cards. The application is a subsection of the company's public website, which displays information about upcoming events, new merchandise, and card tournaments hosted at the store. Additionally, members can:

- Engage in social activities (forums, friend requests)

- Browse friends' card collections

- Make trade requests with friends

- Send feedback to the company (feature requests, bugs, inventory requests)

- Order select cards from the brick-and-mortar store (in-store pickup only), with payment processing handled exclusively through PayPal

The strong customer adoption of Cardstock, along with the store's wide selection of games and involvement in the gaming community, are what drove the efforts to acquire the company and elevate its reach much farther than the regional area it hails from. From a high-level technical perspective, Cardstock consists of a web front end used by external customers to engage in the activities mentioned previously; application servers responsible for brokering communications with the database from the web layer; and a modestly sized SQL Server used to persist members' information, requests, and card

© Josh Garverick 2018
J. Garverick, *Migrating to Azure*, https://doi.org/10.1007/978-1-4842-3585-0_1

inventories. The application itself is written in C#, using a fair amount of boilerplate code with a variety of creative bugfixes sprinkled liberally throughout the codebase.

Andromeda Games has also established a fair amount of technical drift, with on-premises infrastructure hosting their customer-facing software, internal inventory systems, point of sale machines, timekeeping system, and scheduling system used to schedule in-person appearances by professional sports stars for autograph sessions. While GameCorp does have disparate systems that do this work already, members of the technical leadership team want to take a different approach with this integration. Instead of a forced integration with existing legacy systems, the direction is to help lift and improve the back-office systems in an effort to create a modernized and scalable inventory platform with Cardstock sitting front and center for a much larger user base to leverage.

The technology staff at Andromeda has been making modifications to Cardstock since the acquisition, though the output of requested features and quality of the code has not kept up with initial GameCorp expectations. One of the key objectives with the integration project is to position the platform, and its creators, for greater success.

Conducting the Initial Discovery

The first step to determining where the target state of the platform should be will become apparent after an analysis of the existing state of the platform. While it is possible to get a relatively good overview of the core and ancillary pieces that comprise the platform, taking the time to talk with business stakeholders, engineers, product owners, and others will allow for deeper dives into the why and how of the application. Furthermore, cataloging those who produce and consume parts of the larger platform will become very important as we move through different architectural discovery periods. Putting the entirety of this information together in a consolidated place, and highlighting those key pieces of information, is known as baselining (capturing the current state of the platform).

Our first inclination as technical-minded people tends to drive us toward understanding just the technical side of how things operate—inputs/outputs, logical boundaries, database schemas, and so on. That is an important aspect to unearth and grasp, and equally as important is understanding the business or operational need that drives the technical implementations. Some may argue (and rightly so) that the business need is quantifiably more important, as each workstream is in existence to assist in the primary goals of providing value and generating revenue. To venture forward with a semicomplete baseline, without business discovery and input, would certainly sink any effort to gain stakeholder buy-in, improve the operation of the platform, and ultimately gain efficiencies that will lead to more revenue.

A good starting point in any baselining endeavor is to consider the following architectural domains:

- *Business architecture*: Organizational structures, roles, processes, requirements, and more

- *Application architecture*: software components, subsystems, services, messages, and more

  - *Software architecture*: utilizing patterns and practices to construct reliable, maintainable software

  - *Deployment architecture*: combining infrastructure with application components to enable the building, testing, and deployment of software

- *Infrastructure (technology) architecture*: computers, networks, switches, routers, facilities, and much more

- *Data architecture*: structures of data consumed by the platform, produced by the platform, operational data stores, data warehouses

- *Security architecture*: identification of, and compliance with, any regulatory requirements issued by the organization or state/federal/international law

The examples listed for each domain are illustrative and not a comprehensive list. Depending on the organization, there may already be a preferred methodology for discovering, cataloging, and documenting the various architectural domains outlined. Selecting an existing standard for enterprise architecture is always the preferred approach.

For the purpose of this exercise, it is assumed that there is not an existing method of cataloging these architectural findings. While comparing and contrasting enterprise architecture frameworks is well beyond the scope of this book, it is important to have a general awareness of a few of the industry leaders in that department. See the sidebar entitled "Frameworks a Plenty" for more information about different frameworks and the general concepts behind each.

FRAMEWORKS A PLENTY

The very mention of enterprise architecture frameworks can strike fear and loathing in the hearts of many technologists. While traditionally viewed as bulky and "waterfall" in nature, these frameworks can be used to logically categorize different architectural concerns in a meaningful way. While there are many to choose from, a few of the industry leaders are listed as follows:

- *The Zachman Framework*: Considered by many to be the source of the enterprise architecture movement, this classification was devised by John Zachman during his tenure at IBM. The main intent behind the framework was to capture the what, how, where, who, when, and why of information systems. `https://www.zachman.com/about-the-zachman-framework`

- *The Open Group Architecture Framework (TOGAF)*: Based on the US Department of Defense's Technical Architecture Framework for Information Management (TAFIM), TOGAF is meant to provide a structure for describing IT architecture, with the interleaving of parallel architecture streams such as business and security. The primary discovery method is called the Architecture Development Model and is meant to provide an iterative approach for defining baseline and target architectures. `http://www.opengroup.org/subjectareas/enterprise/togaf`

- *Federal Enterprise Architecture Framework (FEA/FEAF)*: A by-product of the Clinger-Cohen act of 1996, the FEA is designed to correlate IT architectural investments by Federal agencies with tangible business value. This framework is also inclusive of security and adds an additional dimension with performance, which is meant to provide an outlet for strategic initiatives and architectural measures/reporting. `https://en.wikipedia.org/wiki/Federal_enterprise_architecture`

- *ArchiMate*: Also managed by The Open Group, ArchiMate is an enterprise modeling framework based on the concepts of the IEEE 1471 specification for software systems architecture. It ties in closely with TOGAF with respect to artifacts, architecture tracks, and nomenclature. `http://www.opengroup.org/subjectareas/enterprise/archimate-overview`

It's important to note that the level of detail, along with the communication tools used to convey the information being captured, can vary from company to company, or even team to team. Using a modeling framework without the overarching documentation included in a complete framework may provide a more agile approach to model development.

As the architect on this project, you decide to follow the architecture domain concepts from TOGAF but not use the full set of document templates and processes. Instead, you decide to move forward with the ArchiMate modeling framework (`http://www.opengroup.org/subjectareas/enterprise/archimate-overview`), which provides a lighter implementation of the full TOGAF framework while still allowing for meaningful details to be captured and presented. In addition, you decide to use Archi, which is a free modeling application that conforms to the ArchiMate 3.0 standard and provides an easy-to-use interface. Archi uses the concepts of view and viewpoint to help encapsulate areas of interest within the model that can be visualized in a diagram. A viewpoint–view relationship is seen as a parent–child in most cases, where a viewpoint could be Capabilities, and the corresponding view could contain information about enterprise capabilities.

Note   While using a lightweight modeling framework can be helpful, it is still important to document the artifacts and components that are found during discovery in a narrative that helps tell the story of the solution you are working with.

Upon learning about your new assignment, you kick things off by conducting a review of the business structure of Andromeda Games. You already have a general idea of the platform based on the initial data sheet that was provided to you by your project manager, and discovering the existing roles should help flesh out the relationships between functional areas within the platform and the business processes they're meant to embody.

After obtaining a company roster, you peruse through the job titles and start to notice some patterns. There is a core leadership team, consisting of the owner/CEO, followed by a director of store operations, a director of technology, and a director of business operations. Underneath each director is a middle management structure, and in the case of store operations, a team of frontline employees. You put together a first pass at a hierarchy chart, shown in Figure 1-1.

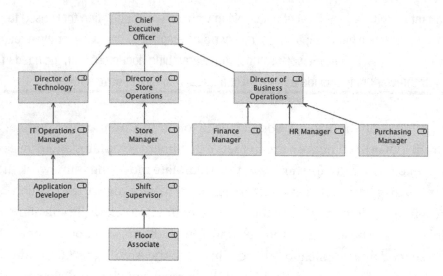

Figure 1-1. *Iteration zero of the organizational hierarchy*

The overall head count is lower in comparison with GameCorp, which leads you to wonder about other roles that may exist at Andromeda without tangible job titles. Typically, smaller companies have employees who wear many hats, meaning they could be fulfilling multiple business roles for the organization. You decide to make a note of this for later exploration.

Getting Details on the Short (and Long)-Term Goals of the Business

You touch base with your project manager and express an interest in getting more information about the business goals tied to the migration. She forwards you a scope document containing information from GameCorp's business partners that outlines the following objectives for the migration project.

- Grow revenue

  - Increase online orders

  - Increase in-store traffic and sales

- Increase market saturation

  - Expand application delivery channels

  - Expand community presence

- Improve process efficiencies

  - Reduce redundant workstreams

  - Automate manual processes

Further to these generalized goals, targets have been outlined in the document to show specific deliverables. While not explicitly laid out in a table format, they are described in slight detail within the scope itself. A target of 15% growth is being expected for online orders, and a 10% increase in store traffic and related sales has been set for the revenue goals. For market saturation, mention is made of a mobile platform application that would address feedback from many existing customers and help expand delivery channels, while community presence is alluded to via appearances by more sports stars and pop culture celebrities, and sponsorships for existing comic book conventions and other trading card game themed events. The last two items are mentioned as much higher level goals to hit, likely due to there being some opportunity to identify manual processes and any potential redundancies. You make a note to pay attention to this last category of goals, as there may be some opportunities to fill in the blanks during the conversations you conduct with folks from Andromeda.

Capturing the goals and targets in a visual state helps to bring some permanence to them, and this artifact can be helpful to others who want a quick, easy-to-digest recap of the main drivers behind this project. Figure 1-2 shows a representation of the goals as they stand, including some influencing relationships between outcomes.

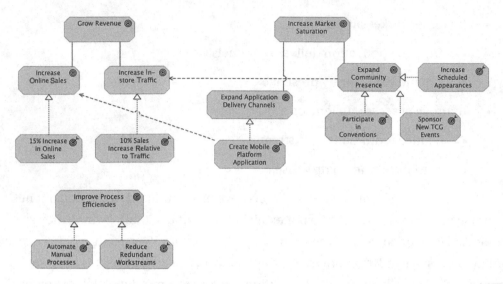

Figure 1-2. *Goal realization view*

Equally as important as the motivations for the business are the stakeholders who help drive and shape those motivations. From the scope document for the project, it's apparent who the stakeholders are:

- Director of Sales, Retail

- Director of Technology, Retail Systems

- CEO of Andromeda Games

- Director of Retail Operations

You catalog the initial stakeholders listed in the scope document for later use.

THOUGHT EXERCISE: STAKEHOLDERS

Given the initial scoping of stakeholders, what other positions could potentially have primary or secondary interest in the success of this project? Could subject matter experts from related service lines be incorporated as stakeholders?

Learning the Business Context
of Application Domains

It's very easy to get overwhelmed by—and lost in—the details of the assignment. Your primary focus is to move the Cardstock application to the cloud, but not to disrupt current operations at any of the store locations. There should be a balance between gathering the pertinent details surrounding the main platform while also making sure to account for any downstream systems, consumers, or users of the platform.

The organization itself is compartmentalized into several areas, each of which has its own workflows, interaction contracts, and needs. In exploring these areas, you could invest a great deal of time in addressing each and every facet of each area, or you could use an existing industry standard reference architecture to help speed up the process. Because you prefer to work smart, you decide to look for some industry standards around retail store management and come across the National Retail Federation (NRF), which has a wealth of reference models that can be used to map to the functional areas that exist within Andromeda Games.

Tip   One of the core concepts of TOGAF is the enterprise continuum, a catalog of building blocks from which an organization can map solutions and applications to help solve a larger problem. Using a model such as the Association for Retail Technology Standards (ARTS) business process model can be seen as leveraging an industry solution, one of several types of solution building blocks. ARTS is managed by the NRF and the Object Management Group. More information about ARTS and the other NRF standards can be found at `https://nrf.com/ resources/retail-technology-standards-0`.

As per the NRF business process standards, there are two levels of business processes that all retail operations generally cover. Using these processes as a guide, and armed with your first iteration of the organization structure, you have the ability to start drawing some relations between these processes and the roles you identified earlier. A summary of the NRF's first and second level concepts can be found in Table 1-1 below.

Table 1-1. *NRF Business Process Model: Levels 0 and 1*

Level 0	Level 1
Serve Customers	Manage Sales
	Manage Orders
	Provide Customer Care
Operate Channels & Shopping Experience	Execute Merchandising Plans
	Manage Channel Infrastructure
	Manage Channel Personnel
	Manage Channel Banking and Cash Office
Market Goods/Services	Track and Analyze
	Message and Communicate
	Develop Customer Loyalty
Manage Merchandising	Plan Goods and Services (Plan Merchandising)
	Manage Pricing
	Plan Presentation of Merchandise and Services
Manage Supply Chain	Manage Inventory
	Manage Transportation
	Manage Warehousing
Source Goods/Services	Develop Goods and Services
	Purchase Goods and Services
	Manage Vendors and Deals
Support Enterprise	Manage Finances
	Manage Real Estate
	Deploy and Manage IT
	Support and Manage Workforce
	Protect and Manage Assets
	Provide and Manage Corporate Services
	Coordinate Plans and Operations

You add the NRF levels to your model in Archi, under your Business Processes folder. You create a subfolder called "ARTS" and place the NRF items within that, to keep them separate from more specific business processes you may discover.

In an attempt to make some sense of the existing roles at Andromeda and the functions outlined by the NRF specification, you put together a mapping diagram with the intent of communicating the relationships between those roles and functions. You start by looking at the roles of finance and HR, figuring those will be more straightforward to map. You make some initial markings to show these roles realizing certain corporate services. Next, you bring in the operations and business (sales) aspects of Andromeda. Most of the NRF functions deal directly with objectives that operations, sales, and support staff would have an immediate impact on. You continue to draw relationships out, paying more attention to the relations being made than the format of the diagram. You end up with a function to role mapping view that is fairly complex (please see the source diagram for more information). You focus on the enterprise support components shown in Figure 1-3.

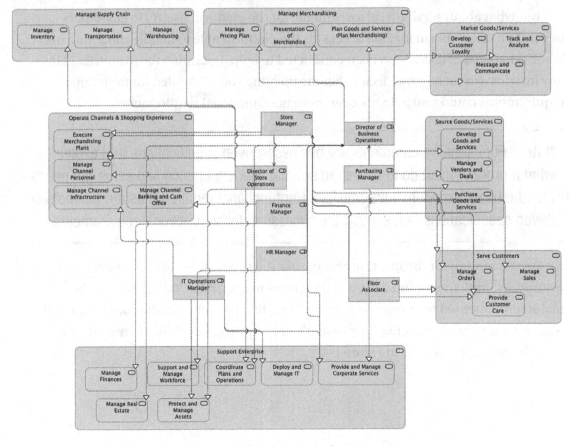

Figure 1-3. NRF function to org role mapping, first iteration

Gathering Functional and Nonfunctional Requirements

The existing platform is not one that is well documented, inclusive of requirements. The major features within the platform were essentially written down with vague specifications in a spreadsheet maintained by the Andromeda back office. As new ideas are presented by employees and customers, they are noted in the spreadsheet, and once every two weeks the developers and operations teams get together to discuss those ideas.

You schedule a meeting with the main business stakeholders as well as the development staff with the intent of talking through the existing features. You've received a copy of the spreadsheet in advance of this meeting, and have started to catalog some of the core features. This, along with notes from your discussion with the business and developers, will be the start of the baseline functional requirements.

But what about service level agreements for the platform itself? Do customers depend on the platform for 24/7 access? Is the platform able to handle moderate user load? What type of testing has been conducted to help determine these metrics? Do any metrics exist at all? You decide that the meeting you scheduled for functional requirements could also help uncover more nonfunctional requirements.

Note   Functional requirements are business-driven specifications that explain what a product must do to deliver an optimal user experience and serve the needs that the users expect to have satisfied. Nonfunctional requirements are technology-driven specifications that support the success of those functional requirements.

In preparation for the meeting, you peruse the spreadsheet again, ordering the features by implementation date, and then by requested date. Taking note of the major implemented features, you put together a first pass at what the core functional requirements should look like, given what's been implemented. You come up with a rough sketch as illustrated in Figure 1-4.

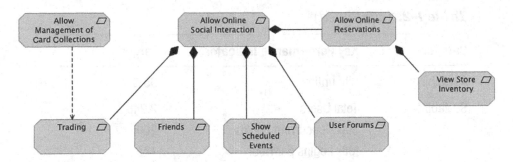

Figure 1-4. *Core functional requirements, first iteration*

In speaking with the staff, you get initial validation that these are in fact the core functional requirements that the system was intended to realize. The operations folks point out that user feedback is an essential part of the platform as well, and you note that accordingly.

You begin to ask questions related to the platform itself. From a baseline perspective, there are no formally recorded nonfunctional requirements. The developers operate on an assumption that anything less than a two-second page load time is not optimal. You ask about user metrics, such as total number of users, logins per hour, peak logins, and user feedback about site performance. You also ask about maintenance and support, unexpected downtime, integration with other systems, and Cardstock's relationship with the Andromeda Games portal. One of the lead engineers begins supplying you with some interesting information, and you notate the metrics as shown in Table 1-2.

Table 1-2. *Baseline Nonfunctional Requirements by Category*

Category	Key Performance Indicator	Target
Reliability	OS Patch Levels	Current
	Mean Time Between Failures	10 weeks
	Mean Time to Resolve	8 hours
Maintainability	Lines of Code	~150,000
	Tech Debt	Not known
Portability	Transition from mobile to PC	TBD
Performance	Individual page load times	<= 2 seconds

(*continued*)

Table 1-2. (*continued*)

Category	Key Performance Indicator	Target
Availability	Site uptime	95%
Scalability	Total Users	2,240
	Max Concurrent Logins	200
	Max Logins per Hour	175
Business Continuity	Recovery Time Objective	48 Hours
	Recovery Point Objective	48 Hours
Operability	Monitoring	Baseline APM metrics
	Site support	12 x 6 support
	Manual to Automated processes	20% / 80%

In many cases, it's clear that you don't know what you don't know—meaning, a few more rounds of pointed questions will need to be answered before you've got a crystal-clear picture on the platform and its relationships to other applications within Andromeda Games. You decide to continue talking to the developers and operations employees regarding the larger application ecosystem.

Discovering Integration Points

In examining a cursory overview of the systems involved with the operations of Andromeda Games, it's clear there are some critical systems that drive the success of the Cardstock platform. At first glance, the core system could be the Cardstock web application. Digging a bit deeper, though, you can find reasons why the retail inventory system might be a core system. Could there be others as well?

Generally speaking, a core system is considered a system or platform that is critical to supporting the business operation. For example, a common scenario used to explain a core system is that of a banking core system—the system that processes real-time and transactional inputs and posts results to accounts in order to support the business effort of managing accounts and generating revenue. With Andromeda, the primary operational focus is on in-store sales.

EXERCISE: CORE SYSTEMS

Supporting the sales efforts of Andromeda Games is not as straightforward as leveraging one platform. There can be several systems of record depending on the function being examined. Let's step through the major functional areas that support in-store sales, with the goal of identifying one or more core systems.

Retail Operations: In-store sales drive the business forward. Without a reliable point-of-sale system, accurately and quickly closing sales becomes a very manual process.

Merchandise/Inventory: Sales would not exist without merchandise to sell. Cataloging the merchandise on hand, in storage, and on order is critical. While the near-time ability to check available stock is important, so is the ability to forecast needs based on prior sales, upcoming promotions, and user-voiced demand. The current inventory system is a custom application written by developers that no longer work for Andromeda. More on this later.

Purchasing: There are several ways to track the procurement of assets, from simple spreadsheets to complex programs. Without an accurate representation of what's been purchased, inventory forecasts can be impacted. This includes store inventory as well as items necessary for the business to operate. At Andromeda, purchasing is tracked through the use of spreadsheets hosted in Microsoft Office 365 and a semimanual process of updating the business office when invoices are due.

Finance: Selling merchandise and collecting payments don't mean much without a way to account for (pun intended) incoming and outgoing revenue streams. At some point, every system feeds or depends on a core financial system. Andromeda currently uses QuickBooks to track its finances.

Given the overview of each major functional area:

- What system (or systems) would you choose as a core system?

- How could these systems potentially interact with one another?

- Is it feasible that all systems could be considered critical to operating the business?

After more productive conversations with operations and development, it starts to become evident that there isn't really one central system that supports Andromeda's operations, but rather several systems that collaborate to reach the end goal of maintaining the business. From an integration perspective, each system plays an important role. The developers provide some insight into the basic integration points that Cardstock interacts with, and you're able to construct a simple interface diagram of Cardstock as shown in Figure 1-5.

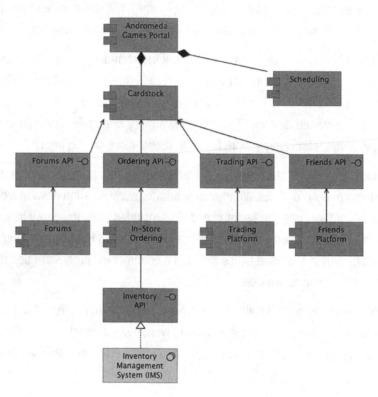

Figure 1-5. *Cardstock interface, component, and technology overview*

The inventory management system is a home-grown database application that was developed in Visual Basic, leveraging Microsoft Access as the persistence mechanism. The application's source code is a bit of a mystery and is actually not maintained anywhere that the current developers are aware of. No attempt has been made to update or scale the existing software for fear of breaking it completely. A newer Web API service was stood up in an attempt to provide a RESTful way to get inventory information, place items on hold for in-store pickup, and adjust inventory counts when in-store purchases occur, among other functionality. There were plans to migrate from Access to a more robust data store, but those plans were not prioritized appropriately.

Cardstock relies heavily on the integration between its main interface and the inventory system's APIs. Without this integration point, there would be no way to generate revenue for the retail operation, making it a critical integration to maintain. Another integration that also helps to drive revenue is Andromeda's scheduling platform, which helps to track and coordinate the visits of famous sports and pop culture icons. This information is consumed by the Andromeda portal and used to advertise upcoming events. Special promotion codes are generated from the website for Cardstock members, and prizes are awarded to individuals who print out and bring that promotional code with them when looking to purchase tickets for an event, or simply to stand in line for a chance at an autograph. These codes are tracked at the store level to determine the draw of Cardstock members vs. the general public. The other platform components (friends, forums, and trading) also provide interfaces, but are integrated with the overall application.

You start notating the systems you're aware of. You add system software nodes to your model for the following:

- Inventory Management System

- Microsoft Access, Excel, PowerPoint, and Word

- QuickBooks Pro

While more will surely follow, making initial notes of these technology components will help with later exercises.

After peeling back the first layer of the onion, you feel ready to start diving in a little deeper to understand what the application components are using under the covers. You continue your conversations with the developers, along with IT operations, to get a better sense of what is written vs. referenced.

Creating and Examining Dependency Graphs

A dependency graph is simply a visual representation of an object's dependencies. An object can be any number of things—a software library, a physical server, a surveillance camera system, and so on. Typically speaking, dependency graphs are used to notate dependencies between software components. Some products (Microsoft Visual Studio Enterprise being one) can generate dependency graphs for you. While handy, these generated diagrams can get a bit unwieldy, especially if the complete graph is laid out showing every relationship. For a first pass, you decide to catalog what you know based on the references found in the source code.

With the help of the developers, you are able to take a look at the Cardstock solution and determine that NuGet is being used to pull in dependencies. This does not account for everything, however. One of the lead developers mentions that a couple of UI components were actually purchased and installed on the developer workstations. They get checked into source control currently and are version static. Another brings up that the friends component relies on the ASP.NET Membership schema, and also uses the mechanics of the Membership functionality to perform authentication and authorization activities. He also mentions the forum module is an open-source library called MVC Forum, last updated in June of 2016.

The trading platform component is the newest of the components and the area of the system that has seen the most active development over the past year. Two of the developers set out to prove they could implement the MEAN stack into the existing ecosystem. The data engine for this component is MongoDB, and the code for the UI is written using NodeJS, Angular, and Express.

Deciding to be willfully ignorant of the npm dependency hierarchy, you put more information into your model and create a dependency graph as seen in Figure 1-6.

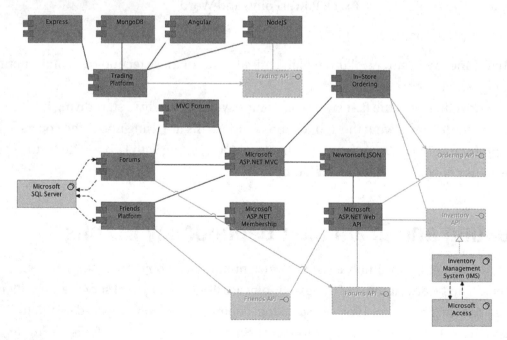

Figure 1-6. *A bare-bones dependency graph*

While not exhaustive, it does give you a start on what needs to be included when building and deploying Cardstock to an environment.

Finding Existing Build and Release Pipelines

During the course of your conversations, you ask about how the software is built and deployed. It doesn't seem as though there's much of a formalized process around that, but you do manage to get some intel that there is a Jenkins server out there. At a minimum, you feel better that there is likely a good chance that continuous integration (CI) builds are executing. Upon browsing through the Jenkins jobs with the help of one of the developers, you note that they do in fact leverage CI for their development branch. The source control management being used is Git, and there is a private Git server where developers push their changes.

Note   A pipeline is a delivery mechanism for software components, typically flowing from one end of a runway (collection of pre-prod and prod environments) to the other. The ultimate goal is to move software through stages in the pipeline, performing tests, obtaining sign-off, and deploying to production.

From a deployment perspective, files are moved over via FTP. Each time there is a deployment, everything is deployed, regardless of whether each item may have changed. There are scripts to run for any database changes, but those are all done manually during the deployment. You decide to ask if they have tried automating any portions of this pipeline, to which a couple of developers replied with "we wanted to, but there was no time." You make a note to revisit this when looking into the deployment architecture for the migrated application.

You are able to identify some servers on which the code is stored, built, and run. The developers give you a rough sketch of each point in the pipeline and you add these items to your model. The baseline view that you construct is shown in Figure 1-7.

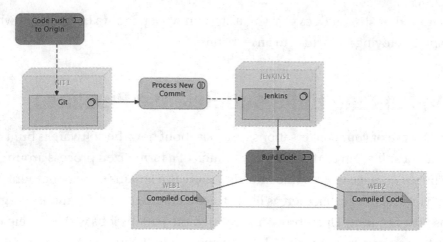

Figure 1-7. *Simple workflow, including servers, showing build and release process*

This does not include any scripts that would be deployed to the database, but you do add an object to your model to account for the DB server. This covers the main application and the MEAN stack application that was developed to manage collections. The main Andromeda Games portal is also deployed to these web endpoints. You make a mental note that there may be too much installed on these two web boxes, and it may make sense to separate this traffic a bit when looking to migrate the web components.

Proactively Seeking Out Pain Points

One interesting feature of the platform is that the forums are used for user discussions, including discussions with certain members of the development staff with respect to features and functionality. Sometimes the discussions are very productive and yield some great ideas for new features. Other times the troll game is strong, and developers get field reports of certain pages being "balls slow" or that a certain user interface is "fugly." While not professional, this feedback is still considered valid and it is ingested by the team with the intent of actually fixing the issues being brought up.

You ask for a list of the top feature requests in order of request amount. With that list, you also request a list of the top user complaints about the platform—nicely worded or not. Some of the items you see on these lists do not surprise you. For example, themes of better performance, mobile support, and payment processing capabilities all seem to jump off the page. The features list is comprised of the following:

1. Ability to pay for items prior to in-store pickup

2. Mobile app/experience

3. Accessibility to preorder/promo items

4. Integrated authentication (Facebook, Twitter, Google)

5. Ability to order and pay for event tickets

For user feedback not related to new features, the list looks like:

1. Web styling needs a facelift

2. Site is slow

3. Image quality of stock items needs improving

4. I can't reset my password

5. Site loses my collection data

You make some notes around the opportunity to tune performance in addition to the gains that have been planned for in the project scope, closely aligning to the feature requests that were supplied to you. Armed with this information, you are ready to go into the next layer of the onion.

Summary

Throughout this chapter, you've been introduced to the team at Andromeda Games, their applications, and some rather interesting information related to their current state of affairs. In addition, you've gained some knowledge about creating an architecture model, using a modeling framework to help categorize different types of architectural assets, and creating views that serve as powerful communication vehicles to business stakeholders and engineers alike.

1. Would you have opted to use the modeling framework chosen in the text? Would you have chosen any framework at all? How would you go about cataloging the information collected, and how would you communicate that outward to the technical stakeholders?

2. In the conversations with the operations and development staff, are there any additional questions you would have asked to flesh out certain details?

3. With respect to the back-office operations, would there be any conversations you would seek out to understand the primary and secondary business processes that are not directly tied to the operation of Cardstock?

4. In the Creating and Examining Dependency Graphs section, there is a very basic graph showing the high-level relationships between application components. What would a more realistic dependency graph look like?

## CHAPTER 2

Domain Architectures

In Chapter 1, you examined the initial makeup of the Andromeda Games platform offerings. Next, you will dig deeper into each of the respective architecture planes that make up the existing solution. But where to begin? You could start with the application architecture, in order to understand the components, frameworks, and patterns used. You could also start with infrastructure, identifying the physical and virtual equipment that makes up Andromeda's core operating platforms. Or, you might want to start with data, as no system will function without the ability to consume and produce data of some sort.

The starting point can be a tough place to take off from, and this task is no exception. Sometimes you will find that you will gather information about more than one area of architecture when delving into a specific domain. For example, looking into application architecture can typically unearth a small to moderate amount of infrastructure knowledge. In the interest of moving forward, you decide that tackling the application architecture is your first stop.

Identifying Primary, Secondary, and Tertiary Components

Application components, much the same as the systems that they belong to, can come in different formats and have various levels of importance. Identifying and categorizing these components leads into some useful exercises that can help you toward identifying service level agreements (SLAs) and single points of failure (SPOFs).

- A primary component is one that is critical to core functionality. A malfunction or removal of this component would critically impact SLAs and/or functionality.

© Josh Garverick 2018
J. Garverick, *Migrating to Azure*, https://doi.org/10.1007/978-1-4842-3585-0_2

- A secondary component is a supporting component that enables the primary component to perform optimally. A malfunction or replacement of this component could adversely impact SLAs/functionality.

- A tertiary component performs noncritical functionality and is generally isolated. A malfunction or replacement of this component should not involve any impact to SLAs, but may impact functionality.

Primary components have the highest risk to the health of the platform if they are not cared for appropriately. In some cases, backbone components like ASP.NET MVC are less likely to cause an issue, as they are tested out before being released into the wild for general consumption. Other components (more often internally developed) could provide core functionality but still pose a high risk through code instability, improper testing, or a lack of scalability. Secondary and tertiary components can still bring risk to platform health, though the level of risk can be easier to deal with depending on the depth of integration with the component.

Using the dependency graph you put together previously, you move through the components you identified and rate them according to the criticality to system health. You also update the metadata of each component in your model to reflect these values, as they can be used to drive different diagrams. The results can be seen in table 2-1.

Table 2-1. *Application Component Matrix*

Component Category	Component Type	Component Name	Manufacturer
Primary	External	ASP.NET MVC	Microsoft
	External	ASP.NET Web API	Microsoft
	External	ASP.NET Membership	Microsoft
	External	Internet Information Services	Microsoft
	External	SQL Server	Microsoft
	External	NGINX	NGINX
	Internal	Andromeda Portal	Andromeda Games
	Internal	CardStock	Andromeda Games
	Internal	Inventory Management System	Andromeda Games

(*continued*)

Table 2-1. (*continued*)

Component Category	Component Type	Component Name	Manufacturer
Secondary	External	Angular	Google
	External	Express	Node.js Foundation
	External	NodeJS	Node.js Foundation
	External	MongoDB	MongoDB, Inc.
	External	Point of Service Software	NEC
	Internal	CardStock Forums	Andromeda Games
	Internal	Friends Platform	Andromeda Games
	Internal	In-Store Ordering	Andromeda Games
Tertiary	Internal	Scheduling	Andromeda Games
	Internal	Trading Platform	Andromeda Games

Documenting Application Collaborations

An application collaboration is any aggregation of two or more cooperating application components. This collaboration helps to set the stage for interactions—behaviors modeled after the cooperation, such as interactions or events. There are several key application collaborations that have surfaced as a result of your research thus far. Primarily you notice the following component collaborations:

- Content Management

- Forum Interaction

- Forum Moderation

- Inventory Management

- Inventory Search

- Online Ordering

- Schedule Management

- Trade Management

- User Interaction

While there are likely many more collaborations among the different applications that Andromeda uses, these are centrally related to the Cardstock platform itself. You enter the collaborations into your model and start to draw out relationships between the collaborations, APIs, and application components. There are many dependencies on the Cardstock application component, based on the relationships you identify. What makes these collaborations important to the platform?

Each collaboration can ultimately lead to the discovery of application events and application interactions. We'll cover interactions in a bit more detail later in this chapter, but we can start to glean some insight into the event structure of these application components. One area of focus is around events related to the inventory system.

Through conversations with the engineering team, you learn that these collaborations you've identified do not manifest in traditional event objects but do take into account that events are triggered—and handled—by the various components. To get a head start on event identification, and with the assistance of the engineers, you decide to employ a technique known as event storming. Event storming is similar in concept to brainstorming, wherein ideas about potential events are offered, recorded, and accepted (or rejected) to ultimately produce a collection of events.

Your event storming session starts off slow but begins to pick up speed once you start challenging the engineers to shout out any events that come to mind. You end up filling a whiteboard with clusters of potential events that could relate to the collaborations you have in your model. Figure 2-1 is a slimmed-down example of the events produced from this session of event storming.

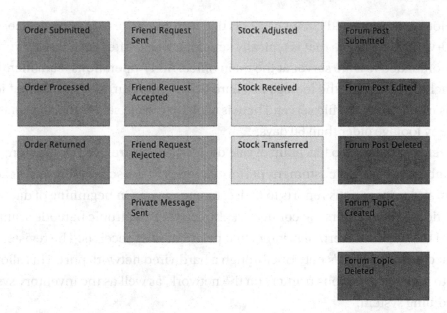

Figure 2-1. *Sample of event storming*

Locating the Components

You are aware of where the components reside within the application, but where does the application itself reside? Bridging the gap between the logical application architecture and the physical architecture starts by finding where the application is domiciled, whether it is a single instance or multiple instances, and what other requirements are impacted by that location (resiliency, recoverability, maintainability).

The portal and Cardstock applications, along with the accounting, purchasing, and other back-office programs, are hosted in the Andromeda main office's server room. The inventory system is a bit different, however. There is a copy of the application that is run from the main office, but each store location has a server running a copy of the application as well. From your conversations with the developers, you've learned that there is a database on each store's server that maintains the inventory information for that store. As long as a network connection can be found, the records from the store will synchronize with the records held at the main office. If that connection is lost, synchronization will occur as soon as the network link becomes available again. It's very important to ensure the store's inventory records are kept as up to date as possible, as this helps employees in locating additional merchandise in the stockroom if the floor location is empty. It's also important to maintain the information from the main office, as that can allow employees to request an interstore transfer or even a warehouse-to-store transfer.

Each location has closed circuit cameras tied into an onsite recording device, which houses surveillance footage that is typically kept for a week. After each weekly cycle, the footage is offloaded to a file server at the main office. An IT operations team member goes to each site, transfers the footage to a hard drive, and returns to the main office where it is moved onto the file server. There is a job on the file server that automatically removes any footage older than 60 days.

Each retail location also has point of sale devices, which are used by the store team members to cash out customers, perform queries to the scheduling and ticketing interfaces, and print various reports to assist store managers in beginning of day/end of day operations. The registers are connected physically to electronic barcode scanners, credit card readers, and thermal printers that print out sales receipts. The registers are also connected to the store's network through a hardwired network port. This allows the registers to connect to various printers on the network, as well as the inventory system and scheduling system.

Through another set of conversations with IT operations, you start to catch wind of some less than desirable application hosting practices. For example, you learn that one of the developers has been hosting the scheduling interface on his desktop computer. You also learn that there is a backdoor web application that allows store managers to peruse and update the inventory records of the main office directly via a password-protected area of the portal. This workaround was put into place due to connectivity issues that the stores faced with a legacy communications carrier that led to unreliable network connections between the stores and the main office. The carrier was replaced, but the web interface remained as a convenient way for managers to check inventory levels, especially from mobile devices.

You inquire about software that is installed on the machines, both at an application and operating system level. While the IT team doesn't have a formal application maturity matrix, it does have a spreadsheet of all paid applications that Andromeda owns, including license numbers and vendor contacts.

Note   An application maturity matrix is a listing of software applications that describes the name, usage, criticality, maintainer(s), business relevance, and other details for each application.

Since most employees have restricted access to install programs, this list is a fairly accurate representation of what could be found on employees' machines. Developers have full administrative privileges on their machines, however, and the IT team knows that the developers have installed a smattering of tools, libraries, and third-party components. What those items are, though, is not something that the IT team is fully aware of. This concerns you and you make a note to gather further information from the developers on what has been installed on their machines.

Constructing a Basic Infrastrucutre View

Taking the information you've gathered, you set out to get a very minimal view of what the infrastructure would look like, including the main office, retail stores, and warehouse. The intent of your first draft is to get a base sense of what's in each location, according to the data you have. You end up putting together a sketch that captures very high-level details. While you know that you don't have all of the actual servers captured, you want to at least get a sense of what the standout infrastructure components are.

Starting with the main office, you sketch out the server room, which has separate machines for the main components of the portal as well as the build infrastructure, source control management, and file server. There are many desktop and laptop computers within the main office, and capturing the fact they exist is important but not critical to what you need for the Cardstock migration. You also make a note that there are several integration points that exist between software-as-a-service vendors and other subsystems—mainly, the procurement platform and the inventory management system. Figure 2-2 shows a first pass at the infrastructure you are able to locate.

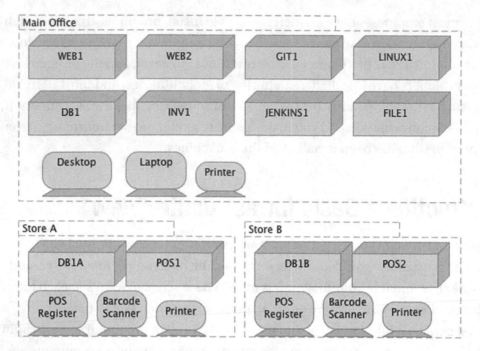

Figure 2-2. *Rough sketch of baseline infrastructure*

Each device shown could have 1 to *n* number of instances at each location. Each node has a 1:1 relationship, meaning each named device has only one instance.

Enhancing the Infrastructure View

The initial construction of your infrastructure view left you with more questions than answers. How should the catalog of devices at each location be captured? What are the technical specifications of each infrastructure component? How are the networking components of each location actually related? Are there details that, while relevant to the view, are irrelevant to the task at hand? Capturing and sorting through these bits of information can be overwhelming but will help establish a better baseline, as shown in the following sections.

Physical Devices

Typically, with physical devices, some system of cataloging is employed to make sure that assets are accounted for and can be studied for potential repair or replacement. Obviously if someone turns in a device saying that it no longer works, a member of the IT staff will be able to assist with fixing or replacing that device (budget permitting). Keeping track of the year an item was purchased can help IT staff be more proactive in capturing potential end-of-life sitauations with equipment. Tracking details such as CPU speed, Cores, and RAM and hard disk size can prove useful in helping to find comparable cloud-based infrastructure.

The IT operations team at Andromeda has managed to keep a fairly up-to-date spreadsheet that tracks the name of each piece of equipment, the serial number, year purchased, date last updated/repaired, and technical specifications such as RAM, CPU cores, disk space, and so on. There are two tabs in the spreadsheet, one for employee devices (laptops, phones, tablets, desktop PCs) and one for internal infrastructure (servers, printers, scanners, barcode readers, point of sale registers, RFID tags, security systems). There are three areas that are of interest to you with respect to this project:

- *Server infrastructure*: rack units, physical and virtual boxes

- *Point of sale devices*: Registers, human interface devices (barcode scanners), integrations with inventory systems

- *Employee devices*: tablets and phones for store employees, and PCs for the engineering staff

The first item is fairly straightforward. In order to host the various platform components, a solid server infrastructure is required. While there are no rack-mount units, the IT operations folks do have several physical machines that serve as the backbone for the back-office systems and the development ecosystem. Capturing the current state for that infrastructure is first on your list.

The second item is a bit more nebulous, as the POS devices are not directly in scope but do interact with the inventory management system, which is in scope. Focusing on the integration points as well as how information is captured at the point of sale does factor into things, especially since GameCorp has an existing POS platform that it prefers. That preferred platform is a bit outdated, though, and there has been talk of wanting to get a fresh take on the POS systems. Part of your hope is that with this project you can introduce a modern platform that makes store employees, systems admins, and developers all happy while still maintaining robust integrations with downstream systems. More on that later.

The last item deals with how employees access and interact with the components of the platform. Cardstock itself is maintained by developers via their laptops, which have certain applications installed and have a higher amount of CPU cores, RAM, and disk space than their nontechnical counterparts. There are a few store employees who have administrator rights within Cardstock to moderate forums, answer inquiries, and take action on users if required (banning for inappropriate actions or content, for example). The store managers have access to the hidden inventory update page from within the portal, and when needed will access that via their smartphones. Store employees also have the ability to search inventory at all locations from within a web browser, but only from machines connected to the store's internal network.

Networking

When thinking of networking, two main ideas may come to mind. One is that of a location and its devices, all able to communicate with one another. Another is that of a set of locations, each able to identify and communicate with devices regardless of physical location. Andromeda has a fairly simple networking setup, wherein each location has its own local area network, and each store can communicate with the main office through the use of a virtual private network, established by the company's Internet provider. Each location also has access to the Internet for critical business functions, but most other traffic is blocked to avoid any potential security issues.

For the purposes of what you are trying to migrate, the local and wide area networks used by Andromeda are not a primary concern. Identifying the components that are in those networks does matter, however, as lifting things out of the ecosystem and putting them into another location could disrupt the existing integrations between software and hardware devices. As an example, moving the point of sale software to a cloud-hosted solution may interfere with the system's ability to connect to receipt printers on-premises. Additional problems could arise if systems that integrate with the point of sale software are located further away, adding latency and potentially impacting the speed of order processing. Figure 2-3 shows a high-level overview of the basic network connectivity between each of Andromeda's locations.

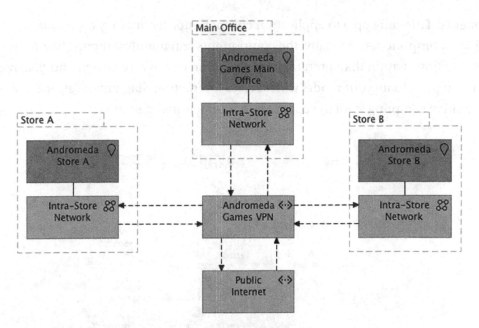

Figure 2-3. *Basic network connectivity, including VPN and Internet*

Your next step in understanding the networking connectivity is to get some baseline details on the type, speed, and quality of the circuits connecting all of these locations together. This information is good to have on hand in the event that you need to integrate services with other networks, such as GameCorp's corporate network or Microsoft Azure. The two stores and main office location all interact over dedicated T1 lines, which offer transmission speeds up to 1.54 Mbps. Each of the T1 connections communicates over a multiprotocol label switching circuit, which in turn communicates with the Internet service provider. You notate this information with the intent of giving it to your infrastructure architect, who will be able to dig in further and give recommendations on target state integration of Andromeda's networks and those of GameCorp.

Seeking Interactions with Applications, Technology and Data

Now that you have identified application and technology architecture components that compose the overall platform, you settle in on fleshing out any interactions that may involve those components and the associated data that goes along with them. An interaction in Archimate terms is a behavior that is carried out by two or more components. This can apply to application components, technology components, or business components. Typically, the components can manifest themselves in the form of functions within that interaction. Through an exhaustive design and discovery session, you populuate your model with several interaction diagrams. Figure 2-4 shows a representative sampling from the application interaction diagram.

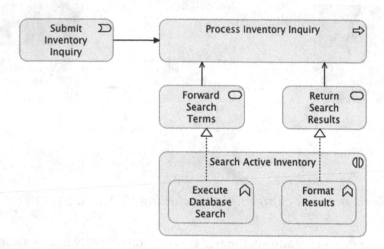

Figure 2-4. *Section of application interaction diagram with event and process*

Tip   Please refer to the Archi metamodel for a complete listing of the application and technology interactions captured.

Determining Information Consistency

Not all information is stored the same way. While this may seem like an obvious statement, the intent of the statement is really to drive understanding about what types of data are being stored for the platform, and what the needs are from a timing perspective. For example, consider the dichotomy of Eventual Consistency vs. Immediate Consistency.

In a platform or subsystem that requires its data to be eventually consistent, there is no rule in place specifying that any persistence of data needs to be done immediately. The target data store can be updated in an asynchronous manner, with varying degrees of speed, based on the functional requirements of that application. Some of those requirements may include a pop-up message being displayed to the end user once the action is completed, with no direct tie to the area of the application that the user may be in at the time.

With immediate consistency, the premise is that any action that means to persist data will do so with no delay and offer a confirmation back to the end user upon completion. Any subsequent queries for that data will result in a dataset that contains the newly created or updated data.

A common way to look at the difference between immediate and eventual consistency is that of real-time vs. batch transactions. In many industries, it is common to allow a set of actions or features to perform operations in "real-time," meaning as quickly as possible. More often than not, this amounts to near-time and not real-time due to latency with the application, infrastructure, or other environmental factors. Any operations that are deemed to be too intensive for near-time processing can be relegated to batch operations, typically run in a scheduled fashion during nonbusiness hours.

That's not to say that batch processing is the same as eventual consistency, however. At a deeper level, eventual consistency works on the premise that information will be updated eventually, but not take such a long time that it does not update until the next day. Normally, operations that fall into this level of asynchrony will take minutes to complete and report back, vs/ batch operations that may take hours and are generally not user initiated.

Most of the data moving between components is considered near-time. It's important to the user experience to have the most accurate inventory listings at any given time, which means that item holds for people who may put an item into their cart via the website should decrement the total on-hand count of an item as soon as possible. There will be edge cases where an online customer may put an item in his or her cart—the last item in stock—and very close in time to that selection, a customer in a physical store location could buy the exact same item. This would lead to an invalidated shopping cart and could result in a somewhat unhappy online shopper. Utilizing the appropriate data consistency level will help to keep the user experience more desirable.

After analyzing the data flows and talking with operations, you arrive at the conclusion that a vast majority of the data being consumed, produced, or persisted is meant to be updated in near-time. A few exceptions would include the prestaging of incoming merchandise from the purchasing system to the inventory system, nightly processing of cash and credit transactions, payroll reports, and sales incentive accumulators.

Go with the Data Flow

Figuring out what data a platform works with is just as crucial as determining whether that data is produced, consumed, or both. While some aspects of inbound and outbound data will be covered in Chapter 3, it is important to at least capture the data flows that manifest between components, subsystems and the platform itself.

Using the application and technical interactions you exposed earlier, along with the general idea of what data transactions exist, you begin putting together a high-level picture of the key data sources, their ingress/egress points, and general timing considerations.

Immediate Consistency

A great deal of the information that the platform consumes, produces, or persists can be seen as immediately consistent. Checking inventory levels at the stores or the warehouse, sending private messages to friends, viewing scheduled events, and even using the secret update page all operate on the assumption that the data involved in these transactions is as up-to-date as possible. You identify data objects that the platform uses along with what components leverage them, starting with registered Cardstock users and working your way out to anonymous users of the public portal. The basic data object you capture can be seen in Figure 2-5.

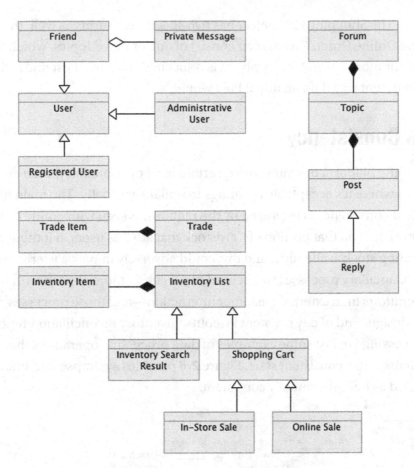

Figure 2-5. *Data objects and relations*

The base object of User has three specializations within the platform:

- Registered User (accesses all areas of Cardstock as well as reads the public portal)

- Administrative User (accesses all areas of the platform and can edit all areas)

- Friend (accesses private messages, friend lists)

The trading platform uses the notion of a registered user and allows for a Trade object to be formed when a trade request is sent from one registered user to another. That Trade object can consist of one or more Trade Item objects. In a similar fashion, an Inventory List object is a base item that contains one or more Inventory Item objects. The Shopping Cart and Inventory Search Result object are two specializations of the

Inventory List. The Shopping Cart object has two specialized forms as well, the In-Store Order and the Online Order. Forums can consist of one or more Topics, which can consist of one or more Posts. A Reply object is a specialization of a Post and is displayed in a slightly different way than an initial Post would be.

Eventual Consistency

While most of the platform operates with a certain level of immediacy, there are some circumstances where it's acceptable for things to update gradually. The main instance where eventual consistency is leveraged by the platform is seen with online ordering. A disclaimer is listed on that portion of Cardstock that advises users that there could be a delay in updating stock availability, and this could adversely impact a user's order. A great deal of ancillary processes run behind the scenes—more aligned with the business operations than external customer interaction—and those processes run off-hours by design. End of day register closeouts, inventory reconciliation reports, and financial processing are just some examples of data processing operations that eventualy bring all systems into a consistent state. Figure 2-6 provides a glimpse into information that is classified as being eventually consistent.

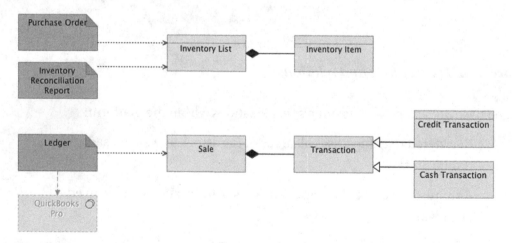

Figure 2-6. *Section of eventually consistent data objects*

Another type of data consistency is related to the system metadata for the platform, who has access to the operations that release the various platform components, and where the plaform is ultimately deployed to. You now turn your focus to peeling back the layer that keeps the lights on—the deployment architecture.

Fleshing out the Build Process (Further)

Initially while talking with the developers, you got a basic sense for how the team keeps its source code maintained as well as how they build and release their software. You decide to dig a bit deeper, though, as the details around the Jenkins jobs are not exactly clear at first glance. You're also not clear about how the Git server is set up.

The Git server is set up on its own machine and is running a local copy of GitLab Community Edition. The developers did not want to use any hosted solutions for fear that they would have issues syncing their code during times of Internet outages. It was initially set up by a developer who is no longer employed with Andromeda, and since everything was working fine, no one saw any need to change that out. There are two engineers who currently have administrative rights on the server, and they manage the maintenance and upgrades for that box.

The Jenkins server is in a similar state, wherein it was set up by the same developer who is no longer with Andromeda. There are a few jobs set up that deal with compilation and packaging of artifacts, but other than that the installation is fairly plain vanilla. There are some plugins installed to accommodate .NET compilation and some minimalistic code metric collection.

You catalog the build jobs for the main portal, Cardstock, and the API layer that allows for integration with the inventory system. Next you move on to the deployment jobs, which outline the various environments used in the pipeline.

Lighting up the Runway

Through your research into the Jenkins instance, you find deployment jobs that are associated with every build artifact. The team uses a central file server to store the artifacts and the Jenkins jobs pull artifacts from that server and move them to the appropriate target environments. While a lot of work is done locally on the developers' workstations, there are two preproduction environments that are used to validate releases prior to sending them to production.

The QA environment is set up so that automated suites of tests can be run against the code, including integration and UI tests. These are typically scripted out through the use of test runner scripts authored in JavaScript and bash shell script where applicable. The Staging environment is set up for members of the business and IT operations teams to test out functionality. Once sign-off is received from the reviewers (typically an

41

email), the code is allowed to be moved to production. Figure 2-7 depicts the baseline deployment runway along with testing interaction points.

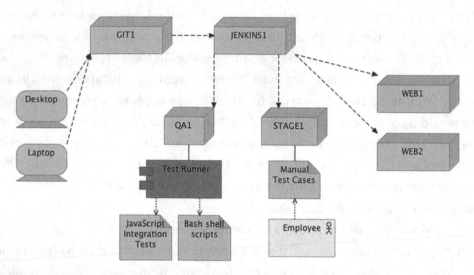

Figure 2-7. *Baseline deployment runway, with orchestration*

From a source control perspective, once code is pushed from a developer's workstation to GitLab, it is deployed to the QA environment and the test runner is triggered automatically. The test runner is designed to execute any tests that are in JavaScript or Bash formats. Once the test runner has finished execution, it sends the results via email to the development team. When a change or set of changes have passed that test run, a release branch can be cut. Once the release branch is cut, the code is moved to staging. Upon successful validation, the release branch is closed out and is merged back into master and develop, following proper GitFlow protocol. Once the merge to master is complete, the code is moved to production and the ensuing commit is tagged with the latest release version.

You finish your notes around the deployment runway and general application lifecycle. Having covered off most of the domain architecture areas for the existing platform, you now turn your focus to the security architecture for Andromeda Games, which will prove to be a challenge unto itself.

Summary

In this chapter, you have examined the existing application, infrastructure, data, and deployment architectures related to Andromeda Games' Cardstock platform. You have been able to identify, catalog, and display the components that make up the platform and its supporting cast. You have put together a series of views within the Andromeda model that capture the information you have uncovered about each of these architecture domains. Metadata about each item and each view have also been captured to facilitate the ingestion of this model by other architects. You have also been able to analyze the components in relation to reliability—or lack thereof. Next on your list of areas to look into is that of security and compliance, something that needs to be right the first time.

EXERCISE: FINDING SINGLE POINTS OF FAILURE

Using the categorized components in Table 2-1 in conjunction with the infrastructure views you've compiled, it's time to work through what potential SPOFs might be present within the platform's ecosystem.

A good place to start the identification process is to look at the components, inclusive of what tier they are in, and ask whether a complete outage of that component would cripple the application. Many of the components in your table wouldn't completely bring down everything related to the platform, but would certainly lead to a highly degraded user experience.

What component(s) can you identify as SPOF candidates? What action(s) would you take to ensure the component(s) identified can be considered resilient and fault tolerant?

CHAPTER 3

Security and Compliance

One of the most important—if not the most important—architectural domains is that of security architecture. As a cross-cutting concern throughout the enterprise, there is likely no component, process, or interaction that does not in some way benefit from or require a certain level of security. From securing application servers to encrypting sensitive data to ensuring users can see only what they are allowed to, security architecture plays a vital part in protecting the interests of end users and system administrators alike. It's vital to keep the broad and short strokes in mind while capturing the current security landscape, and understanding the latest requirements will allow you to enable asset protection, identity protection, systems hardening, data encryption, and other areas that everyone can benefit from.

This chapter is *not* meant to be an exhaustive or authoritative source on all techniques, best practices, and considerations with respect to security architecture. There are plenty of subject matter experts who cover this topic in much greater detail and with a greater amount of clout. The examples and guidance listed within this chapter are meant to guide you as you uncover as much as possible of the security requirements that Andromeda Games currently has for its systems. Where appropriate, notations and links to deeper dives into areas of interest will be provided in order to give credit where credit is due.

Leading in with Expectations

You decide to start by reviewing the security standards and controls that are currently being used by Gamecorp. In your review of the ID10-T procedure document, you find a link to a security questionnaire that is required to be filled out for every application. To your dismay you discover that the questionnaire has 150 questions on it, each of which requires some sort of answer, even if that answer is "not applicable." It seems to have been updated with many more questions since the last time you remember using it for a project.

© Josh Garverick 2018
J. Garverick, *Migrating to Azure*, https://doi.org/10.1007/978-1-4842-3585-0_3

While the thoroughness of the questionnaire seems a bit overwhelming, you know that following it closely will ensure a better migration and a more secure end-user experience. It is broken up into several sections, most of which align with the domain architectures you identified in Chapter 2. The questionnaire starts with data security, then moves to application security, and ends with infrastructure security. There isn't a specific section for deployment security, but you decide to be safe and account for that in your assessment regardless.

THOUGHT EXERCISE

While this example works under the assumption that you will have a set of security standards to compare against, what would you do in the event that no such standards or controls exist? What types of industry standards could you leverage, and where might they be found?

Security Controls

In the realm of security and compliance, security controls are safeguards or countermeasures to avoid, detect, counteract, or minimize security risks to physical property, information, computer systems, or other assets (`https://en.wikipedia.org/wiki/Security_controls`). Having controls that map back to specific requirements under a broader specification demonstrates an intent to comply with the security requirements. Understanding what those specifications are, as well as the applicable requirements, is the first step to setting the table for success when doing a preliminary assessment and gap analysis.

PCI DSS

From previous experience in the retail space, you know that the Payment Card Industry Data Security Standards (PCI DSS), version 3.0, are a must for ensuring protection of consumer payment information in a variety of different transaction scenarios. Normally there are requirements for choosing an approved scanning vendor and a qualified security assessor to audit the implementation of security controls. Being that Andromeda Games fell into the category of small merchant, they were able to get by with using the self-assessment on compliance instead. Table 3-1 illustrates the most recent copy of the self-assessment completed by Andromeda management, along with supporting comments.

Table 3-1. *Self-Assessment Questionnaire (SAQ) for Andromeda Games*

SAQ	Description	Response (Y/N)	Mitigation	Completion Date
A	Card-not-present merchants (e-commerce or mail/telephone-order) that have fully outsourced all cardholder data functions to PCI DSS compliant third-party service providers, with no electronic storage, processing, or transmission of any cardholder data on the merchant's systems or premises. Not applicable to face-to-face channels.	Y		
A-EP	E-commerce merchants who outsource all payment processing to PCI DSS validated third parties, and who have a website(s) that doesn't directly receive cardholder data but that can impact the security of the payment transaction. No electronic storage, processing, or transmission of any cardholder data on the merchant's systems or premises. Applicable only to e-commerce channels.	Y		
B	Merchants using only: - Imprint machines with no electronic cardholder data storage; and/or - Standalone, dial-out terminals with no electronic cardholder data storage. Not applicable to e-commerce channels.	Y		
B-IP	Merchants using only standalone, PTS-approved payment terminals with an IP connection to the payment processor, with no electronic cardholder data storage. Not applicable to e-commerce channels.	Y		

(*continued*)

Table 3-1. (*continued*)

SAQ	Description	Response (Y/N)	Mitigation	Completion Date
C-VT	Merchants who manually enter a single transaction at a time via a keyboard into an Internet-based virtual terminal solution that is provided and hosted by a PCI DSS validated third-party service provider. No electronic cardholder data storage. Not applicable to e-commerce channels.	Y		
C	Merchants with payment application systems connected to the Internet; no electronic cardholder data storage. Not applicable to e-commerce channels.	Y		
P2PE	Merchants using only hardware payment terminals that are included in and managed via a validated, PCI SSC-listed P2PE solution, with no electronic cardholder data storage. Not applicable to e-commerce channels.	Y		
D	SAQ D for Merchants: All merchants not included in descriptions for the previously listed SAQ types. SAQ D for Service Providers: All service providers defined by a payment card brand as eligible to complete an SAQ.	Y		

The next area you look into is the updated requirements framework for the PCI DSS standard. There are 12 requirements listed out for the latest update of the framework, which roll up to six primary goals:

- Build and maintain a secure network and Systems.

    - Install and maintain a firewall configuration to protect cardholder data.

    - Do not use vendor-supplied defaults for system passwords and other security parameters.

- Protect cardholder data.

    - Protect stored cardholder data.

    - Encrypt transmission of cardholder data across open, public networks.

- Maintain a vulnerability management program

    - Protect all systems against malware and regularly update antivirus software or programs.

    - Develop and maintain secure systems and applications.

- Implement strong access control measures.

    - Restrict access to cardholder data by business need to know.

    - Identify and authenticate access to system components.

    - Restrict physical access to cardholder data.

- Regularly monitor and test networks.

    - Track and monitor all access to network resources and cardholder data.

    - Regularly test security systems and processes.

- Maintain an information security policy.

    - Maintain a policy that addresses information security for all personnel.

To keep things consistent, you decide to add the goals and requirements to your Archimate model. Later on, you will be able to map applicable requirements and controls to specific application and technical components within the solution. Figure 3-1 shows a diagram of the goals and primary requirements related to the PCI DSS standard.

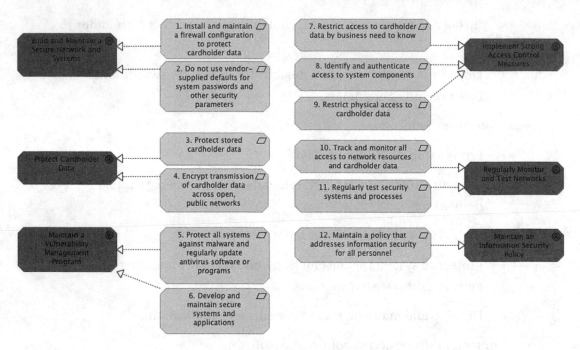

Figure 3-1. *PCI DSS 3.0 goals and primary requirements*

EXERCISE: SECONDARY REQUIREMENTS AND CONTROLS

Using the list of requirements related to the PCI DSS standard (found at https://www. pcisecuritystandards.org/documents/PCIDSS_QRGv3_2.pdf), add the secondary requirements listed in each of the sections to your model. Once complete, create a new viewpoint in Archi that represents the realization of the secondary requirements with respect to the primary requirements shown in Figure 3-1. A realization, in terms of architectural modeling, is a relationship that demonstrates how an object realizes another—meaning, how one object helps to deliver a concrete example of another, more abstract object.

GDPR

The General Data Protection Regulation (GDPR) is legislation that was approved by the European Union (EU) parliament on April 14, 2016. This legislation is meant to bolster existing data privacy and protection laws that had been passed previously, including the Safe Harbour decision as well as the EU–US Privacy Shield regulations.

SIDEBAR: TIMELINE OF EU DATA PRIVACY LAWS

Throughout this chapter, mention has been made of the data privacy laws of the EU, specifically GDPR and its stringent requirements. It's worth understanding how GDPR came to be, and how data privacy laws in the EU have matured over the past two decades.

- Safe Harbour (https://en.wikipedia.org/wiki/International_ Safe_Harbor_Privacy_Principles) was developed between 1998 and 2000, with a focus on protecting data from accidental disclosure or loss. Several key factors were established in this legislation:

    - *Notice*: Individuals must be informed that their data is being collected and how it will be used. The organization must provide information about how individuals can conact the organization with any inquiries or complaints.

    - *Choice*: Individuals must have the option to opt out of the collection and forward transfer of the data to third parties.

    - *Onward Transfer*: Transfers of data to third parties may only occur to other organizations that follow adequate data protection principles.

    - *Security*: Reasonable efforts must be made to prevent loss of collected information.

    - *Data Integrity*: Data must be relevant and reliable for the purpose it was collected.

    - *Access*: Individuals must be able to access information held aboutt hem, and correct ore delete it, if it is inaccurate.

    - *Enforcement*: There must be effective means of enforcing these rules.

- The EU-US Privacy Shield (https://en.wikipedia.org/wiki/EU-US_Privacy_Shield) was developed in 2016 with the primary intent of providing more stringent requirements around transatlantic information flow. The Privacy Shield legislation took the seven principles from the Safe Harbour decision and added the following:

  - More options for EU citizens to file claims: channels are available by both US and EU authorities to submit claims or complaints about data being captured, as well as binding arbitration as a last resort.

  - More monitoring of compliant companies: The US and EU will jointly montior compliance via the Department of Commerce, Department of Transportation, the Federal Trade Commission, and the European Data Protection Authorities.

  - Stricter reporting obligations: organizations that participate in or have participated in the Privacy Shield agreement are required to store data consistent with the regulations, even after withdrawal from the agreement.

- The General Data Protection Regulation (https://gdpr-info.eu/) was passed on April 14, 2016 with enforcement commencing on May 25, 2018. Data collection, retention, correction, and the "right to be forgotten" are all areas receiving more attention.

The driving factor behind the GDPR legislation is centered around the consumer—in this case, an EU citizen—to know about the collection of their data, request all of the data from an organizaiton that has been collected about them, modify any data that is incorrect, object to the collection of data, or request all of that data to be deleted. Additionally, the legislation establishes further rules around what is considered to be personally sensitive information. Much more information about the legislation and its requirements can be found at https://eur-lex.europa.eu/eli/reg/2016/679/oj.

While not all of the 95 articles associated with the GDPR are related to specific security requirements, there are many that are. Mapping those security requirements to controls can be a sizeable feat. Through some research into existing controls referenced by the ID10-T as well as some online sources, you come across an interesting find: the ISO27k toolkit. The toolkit (http://www.iso27001security.com/html/toolkit.html) contains many different reference documents, compiled by the ISO community. One of those documents is a mapping of ISO27k security controls to GDPR regulatory areas. The ID10-T specifically references the controls laid out in the ISO27001 and ISO27002 standards, which gives you some relief knowing that the mapping will serve as a good reference point.

EXERCISE: IMPORT THE GDPR AND ISO27K DETAILS

Similar to the exercise earlier in this chapter dealing with the PCI DSS requirements, import the GDPR security requirements into your model in Archi. Do the same for the ISO27002 security controls that are listed in the ISO27k toolkit documents. Using the mapping document as a guide, create a new viewpoint that establishes the realization paths of the GDPR requirements from the ISO27002 controls.

Are there any areas of overlap between the PCI and GDPR requirements? Are there any common controls found in the ISO27002 collection that can apply to both PCI DSS and GDPR?

After completing the initial entry and mapping exercises, you feel better about tackling the challenge of assessing the existing domains within Andromeda's application stack and cataloging any risk or coverage gaps that may exist.

Identifying Domain Risk Areas

Several of the architectural domains have a bit of overlap with respect to what is being secured, how it is secured, and what controls are in place to ensure compliance. Gamecorp has specific controls in place to safeguard against deviations from corporate security standards. As you begin your assessment of the baseline security architecture, you keep those guidelines close in an attempt to get ahead of what may be a lengthy gap analysis later. You begin to dig into each of the sections outlined in the questionnaire.

Data Security

Gamecorp leverages the concept of CIA when determining the security to be applied to data sources. The acronym CIA represents three points of a triangle, wherein C refers to confidentiality, I refers to integrity, and the A refers to availability. The confidentiality point deals with data that could be considered sensitive—tax ID numbers, account numbers, protected health information, and so on. The integrity point deals with the constructs that allow or deny the data to be edited and to what degree it should be restored in the event of a mistake. The availability point deals with a similar concept to immediate consistency vs. eventual consistency: should the data be available for consumption all the time (highly available) or are there acceptable outage levels around the data being available (generally available)? These three factors are normally used to capture the overall security rating of data. Figure 3-2 shows a basic graphical representation of the CIA triad for information security.

Figure 3-2. *The CIA triad of information security*

Each point of the triad is typically rated on a scale of one to four. While the meaning of the scale could be different, the idea is still the same—the scale is meant to represent a low-to-high scenario. Patterns will tend to emerge when rating different data on these three scales. For example, it's likely that any data that is deemed to be highly confidential will also likely have a high integrity rating as well. In some circumstances, it may be expected that a consumer of that data should have access to it at any time, day or night. This would lead to that data having a high availability rating as well.

Combing through the data types that exist in CardStock, you quickly find that there is not anything being stored in the platform that could be an issue from a compliance perspective. Users are asked for their names and email addresses upon signing up to use CardStock, and address information can be voluntarily provided so that members can receive mailers for special store promotions. Posts to the forums or the trading system are monitored for improper use. This includes violations of the terms and conditions agreement that each member agrees to upon signing up for the service and covers antiharassment, offensive content, and disclosure of personally identifiable information that could lead to more serious consequences.

While this information is not considered sensitive by US standards, the same does not hold true for other countries. Being that Gamecorp has an international presence, along with the statement in the scope document that international expansion is desired once the platform is converted, you decide to look into the data privacy and residency laws overseas. While not immediately necessary, having controls in place to be able to quickly comply with all regulations will be helpful.

You note that user data is adequately secured, and that sales and order information is in good standing as well. There appears to be no issue with finding a way to ensure international compliance either, since the target state in Azure provides several solutions that can meet the needs of data protection and residency, if needed. Now that you have established that the data is classified and safe, you can turn your attention to the application layer.

Application Security

Application security can be seen as a crossover point between infrastructure and data security. There are some areas of overlap, but there is plenty of ground to cover within an application and its related components. Let's explore some of the primary concerns from an application security perspective.

Identity and Access Management

Also referred to authentication an authorization, the notion of identity is a very important and hot topic. Identity theft is an ever-increasing crime, with the majority of thefts related to government documents and bank/credit card accounts. In 2016, over $16 billion dollars was stolen in transactions identified as identity theft, impacting 15.4 million US citizens.[1] Year after year there has been a nontrivial increase of people who have fallen victim to identity theft, and safeguarding users' information is more critical than ever before.

While identity protection can come in many forms, there are typically controls in place to ensure that login information is transmitted, stored and used in a secure manner. In a typical access-based system, audit records are used to track when a user logs in, how long between logins, where the login request is coming from, even when or how often information is changed in the user's profile.

---

[1]Source: http://www.iii.org/fact-statistic/identity-theft-and-cybercrime

Access management can also come in many forms. Some products cater specifically to the identity space, encompassing authorization and authentication. From an authorization standpoint, permissions to access applications as well as access to modify data within that application can be established through the use of roles. Role-based access control (RBAC) is a standard implementation pattern that enables roles to have access to specific functionality through the principle of least privilege. The principle of least privilege states that users should be granted roles that are fine-grained enough to relegate authorization only to areas in which that role must have access. For example, if a user needs to have the ability to read the profiles of others, it would stand to reason that you would not grant that user the ability to edit or delete all user profiles.

CardStock uses the ASP.NET Membership framework to store and process login information. The developers then built an identity model on top of the simple forms-based authentication mechanism to control what users have access to see and do within the platform. Knowing that there will be an integration with Gamecorp's existing business to consumer (B2C) authentication within Azure, you document your findings and note that conversions will need to occur to move the existing user data (including access roles and profile information) into the B2C platform.

Transport and Delivery Channels

Often the means by which an application is available—mobile, web browser, desktop application—is referred to as the delivery channel for that application. There may be many delivery channels in play to reach different target consumers, or there may be one delivery channel that is expected to service all consumers. This is different from the transport, which is more of a lower level technical concern and tends to deal more with ensuring communications to and from the application are able to proceed.

Securing traffic at the transport layer typically involves help from a couple of components. First is the network where the transport operates (infrastructure) is additionally secured by cryptography that obfuscates the network traffic through the use of a secure algorithm. There are different types of cryptographic, or encryption, algorithms, each lending a different type of security to the transports they are employed on. Encryption algorithms are initiated by the protocol upon which the communications occur. For example, secure HTTP traffic (HTTPS) will by default provide an encrypted transport layer. The degree to which it is secure is up to the administrator of the network and the type of application data being accessed. It is much more practical to employ security up front than it is to try to retrofit it onto the transport layer after the fact.

Andromeda's developers and network admins agreed some time ago that using HTTPS was not negotiable for their web applications. It wasn't a huge lift to put that in place, since the internal networks were already running cryptography due to the retailer's need to comply with PCI DSS, the authoritative source on using, protecting, and storing any credit/debit card payment information.

The delivery channel for CardStock, as well as the public portal, is the Internet. A fair amount of overlap exists with securing the transport layer, but additional measures can be taken to secure the application against web-based intrusion and other threats. For example, a common method for compromising websites that use some form of password authentication is a brute force attack. This will usually involve someone writing a script or program that will try any and all permutations of characters in an attempt to "crack" the password for a known account. Measures such as lockouts on a number of consecutive failed login attempts can deter these types of attacks.

Infrastructure Security

Infrastructure is the heart of any company's technology. The networks, devices, nodes, and appliances that are used can all contribute to the success or failure of supporting the business. In some cases, security is inherent in the items being used. An example of that inherent security is the automatic enabling of Windows Firewall with all later versions of Microsoft Windows. On the Linux side, the Red Hat family of operating systems (CentOS and Red Hat Enterprise) make use of SELinux to secure and administer things at the OS level. Even with physical components, security can be inherent with the forced usage of usernames and passwords to access administrative utilities for the devices and even the requirement of secure transports to even communicate between devices. You begin to examine the heaps of printouts, hand-written notes, and rudimentary diagrams supplied to you by Andromeda's IT operations department in hopes of cataloging the baseline infrastructure security view.

Network

Network security is likely the biggest area within infrastructure security, as it looks to secure all traffic coming into the network, leaving the network, and traffic between points on the internal network. Some elements central to network security are also major players with other security domains, as mentioned earlier. In conjunction with cryptography, though, a key part of securing a network falls to the network equipment.

Physical routers, switches, firewall devices, and wireless access points all contribute to strengthening a network from unauthorized traffic.

Andromeda's network equipment is all found to be in excellent shape, both from an aging perspective as well as a compliance perspective. As mentioned earlier, they are required to follow the PCI DSS standards for encryption and protection of consumer payment information. This means the networks are monitored for external threats, secured using 1024-bit certificates, and protected through the use of aggressive firewall policies to ensure only the necessary traffic will be sent and received.

Device

Companies have many options when it comes to what (and how) devices connect to their private network. The two dominant means of access for devices center around company-supplied devices vs. the bring your own device (BYOD) school of thought. In either case, the IT operations and support staff will introduce software of some sort that will sandbox the device, effectively letting it interact only with the things it needs to. Once off the grid, the device can interact with other private or public networks depending on what the user decides to use the device for. Companies will also lean toward drafing policies for using company-supplied devices or BYOD, which can include things like security scans, wiping of non–work-related data, or reclamation of the device altogether.

The IT operations folks at Andromeda subscribe to the idea that devices that are not company approved may not connect to the company network regardless of need. Any phone, tablet, laptop, or PC that is used for work purposes is required to undergo frequent scanning and must comply with all group policies. The group policies cover things like who can install software on the device or what type of software can be installed, access to specific areas of the network, and even size limits on an employee's desktop profile. There is no BYOD program available. This aligns perfectly with Gamecorp's policies, as they also use the same scheme for device compliance, albeit at a much grander scale.

Node

Hot on the heels of device security comes node-level security. Each server that is within the realm of internal infrastructure must have certain security controls in place to avoid issues with unauthorized logins and unauthorized actions being performed on them.

In many scenarios, IT groups will delineate between user accounts and administrative accounts to keep server maintenance, software installation, and other system modifications isolated only to administrative accounts that are allowed to perform these actions. When combined with a solid RBAC implementation, node-level security can be a very effective way to keep unwanted changes off your servers.

Roles and accounts can only cover so much. Servers also need to have appropriate monitoring and protection applied to them to safeguard against external threats, viruses, and malware. In many cases, the combination of a strong antivirus/antimalware agent with a comprehensive monitoring platform will help with real-time protection from intrusion as well as infection.

Andromeda has the standard Windows Defender antivirus and antimalware protection running on all of its nodes and also makes use of Windows Firewall to further limit traffic to and from production machines. They currently use Nagios to monitor their websites and back-end services. From an administrative user perspective, there is no notion of separate accounts for prod access. All developers have full rights all the way up to production machines, as do the IT operations staff. You make a note to address this when developing the risk mitigation for node security, since you know that Gamecorp's policies do not allow for this level of openness with respect to system access.

Deployment Security

While not often seen as a primary risk area, the security around deployments, runways, and environments does come into play. In many smaller organizations, deployments are typically handled not by an IT operations team member, but often the same developers who write and maintain the application. There is an inherent burden that is placed on the developers already, needing to not only write but also take a first pass at testing the functionality as well. The additional responsibilities of also managing the deployment of that code without safeguards or process in place can leave the door open to additional risk. Code meant for one environment could get deployed to production if people are not cautious (or if the deployment is not automated).

Another aspect that can sometimes be overlooked is that of password management. In many n-tier applications, the credentials to a database user, usually one who has data reader and writer permissions, are stored in a configuration file—more often than not in plain text, housed on the target machine. Anyone with node-level access can access the machine, take those credentials, and potentially compromise the database, assuming they know how to access it. Wherever possible, encrypting or obfuscating those values can help protect against username/password exploits.

In the same vein, and tied into the node-level security discussed in the last section, access to the target machines should be very limited. In the Linux world, it is common to use SSH keys to assert authentication and authorization when accessing a machine. In the Windows world, the traditional approach of using Active Directory to federate identity and authorization is a common practice. RBAC leverages Active Directory users and groups to create access groups into which users are dropped. These typically include the administrative accounts referenced in the last section as well.

As stated previously, the developers and IT operations staff have full access to all machines, inclusive of production. Passwords are stored in configuration files on the servers themselves, with no encryption or obfuscation. The Jenkins jobs do help in segregating where code gets deployed, providing a basic level of protection against mistaken deployments. The access to Jenkins, though, is not locked down to a tight group of responsible individuals and could use some additional fortifying. Armed with this information, you move on to the final domain in the security form— software.

Software Security

Securing software is something that tends to rope in a cross-section of all domain security areas because it is a consumer of data, application, infrastructure, and technology security rules. An area that is unique to software, though, is that of open-source software (OSS) consumption. It almost goes without saying that all software consumes some third-party packages that provide frameworks and utilities to application developers. Each of these packages comes with a license for usage and normally has some sort of public presence on sites like GitHub. Community-curated projects have been and continue to be a great additive to new or existing codebases.

Not all OSS libraries are completely billed as no strings attached. Depending on the license under which the library is released, it could bind you or your company to agreements that may not be legally prudent for your organization. For example, the Gnu General Public License (GPL) is one such license—it states that any project that uses the library must also make available, upon request, the source code that consumes the library. OSS management platforms such as Black Duck (`https://www.blackducksoftware.com`) and WhiteSource (`https://www.whitesourcesoftware.com`) will classify OSS contributions using a GPL license as a higher potential risk to a corporation based on the implications of that license.

But package usage and management can be a slippery slope without diligent monitoring. Each package you consume may have dependencies with potential license issues, and those dependencies may have dependencies, and so on. It's best to know what your dependency graph looks like and what the license landscape looks like for that graph. Tools like NDepend can help to root out dependencies within a codebase and make it easier to figure out where potential conflicts could arise from the dependency graph.

The developers at Andromeda do not actively monitor or inspect any of the third-party dependencies they ingest, nor do they perform any type of static analysis to keep an eye on best practices or vulnerability remediation. Though the general opinion of the developers is that they are not doing anything that is really considered to be a "trade secret," there is a worry that any intellectual property could be forced out in the event of inadequate OSS and licensing monitoring.

Having filled out what you feel is a complete picture of CardStock's security footprint and having checked the boxes and filled in the details for the ID10-T form, you are now left to assess the level of risk displayed in each domain, and how those risks can be mitigated either through immediate changes or changes that will be inherently made with the conversion of the platform to Azure.

Mitigating the Risks

Filling in a security questionnaire is a great step toward ensuring compliance, but it should also help you to identify areas where more fortification is required. Some of these areas can be taken care of when switching to more secure hosting options. Relying solely on switching hosting options is not a valid solution to mitigate all risks that are outlined. It's important to not only understand what areas are prone to risk but also how those risks can be resolved.

Risk Register

A common method for cataloging risks is referred to as a risk register. Often seen in more formal or waterfall organizations, creating an initial list of project risks is one of a few primary components to getting a project past the initial gate and into an actionable state. A common misconception about Agile organizations is that documentation is either very lean or nonexistent. It's entirely possible to have a fair amount of documentation and still be able to move in accordance with Agile or Scrum methodologies. Even if the risk information is captured in an informal way, having it captured somewhere is still better than not having it captured at all.

Your initial list of security risks is longer than perhaps you expected, but not the worst you've seen. Each segment is represented in your register. From a data perspective, the potential risk exists for noncompliance with international legislation. There doesn't seem to be a clear way to accommodate things like on-demand data purging, which would be important with GDPR. The risk is low for any issues regarding PCI DSS compliance, as existing infrastructure and application requirements already cover Andromeda for this area.

From an application perspective, transport security is in good shape. The current cipher being used by Andromeda's existing SSL certificates could stand to be updated a bit, since they are using a 512-bit certificate. That is definitely the least of your concerns, however. The outdated ASP.NET membership mechanism is a much larger concern, since it has not been properly curated or updated since its initial usage in the application. This leaves the application potentially vulnerable to attacks. They are also behind on their patching, which introduces more risk.

With infrastructure security, the network is in pretty good shape given the compliance with PCI DSS that Andromeda already has. They do not have any active intrusion or threat detection platforms in place, relying instead on their service provider to monitor this. As the platform is cloud-bound, there will be ways to work around this because the existing service provider will no longer be used. Device and node security are in pretty good shape as well, since Andromeda has a plan in place to avoid bringing in your own device scenarios. The lack of separate administrative accounts is something you do flag as risky, since separation of concern is something that Gamecorp is required to comply with. The lack of this delineation also relates to deployment security.

Software security is the last domain, and you have a large amount of concern around the lack of visibility into what the vulnerabilities and license usage looks like. Not paying attention to what packages are being consumed, along with a lack of awareness around what licenses are in the components being used, could lead to issues down the road. Gamecorp does not allow any components to be used that require license agreements that put the intellectual property of the enterprise at risk.

Risk Mitigation Plan

With the register in place, you move on to make some recommendations that will form the risk mitigation plan for CardStock. The main point you make is that migrating the platform to Azure will satisfy the existing infrastructure security requirements. The following points also come into focus with the plan:

- *Migration to Azure Active Directory Business to Consumer*: this will mitigate the risk of using the ASP.NET membership tables and mechanisms.

- *Implementation of role-based access control (RBAC)*: this will help segregate regular accounts from accounts of privilege and provide clear traceability into who accesses what.

- *Upgrade existing SSL certificates*: this will ensure cutting-edge encryption standards are in place via the use of new 2048-bit GeoTrust certificates.

- *Use of Operations Management Suite and Azure Security Center*: using Azure's product offerings for monitoring and alerting around threat detection, patch levels, machine auditing, and more will shore up the lack of consistent threat detection and overall node maintenance.

- *Static analysis solution*: introducing a method for scanning source code for potential vulnerabilities will help increase the resilience of the software and protect against new and existing threats.

- *Open source analysis solution*: introducing a method for cataloging, managing, and mitigating OSS packages that have risky license models or are vulnerability prone will help bolster platform security and minimize the risk that Gamecorp may be acquiring with the CardStock platform.

Preparing for Regulatory and Compliance Audits

Audits are a fairly common practice for companies that are moderate to large in size. As discussed throughout this chapter, regulations can be imposed on many companies, with more stringent requirements for companies who are in the healthcare or financial sectors of business. Being prepared for the questions an auditor may ask, and having demonstrable proof that controls are being met, will help instill confidence that customer data and company interests are protected. The work you've done to put together the risk register and mitigation plan will move CardStock into a compliant state. Setting up the development teams who will enhance and maintain the platform for success is equally as critical, as it can be easy to slip and cut corners in the interest of getting updates out the door. You feel strongly about striking a good balance of keeping innovation and time to market competitive while also holding compliance in high regard.

Summary

In this chapter, you have explored many different dimensions of security, from data to software and every point in between. You have seen how there tends to be a fair amount of overlap between the different dimensions, centering mostly on identity (authentication and authorization). You have seen examples of regulatory requirements that can lead to more wide-sweeping decisions concerning how data is encrypted in transit, at rest, and in process. You have learned how to formulate a risk register, as well as a mitigation plan that will lead the way to compliance and information safety. Next up, you tackle the initial revision of the operating model—what people, processes, and technologies all come together to create and support the platform.

Given the information and topics covered throughout the chapter, consider the following questions:

1. From a data security perspective, would it have made sense to perform a complete analysis of all data sources within Andromeda? Could there have been potential issues uncovered by exploring the data from other systems and how it may be protected?

2. Would you consider transport security more closely related to application security, or infrastructure security? Why?

3. Are there any futher items within infrastructure security that could be considered prone to risk?

4. During the modeling exercises, were there any techniques or utilities you found to be helpful in importing the requirements?

CHAPTER 4

Operating Models

Regardless of the state of any platform—good or bad—it's important to understand what the operational investment is with respect to how that platform is supported and upgraded. There are many different areas that go into a robust support model. Ensuring that key areas are covered in that model is critical to the success of the support staff in proactively finding and fixing any issues that may arise.

Production support is just one side of a support model. Other considerations that can come into play include:

- Monitoring
- Alerting
- Telemetry
- Patching (OS and application)
- Decision trees
- Escalation paths

Typically, a support model, or operating model as it can also be called, will address the intersection of three main topic areas: people, process, and technology. These topics are also usually referenced when talking about a core definition for many different enterprise or engineering concepts, DevOps being one of those concepts. Defining these intersections, and supplementing them with the considerations previously listed, will help to establish a clear outline for support roles to follow.

It's important to note that with any concept involving those three items, balance is key. In most cases, the easiest point of that triad to gain support for and make decisions about is technology. Solving a specific technical problem with one or more technical tools is a much easier sell than getting a department of 100 software engineers, 30 quality engineers, and varying levels of management to agree on a process at all, let alone a single unified process. Roles within organizations can shift, people can become warm or

65

© Josh Garverick 2018
J. Garverick, *Migrating to Azure*, https://doi.org/10.1007/978-1-4842-3585-0_4

cold to team interactions, and keeping a consistent message among the whole group can be difficult. Having strong and focused leadership endorsing any change is critical to its success. Working with people to define the process(es) used is important not only to the engineering department, but the entire business as well.

The model you intend to outline will focus on the people, processes, and technologies that help to support the core functions of the business. Traditionally, these functions that deliver value are referred to as value streams. Not unlike a process flow, a value stream demonstrates the steps taken to provide value to the end user. Surrounding this value stream are the supporting areas that help to deliver that value. Many different incarnations of this model exist in the wild, and the one that you decide to focus on is the Operating Model Canvas,[1] shown in Figure 4-1.

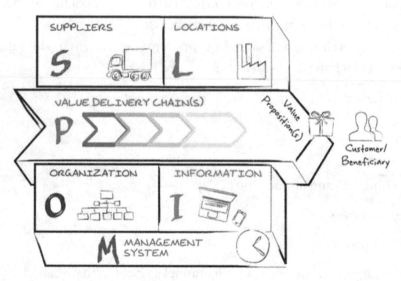

Figure 4-1. *The Operating Model Canvas*

The premise behind the canvas is that it's used to provide a high-level view of an operating model. Details around each of the supporting areas can be found in more robust documentation, but the value stream, and how it's enabled, should be clear to anyone looking at the diagram. Depending on the organization, and the number of value streams that organization provides, the number of these canvases can range from one to dozens.

---

[1]"Operating Model Canvas," Andrew Campbell, Mikel Guiterrez, Mark Lancelott; https://operatingmodelcanvas.com/

The canvas builds upon a set of core concepts that are encapsulated by the acronym POLISM. Below is an illustrative explanation of each concept.

- *Processes*: the work that needs to be done to deliver the value proposition or service proposition

- *Organization*: the people who will do the work and how they are organized

- *Locations*: where the work is done and what buildings and assets are needed in these locations

- *Information*: the information systems that support the work

- *Suppliers*: what organizations provide inputs to the work and what sort of relationships exist with these organizations

- *Management systems*: the planning, budgeting, performance management, risk management, continuous improvement, and people management processes needed to run the organization

When trying to capture or discover what operating models may exist within an organization, it may make sense to start by identifying who the customers are intended to be as well as what the value propositions are that help cater to these customers. From there, identifying the processes makes the most logical sense. After documenting the processes, the other areas can be populated in any order.

Documenting the Existing Support Model

In looking through your existing model and through Archi itself, you don't see anything by way of viewpoint that will capture the canvas approach. However, when trying to add a new view, you notice there is an item that allows you to create a blank canvas, and one that allows you to create a canvas from a predefined template. You decide to create a basic block diagram that is representative of the Operating Model Canvas and its areas. You save the canvas as a template and categorize it under Enterprise Architecture templates. Now, you will be able to create new canvases and maintain the general flow and aesthetics of the template.

As a starting point, you feel it makes more sense to look at capturing the baseline operating model for all of Andromeda. Illustrating the higher level concepts and delivery mechanisms will allow for a better topical transition once more concentrated canvases are created. You touch base with the management team and inquire about Andromeda's mission statement, vision, and value proposition. They direct you to the company's internal website, which lists out the mission and vision prominently on the homepage.

The mission statement posted on the homepage reads:

> *Our mission at Andromeda Games is to provide the best selection of sports memorabilia and gaming merchandise at the best prices through exemplary customer service.*

The vision statement is as follows:

> *We envision the perpetuation of Andromeda's success being attained by leveraging exemplary customer service and continued dedication to the community through the expansion of our services to as many customers as possible.*

The mission statement is clear, concise, and can be easily adapted into a value proposition that intends to serve the customers of Andromeda Games in the purest sense. You take the mission statement shown on the website and translate that into a value proposition to be used as the focal point of the baseline operating model.

Sketching out the Process

Next, you shift your focus to the value stream that can support this proposition. The entry point into that stream starts with the procurement process—purchasing, grooming suppliers and vendors, and coordinating shipments can all fall into this task. Once merchandise is procured, specialists will browse various sources to determine the best market price for each item. Once an item is priced, an image of that item is captured through a digital camera and an asset pack (including the item) is sent to the inventory team. The inventory team looks to see if the item already exists in the system and if it does, the total item count is incremented by one via entering a pending inventory adjustment into the inventory management system. If it does not exist, a new inventory addition is created, which will require the inventory team to upload the picture to the system, enter the relevant details from the asset pack, and mark the item as ready for stock but not generally available for purchase. Depending on the information captured in the asset pack, the item could then be sent to the warehouse for stocking or to the store delivery bin if demand for that item has been recorded at a specific location. Upon arrival at the store, sales associates scan the item to record its new stock location. Finally, as customers come into the store or browse online for merchandise, orders are collated and sales associates tend to the customers' needs. A simple rendering of this flow would look like:

Procurement ➤ *Pricing* ➤ *Inventory* ➤ *Stocking* ➤ *Customer Service* ➤ *Order Fulfillment*

Documenting the Suppliers

Now that the value stream is sketched out, you move onto determining the supporting areas for the canvas. In talking with the business operations folks, you get a general sense of the outlets they use to procure merchandise. In some cases, specific vendors are used and in others, more general intake methods are used. For example, the purchasing lead made mention of two specific vendors that Andromeda orders from:

- Sports Memorabilia, Inc. for sporting goods, autographed memorabilia, and collectible cards

- Wizards of the Coast for trading card game (TCG)-related cards, materials, promotional items, and prerelease event packs

You ask if there are other ways for inventory to come in, and you also learn that customers will come in and attempt to sell TCG or memorabilia items to the store. There is also an involved set of metrics used to determine if there are items selling from certain stores, and online retailers such as eBay or Amazon could be used to get hard-to-find items in a pinch to help satisfy the demand. You make note of these different suppliers in the Suppliers area of the canvas and move onto the next area.

Lighting up the Locations

The Locations area of the canvas seems straightforward. You have already identified that there is a main office (inclusive of the warehouse), and two store locations. You think about any other ancillary locations that could potentially come into play. Is there any location outside of the ones you've identified? Are there any offsite cold storage locations that might house overstock? A quick conversation with the warehouse manager confirms that there are no additional satellite locations that Andromeda manages. You notate the Locations area of the canvas with the locations you're aware of and move on to the Organization area.

Organizing the Organizational Structure

Being that the value stream covers many different facets of the business, you begin the Organization area with some general assumptions around whom the major players are. Obviously, the IT operations staff plays a role, as do the sales associates, managers, and back-office staff. You begin listing out different functional areas of staff that could have an impact on delivering the value proposition. Your first pass covers:

- Technology
  - IT operations
  - Software development
  - Technical support
- Business operations
  - Regional managers
  - Store managers
  - Sales associates
- Back-office or enterprise operations
  - Finance
  - HR
  - Procurement
  - Warehousing
  - Senior leadership

Through some validation with business and technology stakeholders, you confirm your assumptions and notate those org structures in the Organization area of the canvas.

Inventorying the Information Systems

Information systems are likely one of the easier areas for you to work with, since you've classified a great deal of them during the discovery phase. Starting with the obvious, you notate the inventory system, retail point of sale (POS) platform, and procurement system as primary players in this area of the canvas. However, the online portal—the gateway to Cardstock—could also be seen as a system that participates here since it does actively query the inventory system and allow customers to place orders for in-store pickup. Could there also be other enterprise systems that come into play as well? Pricing has a direct impact on finances, and it stands to reason that the finance system could also be seen as a support.

Personnel management is also important to meeting the goal of delivering value, since having an engaged and enthusiastic workforce is critical when seeking to provide the highest level of customer service possible. Tracking hours, goals, development plans, and more all factor into maintaining a healthy workforce. You pencil in HR systems, inclusive of timekeeping, performance management, and discipline management.

Managing Metrics and the System of Management

What controls exist for measuring, monitoring, and improving on the delivery of value to customers? One methodology would be the establishment of (and tracking to) key performance indicators (KPIs) for the business. These can vary by industry, but typically they involve metrics like sales numbers, customer ratings, employee engagement, and so on. Analytics also play a large role in helping to determine what course(s) of action may need to be taken, from simple aspects like inventory reports to more complex areas like stock demand and rotation analysis.

Andromeda does use some standard KPIs regarding sales numbers, loss prevention, inventory rotation, and customer satisfaction. It also employs the use of a "secret shopper," someone who is hired by the company to shop at physical store locations and report back on the level of service. This method of collecting feedback is particularly useful because store associates do not know who or when the shopper will visit, therefore instilling a higher level of consistency with the service levels provided. Customers are also encouraged to provide feedback to the company through feedback boxes in each store location as well as feedback areas on the main portal and within Cardstock.

With the main areas of the model filling in with some detail, you end up with a baseline model similar to Figure 4-2.

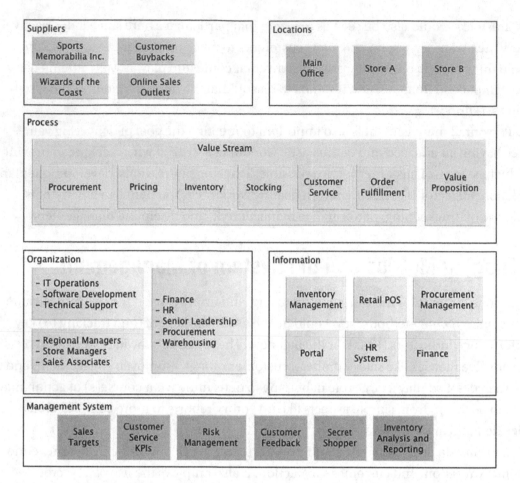

Figure 4-2. *Andromeda's baseline operating model (high level)*

EXERCISE : OPERATING MODEL OVERVIEW FOR CARDSTOCK

In this exercise, you will tackle cataloging the baseline operating model as it relates to the Cardstock platform. To kick things off, you send a note over to the engineering staff asking them to define what their idea of Cardstock is—meaning, what kind of mission statement or purpose does the platform exist for. The common theme that you're able to extract from each response is easily captured using the following value proposition:

"Our goal is to build and deliver a platform in which customers and gaming community members can interact with each other through conversation, trades, and online ordering."

Using the POLISM structure outlined in this chapter and the canvas template found in the downloads section on the operating model canvas, take some time to reflect on what value stream(s) could relate to the value proposition, based on feedback provided by the engineers. Some questions to keep in mind during this reflection:

- What possible suppliers could be involved in the delivery of value?

- Could locations outside of the main office be considered important to the delivery of value?

- What types of information systems would be involved? Are there systems that are not particularly customer-facing that could still play a part in delivery?

- Would any of the bullet points listed at the beginning of the chapter be considerations for the management system section?

Be sure to check the Views section of the model for a sample of what the baseline plan for Cardstock might look like.

Having gotten your feet wet with two operating models, it's time to use those models and further define the support structures, procedures, and tools that will fortify the business. You use the operating model for Cardstock and start in on the details.

Zeroing in on Baseline Details

It's clear after talking with the developers that they do have some procedures for managing the maintenance of the platform. It's also clear that the IT operations team has procedures for maintaining the physical and virtual servers that the organization uses. While not formally written down, these pseudo runbooks are implanted in the minds and calendars of those who run them.

Note A runbook is a set of instructions tailored to a specific task or process that can be followed by an operator, technician, or engineer with reliable and consistent results. This may include day-to-day operations as well as edge cases, such as emergency maintenance.

From the operations side, there are a few standing tasks that occur every month. For starters, the team looks at incoming OS patches and determines whether they need to be applied to the server inventory that Andromeda has. They also receive updates from vendors, such as the POS system, which need to be applied to ensure the business is functional. There are times when the team has to interact with the Internet service provider to upgrade service, ensure quality of service (QoS) for critical business technology, or troubleshoot connectivity issues. For monitoring physical and virtual machines, the team uses Nagios to monitor everything and keep an eye on usage thresholds. All of these areas come with troubleshooting and general maintenance tasks as required.

On the development side, the team is on a regular cadence with releasing patches and updates, following a loose software development life cycle. They also leverage the Nagios installation for monitoring application servers, but additionally incorporate application monitoring via New Relic. While they don't receive updates to firmware or hardware, there are times when components need to be upgraded and doing so could have a nontrivial impact on the platform. Coordinating these changes ties into the update cadence in most cases. Sometimes updates to components are released addressing security concerns, and those require a special amount of attention to ensure everything is on the level. Notifications of these updates can be sporadic, though, as the team does not have a standard method of receiving these updates, instead relying on senior developers to check on components' support pages periodically.

You've already uncovered a few steady-state candidates for runbooks just through talking with each team about business as usual activities. As outlined at the start of the chapter, patching was one of the primary support activities that you wanted to make sure was covered. Monitoring was another area of interest. You decide to take the list of activities you've received from IT operations and come up with the following generalized processes that would encapsulate the tasks they listed:

- Physical and virtual OS patching cycles

- Applying vendor updates

- POS troubleshooting

- Networking, QoS, and telco

- Monitoring platform setup

While not inclusive of all possible processes, this gives you a good starting point for understanding where the IT staff is at with respect to processes that support the

Cardstock platform. From the development side, the patching and monitoring guides are portable enough to be used by the IT or engineering team. There are several other processes that are dev-specific, and you catalog those as candidates for development runbooks:

- Andromeda Portal troubleshooting guide

- Cardstock troubleshooting guide

  - Trading platform guide

  - Forums guide

  - Friend gateway guide

- Andromeda inventory management system Guide

- Scheduling interface guide

Through more conversations with both teams, you start to gather some details about what each of these guides might be composed of. While monitoring and maintenance are definitely covered, alerting and action on those alerts are not completely covered on all fronts. The business-critical functions are covered by the IT operations team, but not as much urgency is placed on the development side because there is no established development operations team. What happens if something goes drastically wrong in the middle of the night? Who gets notified? Is there a clear path to ensure the appropriate party is notified? Clear escalation paths are a requirement to ensure all critical functions can be addressed in a timely manner.

Tracing the Escalation Paths

In most support-based organizations, having a matrix of responsible individuals who can field, triage, and fix issues is essential. There are certainly times when talking about the dreaded "on-call rotation" can cause serious consternation with staff, depending on the team size, the complexity of devices and applications, and frequency of problems. Areas deemed critical to the business should garner special attention and often include off-hours support initiatives. Having appropriate coverage on some sort of rotation is important to ensure that folks are not over-utilized and that the needs of the business are being met.

SIDEBAR: BUSINESS CONTINUITY

A paramount component of any operating model is the understanding of business continuity. Having a solid strategy for keeping resources available and performing optimally will keep stakeholders and customers happy. In many instances, the terms business continuity and disaster recovery are used within the same sentence, and at times can appear to be synonymous. Disaster recovery, though, is the act of maintaining business continuity in the event of a catastrophic datacenter failure. Business continuity itself is ensuring the operation can continue to function if resources are temporarily unavailable. Having a disaster recovery plan is a part of having an overall business continuity plan. Defining what processes and resources are mission critical will help you to put together a proper continuity plan. Understanding what locations are used for primary and secondary datacenter operations will help you to put together a proper disaster recovery plan.

As mentioned earlier, there is a structure in place for the IT operations team. They utilize a traditional three-tier model for support, where the members of the team take turns rotating into level one support. All of the operations staff has company-supplied phones and alerts are pushed to those devices via phone call. If no one answers the initial call, the IT operations manager gets a call. If he does not respond, the regional store manager or the business operations manager gets a call. At this point, the escalation path has been exhausted.

Also, as mentioned earlier, the developers do not have a strict on-call model. They do monitor emails and some alerts while in the office, but after-hours support is not a constant. If they happen to be releasing code and something comes in that they can action, they will take care of it, but the rarity of a production issue being raised via a user, stakeholder, or alert during the same timeframe as a release has not played out for the team up to this point.

Gamecorp's policies for on-call support and escalation policies require all IT operations and developers to support the applications and platforms they work on. Within each team there is a rotation where one person is a primary contact and one is a secondary contact. If both of those do not respond to the call-out, their team lead is notified. If the team lead does not respond, the next call goes to the engineering manager responsible for that team. Given the inconsistency with who responds to support incidents, you note that there needs to be a discussion with Andromeda's stakeholders to discuss the Gamecorp policy and what impact that may have on the development staff.

Collating the Baseline and Target Models

Stitching together the details from your conversations and discovery are not as difficult as trying to draft the target state, especially since you are not completely sure what types of tools and components will be selected to assist in supporting the model. You keep your focus on recording everything you have amassed, understanding that the target model will be a work in progress throughout the design (and likely implementation) of this migration project.

Baseline Operating Model—Andromeda

You begin putting together the pieces that you have collected thus far and have enough in writing to help form the baseline operating model. You understand that it's probably not complete, but the detail you've gathered is more than what was documented before. Using the Gamecorp document template, you adapt it for use with operating models. You then compile the information you have into the model description, making sure to call out each of the runbooks required, the escalation paths for support, the processes used, and all supporting information around the baseline model. Please refer to the reference material included in the downloadable content in the folder for this chapter.

Baseline Operating Model—Gamecorp

The baseline operating model for Gamecorp is a bit more present than the loose collection of policies that Andromeda has. That being said, there are still plenty of areas in which undocumented knowledge about systems, processes, and troubleshooting techniques exists. The core business operating model as it relates to the retail operations is housed in what's called the "ops binder"—a three-ring binder full of photocopied pages that include instructions on how to operate registers, perform in-store and intra-store actions, and what to do in the event of emergencies such as power outages, major storms, even store robbery attempts. The procedures for Gamecorp IT staff, on the other hand, are less organized. In the corporate office, many of the IT and engineering personnel have various Post-It notes with passwords, key sequences, or home phone numbers written on them and stuck to any surface available. Software engineers, as well as IT professionals, are required to support production systems on a rotational basis, and the company utilizes software to manage the notification process when alerts are triggered. While very few diagrams seem to exist for the process flows or escalation policies, you are able to find documents around the procedures for emergency hardware and software maintenance, the ticketing system (used to control and track changes), controls for the datacenter operations, the written flow for level 1/2/3 issues raised within the ticketing system, and some documentation regarding the Gamecorp inventory management system. All of the relevant Gamecorp documents can be found in the downloadable content for this chapter, with many of the main topics being covered at a high level in the sections below.

Beginning the Target Operating Model

At first glance, it seems straightforward that one gap between baseline for Andromeda and the baseline for Gamecorp is the support model for development. Another is the lack of documentation for each of the runbooks that you outlined earlier. You start to add placeholders for integration areas that may crop up due to the use of cloud platform components. In addition, you also find some existing Gamecorp processes that all enterprise development teams follow. Lining up the existing Gamecorp processes with Andromeda's processes (or lack thereof) will also help further identify any gaps that can be addressed.

On-Call Rotation

Invariably, during the course of an application's lifetime, problems will occur. The application may crash during the course of normal use (or stressed use), and someone will need to be available to troubleshoot and fix the issue. Depending on when workloads are run, some of these issues may occur during non-working hours. Having a support staff available to field calls when issues surface is important for keeping customers happy and upholding the integrity of the brand. Planning for that support staff is a critical part of establishing a solid escalation path in the event of such an issue or event.

For a reliable support structure, establishing a rotation for staff so that no one person gets overloaded with off-hours calls is essential to spreading the responsibility and preserving the mental well-being of those involved in support operations. There should also be a depth chart of sorts to go along with each rotation, allowing for one or more secondary contacts in the event that the primary contact is not available.

Communication is another essential part of a well-functioning support plan. From the mechanism used for sending out initial notifications to responders to the policy on the requirements for on-call support, a primary goal needs to be ensuring everyone impacted is aware of the availability of the support structure and the rules of engagement. Furthermore, outlining roles and responsibilities for all parties will help to set expectations and define structure.

The Andromeda team relies very heavily on two senior engineers who seem to be on call perpetually. While there are not loads of after-hours issues, you hear from them that it does take its toll, especially with the knowledge that something could cause them to get called. Sometimes those call-outs require them to call the IT staff, who are not as responsive as the engineers would like. With Gamecorp, the software engineers are generally the second or third line of defense. Identifying the comparable resources within Gamecorp for the Andromeda team to rely on will be an important first step in transitioning to a more self-service model.

Site Reliability Outreach

Some organizations operate with a more traditional operations department, responsible for watching and reacting to infrastructure and application alerts, acting as the first line of defense against larger application and platform problems. In recent years, a newer approach has started to take hold where traditional datacenter operations teams are transitioning into distributed and embedded teams responsible for less generalized efforts and more specific actions relative to an online application or platform. These teams have come to be known as site reliability teams—ensuring the site (typically a website) is operational, available, and reliable.

The term "site reliability engineer" originated with Google, where software engineers were hired to help solve IT operations problems. In an interview with Google VP of Engineering Ben Treynor (`https://landing.google.com/sre/interview/ben-treynor.html`), he talks about the responsibilities of site reliability engineers including "availability, latency, performance, efficiency, change management, monitoring, emergency response, and capacity planning." For many organizations, having all of these capabilities can be a challenge, let alone having one team that can handle them all. Depending on need, certain responsibilities can be sent to other standalone teams (change management, for example). The goal, however, is to automate as many of these responsibilities as possible, establishing reliability in their execution. Other areas, such as change management, can then be incorporated into software platforms that are able to manage the workflow, compilation, and deployment of applications.

Andromeda's engineers tend to fulfill multiple roles, site reliability being one of them. Gamecorp's engineering teams have specialized datacenter teams they can lean on as well as embedded resources in each application team that can work in the capacity of site reliability.

Standardized Response

Having a standard method for the intake, triage, and resolution of issues can greatly streamline any support effort. Equally as important is the notion that a logical, well-defined structure for escalation should be in place to facilitate issue resolution. As discussed earlier in this chapter, Gamecorp uses a three-tier model for responding to outages and issues. The intake process is triggered when an event occurs, whether that is via an alert, user-submitted ticket, call-in from a customer, or vendor reporting an issue. Alerts are triggered based on several points, including application-driven errors, performance metrics, standard up/down monitoring of servers, and drive space limits being reached. Figure 4-3 illustrates the intake, triage, and escalation points for any inbound issue.

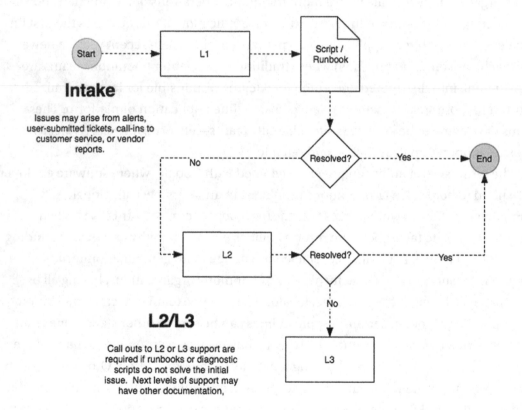

Figure 4-3. *Basic outline of Gamecorp standard L1/L2/L3 support process*

One aspect that is not immediately apparent is that of communication. During each step of the process, there is communication sent to all involved parties notifying them of where things are in the process. While most communication is handled by the ticketing system directly, other communication points are realized through direct contact with the impacted user or vendor. Contacting members of the support team is handled through the use of PagerDuty, an application that aggregates information and sends out phone calls, emails, push notifications, and/or SMS messages to members of a pre-established team.

One area that both Andromeda and Gamecorp need some additional help with is that of log aggregation. While Andromeda engineers know specifically where their logs are stored and how to access them, the Gamecorp datacenter teams have one set of logs for any infrastructure or configuration management issues, and engineers have different locations where logs can reside. Some are application logs stored on caching servers, others are stored on web servers, and some logs are recorded in application databases. Tracking down a full record of what events triggered an issue can be tough without a central way of harvesting that information. Even with a standardized response flow, it can take some time to get to the heart of what really caused an issue to bubble up.

Alert technology is a bit easier to deal with. The main tool used by the datacenter teams is SolarWinds, an enterprise monitoring platform. There are some standards put in place currently by corporate governance that require all servers to have SolarWinds agents installed as a part of the provisioning process. Engineers are responsible for monitoring their application components themselves, however. Some engineering teams have worked out deals with the datacenter teams where alerts that are triggered by the application in question will trigger an alert in SolarWinds. This has drawn some criticism from other teams, as they do not have the luxury of redirecting application errors and alerts to another team first.

There are some options for Azure-based log aggregation, alerts, and monitoring. The Operations Management Suite of products offered by Microsoft allows for the traditional up/down monitoring of resources as well as inventory management, update management (patching), and log analytics by way of log aggregation from multiple operating systems and multiple sources, including custom log ingestion. Azure Monitor also adds to these capabilities by allowing alerts to be captured centrally, and for automated resolutions to be deployed based on those alerts, using Logic Apps, Azure Automation runbooks, and more. Through prior conversations with the engineering staff and leadership, you have laid the groundwork for introducing these tools into the target operating model, allowing for some cost savings as well as a centralized platform for managing resources and applications.

Wrapping Up the Draft

You round things out by filling in the details for the approved platforms used for call-outs, monitoring, alerting, and log aggregation, knowing that more will fall into these categories with the impending migration to Azure. You leave yourself a few to-dos within the draft to make sure you address those newer platforms when getting into the target architecture, as well as a more concerted effort to fold in a structured site reliability team. You make additional notes around potential retraining for employees due to this shift in technology and responsibility, as you have already heard some rumblings of discomfort around moving to the cloud.

Note   The groundwork you have done in this chapter will be expanded upon in Chapter 12.

Summary

In this chapter, you have learned about operating models—what they are, how they are formulated, and who they help. You've also learned a methodology for creating a strawman operating model, which can be helpful during further modeling exercises. Constructing a baseline operating model for the platform and starting on the target operating model are two key achievements coming out of this chapter and will position you for success moving forward. Having gathered critical operating information regarding the steady state of Andromeda Games, you look forward to leveraging your knowledge of the Gamecorp landscape and how that can be used to sketch out a wireframe for the desired target state of the Cardstock platform.

Given the content and exercises in this chapter, consider the following questions:

1. Are there other types of industry-standard processes that could be included in the Cardstock operating model? Can the same be said for the Andromeda operating model?

2. If you were to choose between spending more time on the baseline operating model and starting to draft the target model, which would you be inclined to choose?

3. Being that there are many interpretations of what an operating model should look like, have you come across other examples of these models?

4. Are there any areas in the draft operating model that are being overlooked?

PART II

Planning for the Future

CHAPTER 5

The Wireframe

Having gathered a treasure trove of information from a variety of sources, you now feel as though you can start to look at what the rough target implementation might look like. Embarking on this journey toward a final state is something that you pursue with the understanding that approaches and technology can (and likely will) change. While looking at the nonfunctional requirements will factor into the target design, you can still spend time determining the workloads and appropriate technologies within the cloud that can handle those workloads. Given Gamecorp's up-front investment and strategic vision to embrace cloud-first development, your first stop after reviewing the current reference architecture and the roadmap for Gamecorp's retail operations will be the Microsoft Azure services catalog. Before engaging in further design activities, do a review of common cloud migration patterns as well as the existing architectural landscape that you must integrate with.

Common Migration Scenarios

In the industry, there are typically two patterns that are widely used when moving applications to the cloud. While predominant, they are not the only possible ways to move workloads. Let's take a moment to review the two common scenarios as well as some alternatives that provide additional flexibility.

Case 1: Lift and Shift

This pattern is the most commonly used pattern aside from greenfield development. The sentiment here is that you can perform a one for one move from an existing datacenter to the cloud, leveraging infrastructure as a service (IaaS) to match machines ground to cloud. Often, this approach is seen as the lowest barrier to entry when adopting cloud computing. An interesting thing to keep in mind, however, is that you will likely

© Josh Garverick 2018

J. Garverick, *Migrating to Azure*, https://doi.org/10.1007/978-1-4842-3585-0_5

have differences between your on-premises machines and your cloud machines. Some examples include:

- Memory speeds
- Processor clock speeds
- Processor family (Intel vs AMD)
- Operating system major or minor versions
- Operating system patch levels

Not all of these potential differences will be applicable based on how the shift is planned out, but these items should be taken into consideration because they can affect how application components perform. The risk associated with each difference may vary depending on how wide those gaps are.

Case 2: Greenfield

Greenfield development is everyone's natural desire—a clean slate, no major restrictions, and fresh ideas. The application components developed are also new, starting from the ground up. This approach, while enticing and exciting, can also hold its share of risks. Consider the following points:

- Overwhelming amounts of service choices
- Varying software languages, design patterns, frameworks, and build/release mechanics
- Adherence to industry security standards based on vertical (e.g., healthcare or finance)

Case 3: Hybrid

Another option for those who want to leverage cloud computing but want to ease into the transition is adopting a hybrid approach, meaning some components reside in the cloud and some reside in their existing home on-premises. This presumably lowers the risk of moving all aspects of a platform at once, but can pose challenges depending on the decisions made and components migrated. Some areas to keep in mind include:

- Acceptable network traffic routes
  - VPN over public Internet
  - Direct public Internet
  - Private intranet
- Network assets, such as
  - Internal CIDR address blocks
  - Route tables
  - Firewalls
  - Virtual IPs
  - DNS zone, A, CNAME records
- Expected versus actual latency and consistency

Case 4: Lift, Shift, and Enhance

This option assumes a slightly more adventurous approach, wherein the original concept of lift and shift is applied along with the migration of one or more components to newer platform as a service (PaaS) offerings. Depending on the application's makeup, the front-end components such as web sites, caching layer, and content delivery network could be broken out into components while the remainder of the stack can be moved as-is.

The "Baseline" Target State

Before delving into the future plans that Gamecorp has for its technical landscape, you feel a review of the existing landscape is in order. Some components of Andromeda's applications will be integrating with existing platforms, while others will be considered more isolated and therefore able to operate independently. Knowing where those boundaries lie will be important in later design sessions.

Business Architecture

At a high level, Gamecorp is a traditional hierarchical organization, with a lineup of company executives as well as cascading levels of management and employees in a variety of positions. There is also a board of directors that is responsible for shareholder expectations, since Gamecorp is a publicly traded company on the stock exchange. Major decisions about personnel, purchasing, vendor management, facility management, and more will involve some decision making from the team at the top.

A common set of operational processes are cataloged and followed throughout all locations. While not complete, there are a series of runbooks that describe most major tasks and scenarios that would occur within a large retail-based organization. The stores, distribution centers, and corporate office (mentioned in more detail in the next section) use these processes to ensure quality, customer satisfaction, efficiency, and profitability. These processes align with the National Retail Federation (NRF) ARTS business process models, though there is no requirement to map to the NRF model directly at the corporate level.

One area that does pique your interest is that of loss prevention. Andromeda has a good policy in place to remediate loss due to damage, human error, theft, and defects. Gamecorp, on the other hand, has policies, runbooks, software, and agencies that are directly involved in loss prevention and mitigation. Specific workflows exist for processing data loss, merchandise loss, intellectual property loss, and risk analysis.

Physical Architecture

Gamecorp has 145 retail stores branded as Level Up across the continental United States, and another 15 retail stores cobranded with Level Up in the United Kingdom. Many of the domestic locations are either in or around major metropolitan areas, and Gamecorp's online presence allows for shipments to any customer within the United States, including non-continental states. The locations in the UK will ship items to customers within the UK solely. Stores have the normal stock room, point of sale (POS) registers, location hardware, and network equipment that would be expected at any ordinary retail operation. For security and monitoring, the store locations use a large commercial security company, while the UK locations subcontract out to smaller scale security vendors.

The main headquarters in the United States is located just outside of Denver, Colorado and the company has 16 merchandise hubs strategically located throughout the lower 48.

There are two merchandise hubs located in the UK, with a regional headquarters located in Cambridge, England. The primary datacenter for Gamecorp's US operations is located in Omaha, Nebraska, with a secondary in Chicago. The primary datacenter for the UK is located in London, with a secondary location in Edinburgh, Scotland.

The networks in place for the domestic operations run on standard Multiprotocol Label Switching (MPLS) circuits between all locations and the primary datacenter. There is a dedicated site-to-site virtual private network (VPN) connection between the primary and secondary datacenters for replication and disaster recovery purposes. The same type of connection exists between all locations in the UK and the primary datacenter in London.

Application Architecture

There is a fairly restrictive reference architecture in place for Gamecorp's retail and distribution locations. This standard applies to all locations, domestic and international. From a customer facing perspective, any public websites where users and customers can view or purchase items are hosted via a proprietary content management platform. POS software is the same across all retail stores. Due to exceptions that were allowed during acquisition, some locations still utilize a homegrown inventory management system, while most others leverage a common inventory management system (IMS). There are varying opinions within the lines of business as to whether or not one integrated IMS would be the best option. A fairly standard set of applications in the Microsoft Office suite are used for productivity and business collaboration.

There is an application integration layer comprised of several different types of adapters, enabling the movement of information between systems internally as well as externally. Payment processing systems are points of integration with all retail stores and as such are bound to Payment Card Industry (PCI) compliance standards. There are services that can communicate between internal inventory, purchasing, human resources, and finance systems. There are more services that can move and transform data for various business functions. Another set of services deals with authentication and authorization, allowing internal and external users to perform tasks in limited or wide scopes.

For web-based applications, Internet Information Services is the preferred hosting platform. There are a handful of internal web applications that are hosted using Apache Tomcat, mainly due to the inheritance of legacy systems. The Tomcat-hosted applications are tied to the secondary inventory system that has been carried over by

Gamecorp. For caching and content deliver, Redis is the preferred option. This runs solely on Linux and ties into the OS footprint discussed in the "Technology Architecture" section later in this chapter.

Data persistence centers around Microsoft SQL Server. The preferred version of SQL Server is 2012, though several teams have begun researching 2014 as well as 2016. One group of adventurous developers have even started experimenting with SQL Server 2017 and containerization technology, though you feel this bleeding edge effort is not as relevant to your project as other more stable options.

Data Architecture

As mentioned earlier, some locations within the organization have their own inventory management systems stood up, which forces the use of a data integration layer. This layer transforms the data from the homegrown preacquisition software into a common data footprint that the majority of the company uses for inventory management. There is also a data warehouse built out that serves reporting, procurement, forecasting, and other functions.

A fair amount of data is redundant between the store locations, warehouse locations, and data centers. While sometimes inconvenient due to the requirement of having racks of data storage on-site, this redundancy provides a fail-safe mechanism during power or network outages. Typically, the data updates from a store will go back to the data center that is closest to them. If there is an outage at the store level, the data will be transmitted once the store comes back online. If there is an outage or disruption at the data center, the data can be replicated to another data center, and eventually it will become available in the primary data center. More information about the needs and performance of data synchronization and mirroring can be found in the "Technology Architecture" section following.

Technology Architecture

The physical and technical reference architecture for every Level Up retail store is identical. The same holds true for every distribution center and every corporate or regional office. A master reference architecture has been compiled by the enterprise architects and it is, while comprehensive, rather overwhelming. Every detail from printers to network cables, routers to power management devices, are all accounted for at the store, distribution center, office, and datacenter levels. Some immediately relevant specifications can be seen in Table 5-1.

Table 5-1. *Existing Core Technology Architecture Standards*

Type	Category	Supported	Recommended	Investigating
Operating Systems	Windows (Server)	Windows Server 2008 Windows Server 2008 R2 Windows Server 2012 Datacenter Windows Server 2012 R2 Datacenter	Windows Server 2012 R2 Datacenter	Windows Server 2016 Core Windows Server 2016 Datacenter
	Linux (Server)	CentOS 6.5/7.0 RedHat 7.0	RedHat 7.0	CentOS 7.3 RedHat 7.3
	Windows (Desktop)	Windows XP Windows Vista Enterprise Windows 7 Enterprise	Windows 7 Enterprise	Windows 10 Enterprise
Virtualization Infrastructure	Virtualization Platforms	VMWare ESXi 5 VMWare ESXi 6	VMWare ESXi 6	Microsoft Azure Microsoft Azure Stack VMWare ESXi 6.5
Core infrastructure	Servers – Hypervisor Hosts	Dell PowerEdge R230 Dell PowerEdge R330	Dell PowerEdge R330	Dell PowerEdge R730 Microsoft Azure
	Networking – Routers			
	Networking – Switches			
	Networking – Firewall Appliances			
	Storage – Local			
	Storage – Datacenter			

One of the more interesting aspects of the technology footprint for all locations is that of storage. At the store and distribution center level, a local storage array is used to ensure the information being recorded to the database server is consistent. This means every transaction that occurs within the inventory system is recorded at the local database level and then replicated to a secondary storage location—in this case, the local storage array. In addition, another replication target is established at the datacenter level, which serves as the source of truth for all location data.

In the event of a power outage, each store location is equipped with backup power to allow for processing orders and payments for up to eight hours. Systems will continue to stay in sync until the backup power supply is exhausted. If there is still no power at the location, associates are able to use the mobile inventory companion application to interact with the main inventory system and process payments, though the latter component is rarely used or tested.

Similarly, the distribution centers are set up with a backup power supply, and the same general duration of backup power is applicable. The difference is that if there is a general power outage that extends past eight hours, associates use manual tally sheets to verify inbound and outbound stock adjustments. These tally sheets are then entered into the system once the location comes back online.

There are also standards around human interface devices—barcode scanners, signature pads, QR code readers, and so on. There are two models of barcode scanners that are utilized, one handheld corded unit and one cordless unit. A standard signature pad and payment card interface is used at all store locations in the United States, while another standard unit is used overseas due to availability.

The technology team at Gamecorp has been able to hone its technology footprint so much, that they have a special care package for every new store. Called the SB3 (Small Box for the Big Box), this custom technology kit is shipped out to every new store that opens or is onboarded. It consists of all the necessities based on the technology reference architecture—registers, printers, scanners, payment processing equipment, employee-use computers, and the back-room rack. The back-room rack is a 12U enclosure that incorporates preconfigured Dell PowerEdge servers, patch bays, a 5U APC backup unit, and the local storage array described previously.

Security Architecture

The overall security landscape at Gamecorp is hinged on two main functions: information security and loss prevention. A brief overview of the loss prevention procedures was given earlier in this chapter. The information security team encompasses all corporate-managed information, from vendor contracts to inventory data to payment processing data to customer contact information. Any and all pieces of information are considered protected by the information security (IS) team.

Payment information is especially sensitive. Gamecorp fully supports and complies with the Payment Card Industry's Data Security Standards (PCI DSS), version 3.0. This requires a vast array of controls to be implemented in order to be compliant. Everything from disk-level encryption for data at rest, transport layer security (TLS) version 1.2 compliance as well as HTTP strict transport service enforcement (HSTS) for data in motion, and encryption/decryption algorithms for keeping data encrypted during processing. There has already been a fair amount of chatter internally around keeping these standards upheld once the company starts moving applications to the cloud.

Another area of caution for the company is around personal information stored in the various platforms tied to customer interactions. As Gamecorp has locations in US markets as well as internationally, there are great concerns that personally identifiable information is kept safe and is compliant with legislation such as the General Data Protection Regulation (GDPR), which took effect in May of 2018. Any solution that covers the storage of customer information needs to be compliant with all tenets of any legislation governing the retention, residency, and curation of data.

Closely associated with customer data is the notion of identity, and how that helps (or potentially hinders) compliance with identity protection and data risk mitigation. Gamecorp uses Active Directory along with Directory and Federation Services to ensure internal identities are up to date, and a strong implementation of role-based access control ensures separation of concern and just enough administration rights to internal users. But what about external users? External customers are able to access their identity via the main Gamecorp portal, which uses a custom identity provider tied into the portal. A long-clamored-for integration point has been that of open auth/social media for login and identity management. While on the backlog, it's something the portal team has not had much luck in prioritizing.

Deployment Architecture

Gamecorp uses Team Foundation Server for its build and work item tracking system, along with Octopus Deploy to perform deployments of code both domestically and internationally. Recently an initiative began to migrate the TFS servers, along with all history, to Azure DevOps Services. Azure DevOps Services, as an online software service provider, offers a faster cadence of feature delivery and allows teams to avoid managing and caring for on-premises servers. Gamecorp's developers use a mixture of Git and Team Foundation Version Control for their source control, with the TFVC repositories housing more of the company's legacy system source code.

Each region has its own set of build and deployment agents to provide an appropriate level of segregation between development, testing, staging, and production environments. While not required, it does give applications overseas a consistent deployment experience with those applications hosted domestically. Because the Octopus servers are deployed on Gamecorp's internal network, all existing build agents are also hosted on the internal network, otherwise publishing packages from the public hosted build agents to the internally hosted Octopus server would not work.

As a part of the Azure DevOps Services migration process, there is a plan in place to sunset Octopus in favor of Azure DevOps Services release management. Having both build and deploy managed by the same system will provide transparency into the pipeline and ensure that the same mechanics are used to compile, package and install all applications.

Reviewing the Roadmap

Through a series of project meetings, you learn that the retail operations segment is interested in onboarding Andromeda Games into the mainline systems that all other operations use and that there is a platform conversion in progress to a new POS register system. The conversion of an existing system's information into an existing Gamecorp platform is challenging enough, but on top of that you now have to manage and anticipate how this POS upgrade will impact your project.

Work Breakdown Structure

The roadmap itself is broken down into three major areas of focus: retail operations, technology operations, and development operations. A year-at-a-glance view of the major initiatives for the company can be seen in Figure 5-1.

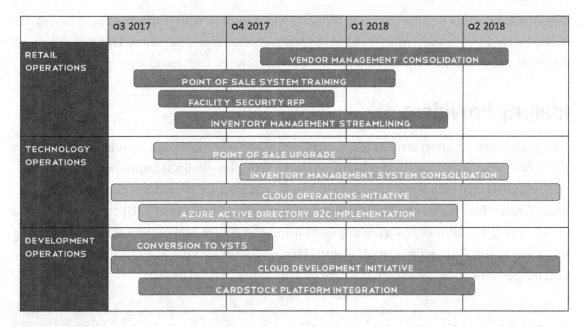

	Q3 2017	Q4 2017	Q1 2018	Q2 2018
RETAIL OPERATIONS		VENDOR MANAGEMENT CONSOLIDATION		
	POINT OF SALE SYSTEM TRAINING			
	FACILITY SECURITY RFP			
	INVENTORY MANAGEMENT STREAMLINING			
TECHNOLOGY OPERATIONS	POINT OF SALE UPGRADE			
	INVENTORY MANAGEMENT SYSTEM CONSOLIDATION			
	CLOUD OPERATIONS INITIATIVE			
	AZURE ACTIVE DIRECTORY B2C IMPLEMENTATION			
DEVELOPMENT OPERATIONS	CONVERSION TO VSTS			
	CLOUD DEVELOPMENT INITIATIVE			
	CARDSTOCK PLATFORM INTEGRATION			

Figure 5-1. *Gamecorp organzational roadmap*

You notice that there are a couple of parallel tracks that look to be mutually beneficial. The POS system training and upgrade start in an offsetting pattern, with training kicking off for pilot locations first, and the upgrade process being implemented at the pilot locations soon after. The cloud initiatives are also complimentary, with the operations and development arms of the cloud migration initiative running across the timeline. Another initiative that Gamecorp is taking very seriously is that of the consolidated identity platform via Azure Active Directory Business to Consumer (B2C). This could potentially impact application integrations depending on whether the B2C integration is deemed as mandatory or if there is a grace period for adoption.

Point of Sale Upgrades

The primary point of sale system is being moved from the in-house IBM registers to using equipment and platform services of Square. Gamecorp was able to broker a rather beneficial deal with Square to get its new POS machine, the Square Register, into its Level Up locations. The integration points with Square's central catalog allow for deeper integration with custom inventory systems, which means the existing IMS can stay in place. This does offer a bit of a wrinkle to your plans, though, as you will need to determine how this Square platform software will integrate with Andromeda's IMS and meet the requirements of folks looking to consolidate all IMS platforms. This register upgrade also involves all scanners, printers, cash drawers, and ancillary supplies.

Identity Providers

Based on outreach from stakeholders, customers, and internal users, a consolidated identity management solution is being pursued. With the planned implementation of B2C, external customers can start to bring their own identity provider with integrations from Twitter, Facebook, and Google. External business to business (B2B) customers can also leverage this identity overhaul by establishing an Azure Active Directory tenant and integrating with Gamecorp's main tenant. This allows for vendor integrations—inbound and outbound—to be established where they have not existed before.

Selecting the Right Services

The service landscape of cloud providers is one that changes often, depending on emerging technologies, market demands, and legal compliance needs. Azure is no stranger to change, and even as you read this text, you fill find that service offerings that may have been listed as being in preview are now fully available. There may be other offerings that are no longer available. Even more services could have changes made to their usage or implementation details, which can cause rework to existing infrastructure or configuration scripts.

In some cases, the selection of infrastructure components is a bit easier than platform components, as you will be looking to match machine to machine as closely as possible. Despite the potential differences listed in the first section of this chapter, selecting machines that have roughly the same surface specs as the machines currently used in production should not pose an immediate problem.

CLOUD SERVICES— GETTING STARTED

Finding resources to get you started on your cloud adventure is not terribly difficult. Sorting through those resources to find the right bits of information can be a bit difficult. Microsoft has a few different online resources that give you everything from a 101-level overview of cloud services to deep dives into patterns and practices used to solve some common problem areas.

- Azure Interactive Experiences (`http://azureinteractives.azurewebsites.net/`)

- Thought Leadership by endjin (`https://endjin.com/thought-leadership/`)

- Azure Architecture Center (`https://docs.microsoft.com/en-us/azure/architecture/`)

The choice is ultimately yours as to the level of detail and guidance that is appropriate. This is not a comprehensive list by any means, and using your own judgment and experience will guide you to the best resources.

Conducting Assessments of Options

In some cases, a component or technology selection is not straightforward. There could be one or more options that can solve a target problem, and each option can present different benefits and challenges. Outlining the problem statement along with potential options to solve that problem sounds like an easy enough task, but when faced with complex requirements or operating conditions, this can be more involved than one may think.

A good assessment of options should be comprised of the following sections:

- Description of problem/opportunity statement

- Review of key functional requirements related to the statement

- Review of key, nonfunctional requirements related to the statement

- Description and diagram of each option being presented

- Matrix with pros and cons for each option

- Final presentation matrix (heat map, categorical ratings, etc.) with proposed solution

- Next steps

Composing and delivering an assessment can take many forms. In many cases, it is most beneficial to condense the information gathered in the sections listed previously into a document or slide deck that can be easily delivered to and digested by all stakeholders.

There are a few areas of your proposed wireframe that have more than one possible solution, based on the research you've done into the service offerings that Azure has. To ensure the business has the information it needs to make an appropriate decision in each case, you list out the areas in question and start the assessment process for each one.

- Eventual (and durable) consistency for inventory information

- Current and future POS system integration

- Platform integration with social media and other OAuth identity providers

---

ASSESSMENT: INVENTORY INFORMATION CONSISTENCY

The requirement around eventual consistency for the inventory data is listed out as needing to be consistent within five to ten minutes of a transaction. A transaction, as defined by the business, could consist of a finalized purchase, an item hold based on a customer's shopping cart, a stock update when fulfillment has entered inventory into the system, a store-to-store transfer (sending or receiving), or a warehouse-to-store transfer (sending or receiving). In the case of stock transfers, the system must be consistent based on the current state of the transaction and not the intended end state. For example, a manager performing an intrastore transfer would decrement the item count for an item and that part of the transaction would have to adhere to the five- to ten-minute consistency SLA. The same would hold true for the completion of the transaction once the receiving store enters the item into stock. The nature of the SLA defined is more to set customer expectation than anything else—the majority of transactions update the data store within seconds of a transaction occurring.

As a first pass, you put together a proposal for the use of an event-driven, messaging-based integration layer that would interact with the existing Gamecorp inventory system. The idea behind creating a new integration API was to allow for greater flexibility if an instance arose where a new inventory system was introduced.

An example assessment for this exercise can be found under Assessments > Data Integrity.pptx.

ASSESSMENT: POS SYSTEM INTEGRATIONS

Knowing that a pending POS system upgrade is on the horizon, you begin to think through the various ways that an extensible API could be placed in alignment with that, or any other, system. While you do not have any direct impact over what hardware or software is selected or implemented at the store level, you do have a need to integrate with that software from an inventory management perspective. The POS project has also taken a dependency on your project to get that integration working, since the software being used by the registers will interface with the existing and soon-to-be inventory systems.

Functionally, the integration layer would need to be able to ingest the information from the new point of sale software (in this case, Square), the existing Gamecorp inventory system, and the data warehouse.

An example assessment for this exercise can be found under Assessments > POS Integrations.pptx.

ASSESSMENT: IDENTITY MANAGEMENT INTEGRATIONS

The use of, and integration with, external identity providers is a technical use case that has gained a lot of momentum over the past few years, and shows no signs of slowing down from a popularity or adoption perspective. Having the ability to use an existing identity that you own and control as the point of authentication into another system is an attractive option for many users. Fewer passwords to manage, more integration points, and ease of use are all seen as benefits to users with portable identity management providers. While not trivial, social media and other portable identity solutions are easier to integrate than ever before, and in some cases consumers expect companies to offer authentication into an app or website through one of these methods.

The platform authentication for Cardstock is a homegrown derivation of the ASP.NET Membership provider. The developers at Andromeda have been working toward standing up IdentityServer, an open source identity and token management system. The implementation has not yet been kicked off, but there is a sense that it should be the preferred approach for upgrading the user authentication experience. You have voiced some concerns over this approach, as it has the potential to duplicate work that is already occurring with Gamecorp's implementation of B2C, and it also introduces extra ownership cost in having to maintain the servers on which the solution is deployed.

An example assessment for this exercise can be found under `Assessments >`
`Identity Management.pptx`.

Reviewing Assessments with Stakeholders

A critical piece to conducting and compiling an assessment of options is the delivery of
that assessment to the stakeholders who will ultimately benefit from that assessment.
These stakeholders also hold the approval power for your proposals, so ensuring
that everyone clearly understands the information being presented is of tantamount
importance. There will be situations where the outcome of an assessment (the
suggested solution) will not be accepted, and another solution will be selected instead.
Anticipating cases like this, you should aim to present solutions to stakeholders that you
want them to approve. Even the riskier, more expensive options should be tailored to
achieve the overall goal and should not be extraordinarily painful to adopt or implement.

Another important aspect of reviewing an assessment is to carefully consider your
audience. The amount of information contained in a single assessment of options
could potentially be overwhelming to nontechnical stakeholders. Conversely, there will
be stakeholders who are very technical and will require more information about the
composition and implementation of your proposed solutions. It may be more beneficial
to have two separate presentations: one meant for a general audience and one meant
for a technical audience. Keeping everyone's attention while presenting this type of
information can be challenging, and being selective about the information used can
assist in delivering a concise message.

You schedule three meetings to cover the assessments you've conducted with
the stakeholders who will be impacted. As these solutions involve staff from both
Andromeda and Gamecorp, you decide to present a business-focused approach to each
assessment and supplement that presentation with technical data sheets. Taking this
approach should afford you the opportunity to move through the presentation with few
interruptions and still offer technology-minded individuals the information they will be
interested in.

The first session you present is the assessment of possible POS integration options.
You've already uncovered the integration points that Andromeda leverages to talk to its
own inventory system, and through the documentation from the Square Connect site,
you also have the general interface for communicating with the catalog used on the back
end by Square products.

Going Through Peer Review

With your assessments complete and presented to the business, you are now ready to compile the blueprint of your proposed solution. Once that compilation is complete, you are required by company policy to go before an architectural review board to ensure there are no technology choices or pattern implementations that would deviate from Gamecorp's reference architecture or expose the company to outside risk. Preparation for this step is key, as there have been times when colleagues of yours have gone through review and had to re-do their approach completely. Between the work done to prepare the assessments and the amount of mapping you have attempted to perform between Gamecorp's standards and the desired end state, you approach the peer review with cautious optimism.

Note   While not every company has a full architecture staff or mandates a peer review of design, it is always a good idea to get input on your design from peers. The more variety of experience those peers have, the greater the chance of receiving valuable and actionable feedback.

After reviewing the work you've done, the peer review group informs you that some things have changed with respect to the requirements around diagramming and, more specifically, modeling. Technical leadership has decided that the Archimate framework is not something they will be moving forward with, as consensus is that maintaining metamodels at that scale would be insurmountable. While the information you captured is very good, it will likely not be used aside from you and possibly your team. Leadership has also decided to go a different direction with diagramming and has picked up the open-use program Draw.IO, which offers a desktop and web interface. You will not have to recreate the diagrams done in Archi, but new diagrams will need to be done using the approved interface.

You find this to be very disappointing, given the amount of effort spent to put together the details behind this view of Andromeda Games. You know that no guidelines were given to you regarding what program should be used to capture the project details, and you had conversations with your supervisor about the use of Archimate and the benefits you could see with a larger implementation of the framework.

From an architectural perspective, the blueprint you presented for the platform stood up to the questions asked by the review committee. Your choices along with the backup information shown via the assessments you completed helped the review committee to understand what decisions were made, and how they were arrived at. An example of an architectural blueprint can be found in the downloaded content, specifically under `Assessments > Blueprint.pptx`.

Summary

In this chapter, you have gone through a variety of exercises meant to identify where your project lines up with the overall goals that Gamecorp is interested in over the next few quarters. You have reviewed common cloud platform migration scenarios, the existing landscape of architectural components, timelines and roadmap items, cloud service catalogs, and use cases for common components, identifying and performing assessments of options to determine the best approach for a problem, going through and processing peer review and iterative approaches to updating the target state's initial design. As you have likely surmised, this will only be the first of many such iterative sessions you encounter, with developing the final target architecture being the end goal. Designing appropriate and attainable transition architectures is just as important as designing the most effective end state possible. Next, you look forward to digging into more options and information surrounding capacity for all of the platform components.

Considering the content you've covered in this chapter, please reflect on the following questions.

1. Given the approach that was selected for the migration strategy, and the potential complications that may arise, have all of the risks introduced by this selection been mitigated? Would another approach have been more appropriate for the platform migration?

2. Were there any areas you found to be lacking detail in the review of the Gamecorp architecture landscape? If so, what would you have wanted to have information about? How would you go about obtaining that information?

3. During the initial cloud service catalog review, is it more important to select components that are appropriate to use and are cost-effective? Does (or should) developer adoption factor into this decision? Should operational support also be considered?

4. Do you feel that the assessment process undertaken is too formal, or not formal enough? How would you approach documenting and analyzing the requirements for each assessment performed?

5. Is there a way in which you could get away from having different "versions" of the same information for different audiences? Is the reason for tailoring the message to stakeholders more of a preference or a necessity?

6. Reflect on some of your experiences with peer review sessions and/or architectural review board sessions. Are there examples that come to mind of good, constructive feedback that helped shape your path forward? Can you think of examples where feedback or review sessions did not go as planned? If so, how did you adjust or compensate for the outcome?

CHAPTER 6

Capacity Planning

The process of capacity planning takes on many meanings, given the lens you're looking through. As a part of the larger solution analysis, planning for system usage and growth covers more than the mainstays of database storage and application expansion. Capacity can relate to network usage, application components (and their limitations), satisfaction of nonfunctional requirements, even infrastructure composition and scaling. There will be two main questions that should be asked of each capacity planning area throughout this chapter:

- Are there any limitations to the approach or component being considered (cost, time, max connections per second, etc.)?
- Can this approach be scaled out to meet regional needs, and scaled up to meet baseline usability requirements?

Tip Knowing your limitations is essential when planning, testing, or implementing any solution in the cloud. See `https://docs.microsoft.com/en-us/azure/ azure-subscription-service-limits` for more information on what you can (and can't) do with cloud components in Azure. Keep this link handy as you move through each of the exercises in this chapter.

Network Architecture

The physical networking layer is one that fortunately you don't have to be too worried about. In the existing datacenters, the technology team is responsible for ensuring that everything is wired appropriately, that every device has electricity, and that raw data streams are able to travel into, within, and out of each datacenter. Compliance with telecomm standards, electrical standards, and any other physical construction standards

© Josh Garverick 2018
J. Garverick, *Migrating to Azure*, https://doi.org/10.1007/978-1-4842-3585-0_6

are all taken into account through this team in conjunction with vendors and outside contractors.

With transitioning to Azure, these concerns do still come into play, but are not in scope for the type of change you are looking to make. Understanding the target state of these connections does impact how your application will run in relation to others within the organization. For example, the makeup of the network circuits from Gamecorp's datacenters to the ExpressRoute entry points determines how much available bandwidth exists. If those circuits are too small, traffic from ground to cloud and back again will be adversely impacted. If they are too large, they may be underutilized and would incur additional maintenance and usage charges, some of which could be significant.

Laying the Groundwork

The network layer is the culmination of the physical pipes that allow raw data bits to be passed from place to place with the interfaces that determine unique MAC addresses to form a network of cables, routers, switches, and network cards that all behave as one collective.

Figure 6-1 shows a representation of how customers can connect to various Microsoft resources through methods such as peering. The sections that follow will describe what those methods entail, as well as things to consider when choosing what method(s) to use.

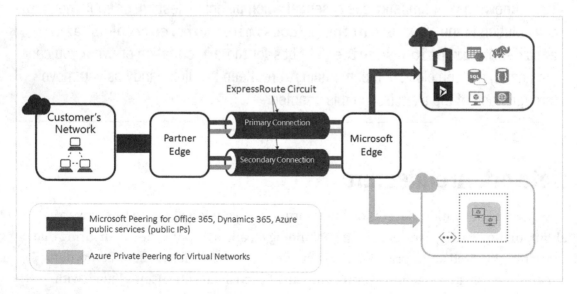

Figure 6-1. *Microsoft ExpressRoute connectivity example*

Network Peering

Network peering refers to the practice of directing traffic over a specific network circuit in order to maintain a dedicated connection to select resources. There are three types of peering that come into play when looking to connect with Azure-related resources:

- *Public peering*: This peering type allows for direct connections to public resources and address spaces (typically platform-as-a-service components) over an established and dedicated circuit.

- *Private peering*: This peering type allows for direct connections to private resources and address spaces over an established and dedicated circuit.

- *Microsoft peering*: This peering type allows for direct connections to software-as-a-service offerings from Microsoft, such as Office 365, Azure DevOps Services, Dynamics 365, and more.

When talking with your network architect, you learn that there are certain circumstances where peering connections are beneficial and others where a direct over-the-Internet connection is more beneficial. For example, peering can help when traffic needs to absolutely follow a known and secure path. An unanticipated side effect of that can be seen in latency, especially if the circuits connecting the datacenter and the ExpressRoute connection point are not big enough. He also mentioned that the peering options selected (private and public) were selected to offer connections to Azure-based assets, with an interest in looking into Microsoft peering further down the road, should corporate consumption of those services increase.

ExpressRoute, the Backplane, and the Edge

As seen in Figure 6-1, ExpressRoute in concept is a paired connection between a partner provider's network and Microsoft's internal datacenter networks, often referred to as the backplane. On either side of that paired connection is what's known as the edge—sets of routers that will direct traffic to or from specified locations. Think of edge routers as the border crossing plazas between countries. There are typically lanes for traffic to go through, and each lane has a checkpoint where a government official will ask where you're coming from (origin), what the nature of your visit is, how long you will be visiting, and where you will be going (destination). In addition to gathering that information about an incoming connection, the edge routers will direct the traffic over the ExpressRoute network connection to the Microsoft edge routers, where a similar validation and exchange will occur. From the Microsoft edge routers, traffic is directed to its final destination.

A common misconception is that a connection to ExpressRoute is a fastlane to the cloud, with gigabit transfer speeds and lightning-fast response times. While that type of result can be attained, it is often at a considerable cost to the company implementing that connection. A requirement for accessing the ExpressRoute circuit is that a business works with a partner provider to establish a dedicated network circuit between the wide area network of the business and the partner provider's edge routers. From there, the traffic routing can be done with the components previously mentioned. Not planning for additional network traffic and selecting smaller bandwidth pipes from your business to the provider's routers can hamstring you later if there is any expectation of reduced latency, especially in hybrid workflow scenarios where cloud and on-premises machines are involved in performing work that requires a near-time response rate.

DEMYSTIFYING CONNECTION TYPES

At its core, networking is a fairly simple concept—one location can connect to another through a series of different equipment, such as routers, switches, cables, or wireless access points. We are used to being connected to some sort of network wherever we go in today's world. When it comes to connecting large networks of assets together, however, there are a few standard ways in which those connections can be made, such as virtual private networks (VPNs) and virtual network to virtual network. The addition of concepts such as ExpressRoute can help complicate those connection types. Let's take a moment to explore these connection types in relation to how they work with Azure hybrid traffic scenarios:

- *Colocated at Cloud Exchange*: This option connects to the cloud via a shared virtual cross-connection with an existing cloud exchange, meaning a shared connection with other consumers. A Layer 2 cross-connection or managed Layer 3 cross-connection can be utilized in this model.

- *Point-to-Point VPN*: This option connects the cloud to a single location or datacenter. Traffic is managed via Layer 2 connections or Layer 3 connections.

- *Any-to-Any VPN (IPVPN)*: This option connects a corporate wide area network (WAN) to an Azure location or locations. In this model, Azure will appear to be an extension of your core network, with resources created in Azure taking on the same characteristics as resources created within core network segments. Traffic is managed using managed Layer 3 connections, typically over MPLS circuits offered by IPVPN providers.

For more information about ExpressRoute connection types, see `https://docs.microsoft.com/en-us/azure/expressroute/expressroute-connectivity-models`.

Peering Routes and Custom Routes

Route tables are another construct that allow for the definition of advertised network routes—that is, a description of the next logical location in a network that traffic should flow to, given its advertised destination. Normally when accessing Azure components in a nonwork setting, your traffic goes over the public Internet. The route tables associated with connections to Azure specify that traffic with a destination of a public Azure IP will be directed to the edge router associated with that resource from the egress point on your Internet provider's network. While a more direct connection, it can vary in speed and saturation due to the provider's bandwidth allocations, contractual throttling, number of users on the network, and other technical factors.

Ingress Points and Load Balancing

Choosing the right type of load balancer for your use case can mean the difference between simple routing and complex algorithmic routing. There are three main components available to you in Azure, each with different requirements and use cases.

- *Application Gateway*: The Application Gateway can handle simple round-robin distribution of TCP traffic akin to Layer 4, along with more complex routing algorithms depending on need. The benefit to using an App Gateway comes via the configuration aspects. You can configure a web application firewall with little effort. You can offload SSL certificates at the App Gateway, as you can with any physical or virtual load balancer appliance. Network address translation, custom routes, and scalable throughput instances can be leveraged as well.

You can map specific, fully qualified domain names to an App Gateway, with a hard cap of 20 per gateway. This does not include the mapping of root domains and does not accept wildcards in those mappings. You can upload wildcard SSL certificates to the gateway, however.

- *Azure Load Balancer*: The Azure Load Balancer is another software-defined networking construct that truly caters to protocol-level routing only. Simple functionality like network address translation (NAT), front-end IP address configuration, back-end pool configuration, and health probes all exist with the Azure LB. This component can be used for internal or external load balancing but does not support SSL offload or complex routing definitions. You can, however, map a root domain to the front-end IP address via DNS records, should you need to.

- *Third-Party Virtual Appliances*: These come in many different sizes, supplied by several vendors. Some examples of vendors in the Azure Marketplace who offer virtual firewall appliances include Checkpoint, F5, NetScaler, Kemp, and Barracuda. Some of these offerings also fall into the realm of what is known as a next-generation firewall, covering additional security concerns such as packet inspection, intrusion monitoring and detection, as well as settings to establish quality of service for network throughput to critical functionality and platform components.

EXERCISE: NETWORK LAYOUT

Having reviewed the various network components that Azure has to offer, you are now tasked with coming up with a capacity plan for the networking aspect of the platform, inclusive of the portal. Gathering information from Gamecorp's infrastructure engineers, you have a good overall idea of where the existing networks are and what they are composed of. Given your involvement in the security assessment, you also know that constructing a PCI compliant network reference is essential. Using the reference architecture provided by your contacts in infrastructure, you start to piece together the shell of your new network.

Please answer the following questions using the materials supplied in the downloaded content as well as the preceding text. Any source code or other supplementary material referenced by the author in this book is available to readers on GitHub via the book's product page, located at `www.apress.com/9781484235843`. For more detailed information, please visit `www.apress.com/source-code`.

- You notice that the network on which the existing CMS installation resides is abundant with free IP space but caps out at 250 total addresses. The datacenter networks are provisioned in a traditional DMZ and Core setup, with firewalls separating the DMZ from the Core, and the DMZ from the outside world. What would be an appropriate way to split up the network segments to minimally mirror the existing datacenter, and optimally mirror a PCI compliant network stack? What types of IP address configurations would work best to accommodate the infrastructure for Cardstock and for the portal?

- Your requirements indicate that the external web traffic is required to be encrypted, and that SSL offloading needs to be performed. You also note that peak traffic for the portal has been benchmarked at 5,000 concurrent sessions against the application while hosted in Gamecorp's primary datacenter. What routing component would best handle these requirements? How would you configure this component to be equipped to deal with traffic patterns such as these?

- The existing datacenter footprint in the United States is straightforward, as is the footprint in the UK. To mirror the existing primary/secondary circuits that are in use by Gamecorp's existing datacenters, corporate networking has set up two peering circuits for each geographic region. For the ExpressRoute circuit size, each circuit has been set up to handle 200 Mbps on each peer. Will the design by Gamecorp's network engineers support the expected throughput of the applications you are migrating? Why or why not?

Exploring Storage Options

Storage is another major area in which you spend some time. Understanding the need for storage (file systems, assets, virtual disks, tables, queues, and so forth) is critical for the existence and performance of the platform. Depending on current usage statistics and projections for future growth, weighing out the sizing as well as the locations of storage for the platform will be an important endeavor. There are several different aspects of how information is stored that will factor into your decisions.

First, you need to get a sense for the overall footprint of storage needed for the existing applications to run. This includes assessing the current file structures of the database servers, the disks on which the VMs currently run, the host hardware specifications (hard drive, direct attached storage, network attached storage, storage area network), and the locations in which they run. Specifics, even down to whether the disks are solid-state drives (SSDs) or more traditional mechanical hard disc drives (HDDs), will come into play.

When sizing out storage options in Azure, you can choose between standard storage (akin to HDD) or premium storage (akin to SSD). This will apply not only to OS and data disks for virtual machines but also for storage accounts. You can also choose redundancy options with those storage media as well. There are several different tiers of redundancy with storage accounts in particular.

- *Locally redundant storage (LRS)*: This storage type will create a total of three instances of your storage account within the same datacenter.

- *Geo-redundant storage (GRS)*: This storage type will create copies of your storage account in the datacenter you selected as well as another datacenter located in another geographic area. This option uses paired datacenters for redundancy, vs. availability zones which are a macro level grouping of geopolitical areas.

- *Zone-redundant storage (ZRS)*: This storage type will create copies of your storage account in the datacenter you selected as well as other locations within Azure availability zones.

- *Read access geo-redundant storage (RA-GRS)*: This storage type provides read-only access to the data in a secondary location, in addition to geo-replication across two regions.

There are significant differences between how standard storage and premium storage are billed. Standard HDD storage allows you to dynamically reserve up to a certain size but will only bill you for actual space used. Premium SSD storage will reserve and charge for the entire size—if you request a 512GB SSD drive, you will pay for it fully, regardless of how much actual data you have stored on it. In addition, depending on the tier of storage you select, you will be charged higher rates for performance and redundancy.

Another aspect to keep in mind is that of managed (Azure-curated) vs. unmanaged (customer-curated) disks. Traditional virtual hard drive (VHD) storage is considered unmanaged, as the system administrator or other responsible engineer is responsible for sizing, managing backups, managing a business continuity strategy, and so on. Managed disks are less maintenance intensive but come with the trade-offs of not being more than locally redundant, and they are subject to additional backup and maintenance fees.

Because downtime for either the portal or Cardstock IS not something that the business is willing to tolerate, it's important to set up redundancy to prevent unplanned outages. To ensure business continuity and to play to the strengths of the primary and secondary circuit locations, you initially look at using GRS for any data needed by the platform that is not already captured by a persistence layer. In most cases, having locally redundant storage for virtual machine hard disks is acceptable, as the plan is to have the infrastructure captured as code, so recreating an environment in the event of a regional outage or disaster would not be too taxing.

EXERCISE: STORAGE LAYOUT

You start to review the technical notes from the Andromeda IT team about the servers on which the main applications are installed. For the Git and Jenkins servers, each physical machine has two 5,400 RPM hard drives in them, each with a capacity of 200 GB. For the production web servers, as well as the inventory system, the storage array that is used consists of ten 7,200 RPM hard drives, each with a capacity of 500 GB. The overall usage of that array sits at around 75%. There is a separate file server, with a separate storage device, that contains about 2 TB of data, mostly in the form of spreadsheets, employee file shares, and integration files used during the procurement and accounting processes.

On the Gamecorp side, the portal is running in a load-balanced web farm with six identical web boxes. Each of those boasts a 320 GB virtual hard drive. The database files for the portal application is located on a single SQL Server instance, with SAN replication occurring every 30 minutes. The storage on the SQL Server totals 6 TB, with about 45% of that allocated. The SAN reserves a buffer of three times the size of the database's full backup, which typically runs around 250 GB.

Given these details, as well as the information you can gather from the machine assessment worksheet included in the downloaded content, please answer the following questions:

- What is the total need for locally redundant storage, based on the specifications of the existing environments?

- If applicable, what would the GRS tier be used for? How would that be sized in relation to the other storage needs?

- Given the varying nature of items being stored, are there other options that can be used in lieu of Azure storage accounts?

- Given the trend information supplied by the infrastructure engineers for Gamecorp and Andromeda, what degree of flexibility would be required for machine storage? For file storage?

Application Architecture

Managing limits in application components or cloud platform offerings is an additional way to determine capacity for the platform and what that looks like from a vertical and horizontal scaling perspective. Looking to items such as App Services, Functions, Event Hubs, Logic Apps, and Container Services for ways to address the needs of a distributed system with multidimensional data and the expectation of asynchronous message digestion can muddy the waters some, as each component has its own set of pros and cons. You look into the backbone of the platform's component structure first, examining messaging and transactional processing needs.

Event-Driven Architecture

Cardstock has already embraced the notion of event handling and processing within its confines. The portal, on the other hand, is much more procedural and linear in its workings. The gray area that exists at this point is that of the integration layer between the new POS inventory control set (Square's inventory APIs) and the proprietary inventory management system. Through the assessments you conducted earlier in Chapter 5, you learned that the need for real-time or even near-time consistency between the Square POS inventory catalog and Gamecorp's IMS is less important than ensuring the Square catalog is updated and as current as possible. The IMS is viewed as needing eventual consistency with the Square catalog, and it serves as more of a reconciliation and reporting source than an online transactional system. While there are a few exceptions to that rule, it allows for planning out a store and forward approach to moving information updates from place to place.

A common pattern that can be seen in many implementations of event-driven systems is that of data duplication. In a system with independent domains, each domain will store information that is relevant to its operation. This information could be stored in another domain for other operations, and so on. This can lead to increased storage needs depending on how much duplication is actually being done.

Container Registries and Container Services

Given the drive toward using a more containerized approach to delivering Cardstock to its users, you look to utilize Azure Container Services (AKS) and Azure Container Registry. The current needs of the Andromeda team, along with expressed interest from other lines of business, leads you to believe that consumption of this service would be rather popular. To ensure higher availability of the service to distributed development teams, you review the product SKU comparisons listed in Table 6-1. More information about these SKUs can be found at `https://docs.microsoft.com/en-us/azure/ container-registry/container-registry-skus`.

Table 6-1. *Azure Container Registry SKUs and Features*

Resource	Basic	Standard	Premium
Storage	10 GiB	100 GiB	500 GiB
ReadOps per minute[1, 2]	1k	300k	10,000k
WriteOps per minute[1, 3]	100	500	2k
Download bandwidth MBps[1]	30	60	100
Upload bandwidth MBps[1]	10	20	50
Webhooks	2	10	100
Geo-replication	N/A	N/A	Supported (preview)

[1]*ReadOps, WriteOps, and Bandwidth are minimum estimates. ACR strives to improve performance as usage requires.*

[2]*Docker pull translates to multiple read operations based on the number of layers in the image, plus the manifest retrieval.*

[3]*Docker push translates to multiple write operations, based on the number of layers that must be pushed. A docker push includes ReadOps to retrieve a manifest for an existing image.*

Azure Container Services are the hosted orchestration and clustering pieces that allow for containers to be run, monitored, and scaled using a common orchestration platform. When looking at containerizing parts of the platform, one of the areas brought up by the engineers was that of full container isolation—meaning no formal orchestration or network bounds. Using this feedback, you research Azure Container Instances, which are isolated runtimes that allow containers to be hosted with truly no visibility into the underpinnings of the host. After consulting with information security, you decide that the first iteration (and perhaps several subsequent iterations) will deal with the container service, with container instances on the docket for further research.

EXERCISE: COMPONENT LIMITATION AND CAPACITY ANALYSIS

Given the hybrid approach you are taking with how the portal and Cardstock are using infrastructure vs. component services, it's time to look into the components that you have selected and how those components support the transactions you're about to put them through. Using the link provided in the beginning of the chapter for Azure component and subscription limits, along with the transactional data you have already accumulated, pull the limits for the following component choices:

- Azure Service Bus

- CosmosDB

- Azure Container Services

- Azure Container Registry

- Azure Web Apps

- Azure Logic Apps

- Event Hubs and Event Grid

After marking your observations, please answer the following questions:

- Are any of the components you've selected unable to meet the demands of your solution as it stands today?

- Are there other considerations to take into account (pricing tiers, performance SLAs) for any of these components?

Data Architecture

Capacity as it relates to the data architecture of the platform is less about the need for specific data structures and more about the actual storage and throughput capabilities. In order to appropriately allocate resources for use by application components, Azure comes with the notion of units for measuring how much (or little) can be used. A common theme across these units of measure is a composite of CPU, memory, and I/O transactions per second (IOPS). In the case of Azure SQL, this is measured in database transaction units (DTUs). The exception to this is in the case of Azure SQL Managed Instances, which uses a different calculation method to determine consumption and cost. More information on DTUs can be found at `https://docs.microsoft.com/en-us/ azure/sql-database/sql-database-service-tiers-dtu`.

There are some great resources available for helping to properly scope out and plan for database usage in Azure:

- *Azure SQL Database Transaction Unit Calculator*: This allows you to not only calculate the required DTU tier for standard Azure SQL databases, but will also allow you to calculate the same for elastic instances. `http://dtucalculator.azurewebsites.net/`

- *CosmosDB Capacity planning tool*: This will analyze the existing JSON structures you are looking to store and will calculate the request units needed to ensure performance and appropriate storage. `https://www.documentdb.com/capacityplanner`

EXERCISE: DATABASE CAPACITY PLANNING

Using the capacity calculators previously listed, along with metrics you have collected from existing SQL Servers in Andromeda's and Gamecorp's datacenters, you can now move forward with gathering information on the data structure and performance needs.

Another aspect that falls within data architecture that can be overlooked is that of data warehousing, analytics, and reporting. Both operational and transactional data stores will have certain requirements for storage, IOPS, availability, and presentation. Not to be left out, Azure SQL Data Warehouse uses data warehouse units (DWUs) to determine service level, consumption, and cost. A full breakdown on the structure of DWUs can be found at `https://docs.microsoft.com/en-us/azure/sql-data-warehouse/what-is-a-data-warehouse-unit-dwu-cdwu`.

For large-scale platforms, running reports and performing complex analytic queries against a near real-time, transactional data store is not considered best practice. In fact, it's not considered good practice at all. Software architecture patterns such as command query responsibility segregation (CQRS) aim to split this aspect up within an application by tailoring the data stored—and returned—so it is optimized for the desired behavior.

From a reporting perspective, it is important to examine the presentation platform being used as well as the implementation details of that platform. In the case of Gamecorp, a corporate decision was made to leverage PowerBI to provide business intelligence resources. There are different ways in which PowerBI can be implemented, dependent on the features of the suite that are required as well as where the data sources are located.

There are some great resources available relative to capacity planning for data warehousing and for business intelligence:

- *SQL Data Warehouse capacity limits*: This site explains the upper bounds of the data warehouse offering in Azure. `https://docs.microsoft.com/en-us/azure/sql-data-warehouse/sql-data-warehouse-service-capacity-limits`

- *Azure Data Lake store*: This site will show a comparison between Data Lake and Azure Storage for the storage and processing of big data sets. `https://docs.microsoft.com/en-us/azure/data-lake-store/data-lake-store-comparison-with-blob-storage`

- *Capacity planning for PowerBI Server*: This site will give best practices around adequately planning resources if you are intending to use the VM-based PowerBI Report Server. `https://docs.microsoft.com/en-us/power-bi/report-server/capacity-planning`

Backup and Recovery

A final consideration in capacity planning for the cloud can be that of backup and recovery. As the storage planning section outlined earlier, you will need extra storage space to account for backups and backup retention. But what about VM recovery options? While not everything in the platform will require infrastructure-as-a-service components, there will be items at the portal level that will. You begin to look into Azure Backup and Azure Site Recovery as options for providing a disaster recovery solution for the portal, and hopefully other solutions going forward.

Through some initial research you find that Microsoft offers a capacity planning worksheet (see `https://docs.microsoft.com/en-us/azure/cloud-solution-provider/migration/on-premises-to-azure-csp/asr-capacity-planning`) specifically tailored to site recovery.

EXERCISE: AZURE SITE RECOVERY— CAPACITY PLANNING

After finding and downloading the spreadsheet from the Microsoft site listed above, you begin to review the details you've collected and plug them into the spreadsheet to start the planning process.

- Using the Quick Planner, enter the information requested and make note of the results.

- For a more in-depth experience, use the Detailed Planner. For the purpose of this exercise, though, it is not required.

- Compare the output of the spreadsheet to the information you've already calculated. Are there any significant differences between your numbers and the spreadsheet?

Summary

Through your trip across the various planes of architecture, you have taken a journey through the platform and looked at areas for capacity. You have learned where to gather information from existing infrastructure as well as new infrastructure. You have learned how different product offerings in the cloud can yield different capacity and throughput based on SKU. You have examined different application and infrastructure needs and seen how capacity planning is much more than how many servers and disk drives a platform might need. Keeping what you have learned about capacity in mind will help as you move to your next area of reflection, application and platform performance considerations.

Based on the topics covered in this chapter, please reflect on and answer the following questions:

- Are there any areas that could have been covered when looking into the needs of the platform?

- Could the spreadsheet shown in the disaster recovery exercise have also been used initially to help perform the full capacity analysis for storage and bandwidth usage? Why or why not?

- During the database capacity planning exercise, did you evaluate the cost for the Azure SQL offering vs. any other contenders, such as VM-based SQL Server and Azure SQL Managed Instances? Why or why not?

CHAPTER 7

Performance Considerations

During the design and eventual maturation of a platform, decisions are made to implement functionality in ways that, given the resources available, make the most sense to solve the problem at hand. There are plenty of times when planning for performance can be an afterthought, especially when trying to release a minimum viable product (MVP) to market. Depending on how a platform is initially engineered, there can be less difficult ways to "back in" performance gains. Most applications that are moved through the MVP stage and have functionality rapidly bolted on to meet consumer or stakeholder demands can run into problems accommodating extra requests while maintaining a consistent user experience. When considering the overall performance of a solution, whether in the cloud or on the ground, several aspects can come into play. These aspects include:

- Geography
- Network traffic and latency
- Application behavior under load, stress, and chaos
- Component use cases and limitations
- Data transformation, querying, and rendering

While not exclusive, the areas mentioned are typically game changers when looking to maximize performance. There are plenty of areas in which software patterns and best practices can be examined to look for additional performance gains. The immediate focus of this chapter will be on the items listed, though, since these can be new to many who are looking to embrace cloud-based platforms. Choices that are made in each of these categories will drive the success of your platform, sometimes in spite of how well you may performance tune your business (and execution) logic. The first area we will examine will be physical location, or datacenter geography.

© Josh Garverick 2018
J. Garverick, *Migrating to Azure*, https://doi.org/10.1007/978-1-4842-3585-0_7

The Impact of Geography

With presence in 54 regions around the world, Azure datacenters outnumber both Amazon and Google combined (Figure 7-1). Finding a datacenter near a center of business or concentration of customers is less likely to be an issue. That's not to say that the regions available will solve all problems, as there may still be issues with infrastructure or platform latency depending on how a solution is put together.

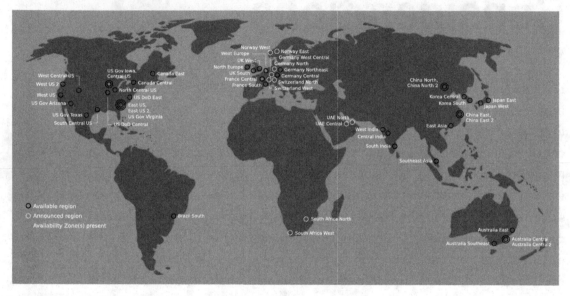

Figure 7-1. *Map of Azure regions (available and planned), July 2018*

In addition to considering regions for geographic proximity, it is also important to keep data residency requirements in mind when looking for datacenters to host infrastructure or platform components in. These generally come into play when dealing with legal and compliance requirements around data security. Many countries have strict data residency requirements, and some even mandate that applications cannot be hosted or accessed from outside the country's networks. In cases where complete isolation is required, Microsoft has established exclusive datacenters that are compliant with residency and access needs. Examples of countries where this level of isolation is a necessity include:

- Brazil

- China

- Germany

Note   Brazil is the only region in the Azure ecosystem that does not have a mapped secondary datacenter in the same region. Brazil South currently maps back to South Central US for its business continuity/disaster recovery needs (`https://docs.microsoft.com/en-us/azure/best-practices-availability-paired-regions`).

Knowing where your target audiences are located helps in planning for what datacenters should be targeted for implementation. Knowing the reliability of those datacenters and the available services at each can help in the planning process for implementation. Tradeoffs can be made with respect to datacenter location, network latency, and component availability if the first choice in datacenter locations is not as reliable as you may prefer. Keeping these tradeoffs top of mind will help you to choose the right location with the appropriate component availability and acceptable network throughput. What is deemed acceptable network throughput, though? Let's dig into that question a bit more to learn more about anticipating—and planning—network traffic.

Anticipating Traffic Patterns

Every application has what it considers to be a normal flow of user traffic. Some consider a few users per day to be normal; others consider hundreds of users per hour to be normal. As mentioned in the previous section, geographic placement of application components can contribute to network latency, depending on the location of the user(s) in question. Just as there are assumed steady-state traffic patterns, there can also be patterns that can push the boundaries of the application and network capacity.

Gamecorp has relatively fresh baselines for user traffic on all externally-facing sites. Andromeda, however, has never really tested their average throughput for user traffic. Before going any further, you decide to look into what it would take to capture a baseline of the platform.

You meet up with the engineering team once again, and ask some targeted questions about times they have seen the application working harder than normal to keep up. Were there any periods of time where usage was markedly higher? Were there any user demographics captured that could lead to discoveries about traffic concentration? Could any conclusions be drawn from sales initiatives or special trading card game events and accompanying usage statistics?

Performance Under Load

The first area you decide to explore is that of the application's performance under load—additional traffic to the site that is outside the normal anticipated range of concurrent users or transactions. Tools like Apache Bench, SoapUI, LoadUI, and more can be used to test and capture information about site throughput. Capturing performance at expected or average thresholds will help to drive any future analysis regarding areas of the platform that have improved or degraded performance.

To help gather metrics about major endpoints, you decide to put together a framework that will generate a suite of integration tests. These tests will run Apache Bench to gather load time statistics, report findings, and store the data in a datastore to allow for trend analysis. In order to do this, each API route will need a couple of different test types to ensure an appropriate variance:

- A "standard" accessor, assuming a general interaction with the API

- A "light" accessor, assuming a smaller than average interaction with the API

- A "heavy" accessor, assuming a larger than average interaction with the API

After completing the initial analysis, you are now ready to begin crafting the mechanism for gathering benchmark data. Your goal is twofold: provide a fast means to accumulate benchmark data, and a way to visualize that data to help identify trends. You find some great examples of Docker-based tooling from one of the open source community's most active members by doing some initial online searching. Visiting her GitHub account (`https://github.com/jessfraz`), you find a wealth of information as well as Dockerfiles for several utilities. One of those is a Docker container built from Alpine Linux with Apache Bench installed. Using this newfound information, you produce a to-do list for implementing this testing solution:

- Set up a container using `jess/ab` for small, medium, and large testing sets.

- Set up a script that will capture the output from each individual API test and place it into a file, and upon completion, zip all of those files up to create one object to send to the cloud.

- Set up a container from `azuresdk/azure-cil-python` to upload the results of your test runs to a storage account.

- Set up an Azure Function app for processing files into Cosmos DB document storage.

- Add reporting from PowerBI for visualizing the data from CosmosDB.

- Create an embedded report from the Power BI visualization that can be displayed on a dashboard.

You also sketch up a rough diagram of how the solution might look when using all components. Figure 7-2 illustrates the initial design.

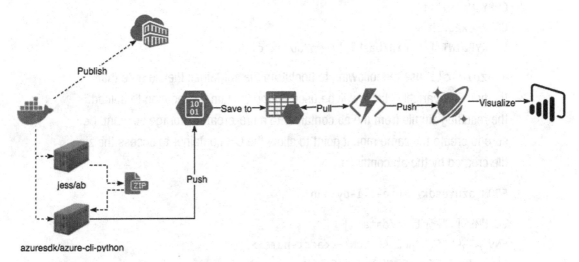

Figure 7-2. *API Testing solution overview*

EXERCISE: THE APACHE BENCH API TEST SOLUTION

While the individual components of this solution do not seem to be overly complicated, making this all work together will prove to be a bit more challenging than you first thought. Following the checklist you put together, you start assembling the components and testing out the solution.

1. Create a new folder for your solution on your file system named `ab-api-tests`. Inside of that folder, create folders for your major component types: `docker, functions, reporting`.

2. Within the Docker folder, create directories for your containers: `ab`, `azure-cli`, `mongo` (for local persistence testing), and the Function app. Within each of the new directories, create a new Dockerfile:

3. In the Dockerfile for the custom `ab` container, use the following to bootstrap the container:

```
FROM jess/ab
RUN apk --update-cache add bash python libffi openssl gnuplot
curl zip
VOLUME [ "/opt/ab/data" ]

WORKDIR /tmp/ab

COPY Urls.txt .
COPY exec.sh .
ENTRYPOINT [ "/bin/bash","/tmp/ab/exec.sh" ]
```

4. In `azure-cli`, use the following to bootstrap the container. Please note that the two ENV variables listed will be used during container execution to upload the resulting zip file from the ab container to a pre-created storage account. Be sure to create the same mount point to allow the CLI container to access the zip file created by the ab container.

```
FROM azuresdk/azure-cli-python

VOLUME [ "/opt/ab/data" ]
ENV AZURE_STORAGE_ACCOUNT=<<acct-name>>
ENV AZURE_STORAGE_KEY=<<SAS KEY>>
```

5. For testing purposes, create a file called Urls.txt that contains the route of each API you'd like to test. Ensure it is in the same directory as the ab Dockerfile. Enter two or three test URLs into that file.

6. Construct a bash script that will execute the Apache Bench tests and save the output along with a file that contains information about the URL being tested, the name of the data file, the unique ID of the test run, and the timestamp for when the test was run. Name the file `exec.sh` (as mentioned in the Dockerfile in step 3). Allow the file to accept the number of requests to use along with the number of concurrent requests to use. The script should read similar to the following:

```
#!/bin/bash
timestamp(){
    date "+%Y-%m-%d %H:%M:%S"
```

```
}

getrunid() {
    python -c 'import uuid; print str(uuid.uuid4())'
}

echo "${2} concurrent connections requested"
echo  "${1} requests requested"
i=0
rm /opt/ab/data/links.txt
touch /opt/ab/data/links.txt

runtime=`timestamp`
runid=`getrunid`

while IFS= read -r line
do
    ((i++))
    ab -n $1 -c $2 -r -g "/opt/ab/data/out${i}.dat" $line
        echo "${line},out${i}.dat,${runid},${runtime}" >> /opt/ab/
        data/links.txt
done < "./Urls.txt"

cd /opt/ab/data

zip "${runid}.zip" o*.dat
zip "${runid}.zip" links.txt
```

7. Create a storage account in Azure that will house the uploaded zip files. You
    may use PowerShell or the Azure CLI to perform this task. An example of the
    Azure CLI command is shown as follows:

    ```
    az storage account create -g <<RESOURCE_GROUP>> -n <<STORAGE_
    ACCOUNT_NAME>>
    ```

8. Build the Docker image by going into the ab directory and typing:

    ```
    docker build . -t ab:latest
    ```

    Do the same for the azure-cli directory, changing the name of the tag from
    ab to azure-cli. Be sure to update the Urls.txt file with valid URLs to test
    against.

9. Experiment with a few configurations of requests vs. concurrent requests by starting the container with the following command and replacing the requests and concurrent requests numbers as you see fit:

```
docker run -d --rm ab:latest -v ~/ab:/opt/ab/data ab 500 500
```

What findings do you come up with when testing this container out locally? Do the data files get created properly? Are you able to look at the data output that Bench creates?

Now that you have the basic mechanics related to the benchmark tests complete, you can move on to constructing the function that will extract the data files and metadata file from the zip archive and prepare them for a slightly more structured format in CosmosDB. You classify the data model by looking at the components being captured. For starters, each URL group (the contents of the Urls.txt file) is considered a test run. Each test run has a unique identifier that will tie all of the data together. The results of each URL test will be stored in a tab-delimited data file, specified by the command arguments to the ab utility. You decide to leave these files as-is, since the formatting is already taken care of by Apache Bench.

You need a construct for tracking all of these test runs, along with what URL is associated with them, since the output from Bench does not include the URL being tested. You sketch up a metadata class called RunOutput, which holds some key data for the overall run as well as a collection of URLs being tested, and a collection of run objects (RunInfo) that contain the URL and associated results from Bench. Figure 7-3 illustrates the class representations and the flow of that information (the collection of RunInfo objects) to CosmosDB.

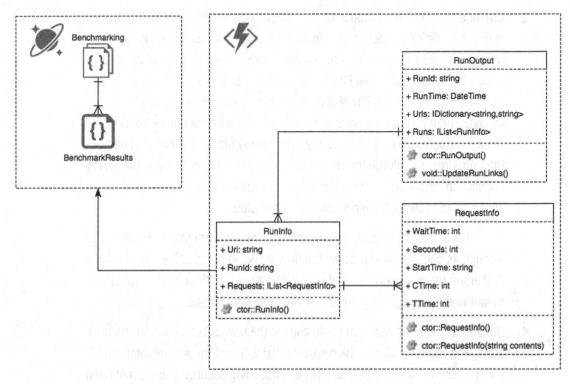

Figure 7-3. *Class and collection relational diagram*

EXERCISE: THE AZURE FUNCTION IMPORT ENGINE

To get started with the second part of this solution, you focus not only on the function that will be executing but also the data source it will be writing run information to. Continuing to follow your checklist, you set up the components you need for phase 2.

1. Create a new CosmosDB instance in your Azure subscription with support for the MongoDB APIs. This will come into play when setting up local containers for testing prior to running in Azure. Create a database called Benchmarking, which will be where run results will ultimately live. Then create a collection called BenchmarkResults, which will be the collection comprised of each test run's results.

```
az cosmosdb create -g <<RESOURCE_GROUP>> -n <<COSMOSDB_NAME>>
--kind MongoDB
az cosmosdb database create -g <<RESOURCE_GROUP>> -n <<COSMOSDB_
NAME>> -d Benchmarking
az cosmosdb collection create -g <<RESOURCE_GROUP>> -n
<<COSMOSDB_NAME>> -d Benchmarking -c BenchmarkResults
```

2. Create a new Docker Compose file to perform local testing. The file should include references to MongoDB (mongodb), the MongoDB client (mongoclient/mongoclient), an Azure storage emulator (arafato/azurite), and to the Azure Functions runtime (microsoft/azure-functions-runtime). The MongoDB client will allow you to visually validate when records are written, ensuring that the function is performing the appropriate action. Be sure to map the default MongoDB port as a pass-through. Create a volume for the MongoDB client container to allow persisting connection data locally between sessions and create a volume for the Azurite container to allow for local persistence of test blobs.

3. Construct an Azure Function that will pull in a zip file from blob storage, cycle through its contents, and process the files. It should process the links.txt file to gather information about the test runs and associated URLs, and the data files to gather the raw figures related to the Apache Bench tests.

4. Update the local.settings.json file to change the connection string for the blob storage account to point to the container that will host the Azurite instance. If you are testing locally with MongoDB and not using security, you will not need to provide an account key in the connection string.

    ```
    "AzureWebJobsStorage": "DefaultEndpointsProtocol=https;AccountName=<<ACCOUNT_NAME>>;AccountKey=<<ACCOUNT_KEY>> "
    ```

5. Open the zip file using a .NET library of your choosing. For this example, the SharpZLib library will be used. Loop through the contents of the zip and execute on each object as long as it is a file.

    ```
    using (ICSharpCode.SharpZipLib.Zip.ZipInputStream str = new
    ICSharpCode.SharpZipLib.Zip.ZipInputStream(myBlob))
        {
    ZipEntry entry;
            while ((entry = str.GetNextEntry()) != null)
            {
                if (entry.IsFile)
                {

                    . . .

                    }
            }
        }
    ```

6. Next, read the contents of each object stream into a variable and analyze the file contents in memory.

```
{
    size = str.Read(array, 0, array.Length);
    if (size > 0)
    {
        contents += new System.Text.ASCIIEncoding().
        GetString(array, 0, size);
    }
    else
    {
        break;
    }
}
```

7. Construct the data objects from the file structures output by Bench by passing in the line data to the constructor.

```
var req = new RequestInfo(items[i]);
info.Requests.Add(req);
```

8. When complete, allow for the removal of the blob from the storage account.

```
CloudStorageAccount storageAccount = CloudStorageAccount.Pa
rse("DefaultEndpointsProtocol=https;AccountName=<<ACCOUNT_
NAME>>;AccountKey=<<ACCOUNT_KEY>>");
// Create the destination blob client
CloudBlobClient blobClient = storageAccount.
CreateCloudBlobClient();
CloudBlobContainer container = blobClient.
GetContainerReference("ab-test");
var blockBlob = container.GetBlockBlobReference(name);
if(blockBlob.DeleteIfExists()) {
    log.Info("Deleted source blob.");
} else {
    log.Warning("Could not delete the source blob.");
}
```

9. Send the aggregated results to the CosmosDB (MongoDB) instance by returning the collection of RunInfo objects from the exiting function. The output sink will store the data in your target data store.

Test out your processing engine by running docker-compose build && docker-compose up, then executing one of your ab test containers. You will see the tests execute, the zip file get created, and the Azure CLI upload the zip file to the blob storage account (in this case, the container).

The first data point you work to collect is what the expected level of concurrency is—that is, the count of how many users accessing the site at the same time. Based on the traffic analysis you performed, you see that the mean number of concurrent connections appears to come in at 500. Next, you start with a baseline of 10,000 requests to give the benchmarking an appropriate place to start. You run through a few different URLs to get a sampling of different functionality, and now have enough data to focus on building the visualization tools for the benchmarking data.

EXERCISE: POWER BI AND COSMOSDB

In this exercise, you will explore the PowerBI interface and its connection with CosmosDB. Using the visualization tutorial for PowerBI and Cosmos found at https://docs.microsoft.com/en-us/azure/cosmos-db/powerbi-visualize, along with the data renormalization concepts found at https://docs.microsoft.com/en-us/azure/cosmos-db/odbc-driver, explore the data you have collected so far with the previous exercises. Experiment with different visualization techniques and database queries.

1. What visualization techniques were you able to try out, and of those, which worked the best?

2. Is there a mechanism for sharing the visualizations you've created with other users? Can they be displayed within other applications?

3. After using the query editor to pull information out of the CosmosDB instance, do you notice any performance issues? Could the persistence layer have been another type of datastore? Why or why not?

Performance Under Stress

The second area to explore is that of the application's performance under stress—excessive traffic and transaction processing that can cause errors to surface, site processing time to slow, or a combination of both. Benchmarking individual API calls can be very useful to help tell the initial story. Moving forward with more complex testing scenarios, however, you feel it's best to look into some alternatives for more real-world use cases.

There are as many tools in the market today as there are use and edge cases for any application. Some are designed for ease of use, while others are designed for versatility and complexity. Regardless of the tools you choose, there are higher level categories into which these products fall. Let's take a moment to review those categories and some examples of each:

- *Functional/integration testing*: The main goal of tools in this category is to verify the functional aspects of the test subject. Typically, this includes integration testing, as a good way to validate functionality is working as expected is to use a representative test subject composed of the actual components. Examples of functional or integration testing tools can be seen in Specflow (leveraging Gherkin and Cucumber).

- *User interface testing*: Also known as Coded UI or Record/Playback testing, tools in this family tend to focus specifically on validating use cases where the user interface dictates the flow. While very good for capturing usage-based cases, any change to the UI will create a need to update the test(s), and maintenance can be overwhelming if many changes are made to the UI.

Use the example in the last section to build on the automation, showing how increasing the concurrency and max requests will give different results.

EXERCISE: TURNING UP THE HEAT

Having established baselines in the last section, it's time to turn things up a bit. You decide to work with three different scenarios to determine what the breaking point of the test suite, and ultimately the application, would be. The first is a conservative estimate, using a factor of 1.5x to test with. The second is a midrange estimate, using a factor of 2x. The final case is an extreme, using a factor of 3.5x.

Using the benchmarking rig you set up in the last section as a guide, along with the functional tests you have created, execute each of the test run cases listed in the previous paragraph. How do the results and visualizations compare with those of the baseline executions?

Performance During Chaos

The final area you look into is that of chaos engineering—intentional actions that cause platform components to fail and reveal how durable a system or application can be. Knowing that development teams that you've worked with at Gamecorp do not always keep resiliency top of mind, you look into some ways to test out random failures and whether or not those failures cause full system outages or only affect the components in isolation.

Note   The term "chaos engineering" was coined by Netflix as an approach to test the resiliency and reliability of their Amazon Web Services (AWS) application components. An application dubbed Chaos Monkey was the first of several utilities that Netflix wrote and used to perform these tests. It is written in Go and freely available via GitHub at `https://github.com/netflix/chaosmonkey`.

More robust components such as Service Fabric have built-in capabilities for testing chaos scenarios. Given that your design does not leverage this type of component, you will have to work with engineers to come up with a set of tests that will give the same level of chaos to test against. Before anyone can begin exercising chaos tests on the platform, a couple of things need to be taken into consideration. For starters, you will not have the ability to bring up (or down) any components controlled by outside vendors. The Square APIs cannot be directly forced to act as though they are not there. In a case such as this, an abstraction layer will be needed to simulate what would happen if the portal or Cardstock were unable to interact with the inventory back end.

Telemetry has to be spot on as well. Taking down parts of the platform, regardless of size or relative importance, should not occur without logging at the application layer as well as the infrastructure layer. Not having an appropriate level of auditing and tracing will lead to mystery failures, and stakeholders have zero vested interest in being told that "something" happened without any idea of what that something was, much less how to prevent it from happening again.

There needs to be a clean method of interaction with this abstraction layer as well—one that can seamlessly switch between the desired integrated state and one that is not integrated.

EXERCISE: RELEASE THE KRAKEN

To get started, you work with the engineering team to determine where the best points in the platform would be to abstract out—meaning, the Square APIs, the internal applications, and the event registration system. For each of the abstraction layers, be sure to identify whether or not the entire API is required, or if a subset will do given the scope of integration.

1. Reverse engineer the existing infrastructure into an ARM template and determine areas that could fall victim to random, or even planned, outages.

2. Detail out each interface that needs to be abstracted. Note the methods that need to be accounted for. What approach do you feel would best encapsulate the desired outcome of simulating random start/stop sequences for each API?

3. Being that some resources are VM dependent, and therefore network dependent, are there ways to change the flow of network traffic to simulate broken or slow connections?

4. Using the business process flows you captured during the earlier chapters, identify critical business operations and areas of potential disruption that could come from outside the platform.

5. With these scenarios and components documented, put together scripts that will simulate the outages and intentional chaos you've identified. What types of issues show up? Are certain types of disruptions more damaging to the integrity of the platform? The operation?

It is possible to identify and isolate components that will handle specific load-based, stress-based, and chaos-based situations with grace. Working with the engineering teams from Andromeda and Gamecorp, you document your findings based on the performance and stress tests you've built thus far. Your next focal points will be that of platform components, and limitations that could change your initial design.

Considering Component Use Cases

A common perception of cloud components is that they are innately and infinitely scalable—often with little credence given to the actual use cases the components were designed to service. The notion that these components can scale automatically and quickly can lead to surprises later when performance is not as good as people anticipated it would be. For example, many implementations that involve infrastructure-as-a-service components are fairly static by nature. A single virtual machine will not automatically resize itself if it detects an abnormally high usage of memory or processors. In fact, resizing a virtual machine will cause the machine to reboot, effectively killing any in-process transactions on that box. Virtual machine scale sets (VMSS) are a platform component offering that allows for certain degrees of auto scaling depending on thresholds you set, but even then, the machines follow a standard specification and will only horizontally scale.

Building on the information you gathered in Chapter 6, you start to drill further into the relative and absolute limitations of each of the platform components you've selected.

Application Gateway

The application gateway component is the entry point into the presentation layer and the gatekeeper for communications with the platform. From a convenience and cost perspective, it is an attractive option in the managed component space. Simple and complex load balancing scenarios can be carried out using this device, and enhanced protection can be realized using the web application firewall (WAF) functionality included with larger SKUs of the gateway.

Basic functionality for an application gateway, regardless of SKU, is split into a handful of components:

- *Back-end pool*: a collection of one or more target network locations, which could be virtual machines, App Services components, etc.

- *Front-end IP*: the public facing address that DNS will use to route requests to the gateway

- *Rules*: Rules will determine what traffic is permitted to pass through the gateway. Basic rules pertain to ports and protocols (HTTP/S), while multisite rules can include multiple fully qualified domain names. This helps when routing requests to back-end web servers expecting a specific domain in the request header (e.g., vanity URLs). *Note that multisite rules support up to a maximum of 20 FQDNs.*

- *Listener*: A listener will tell the gateway to be aware of requests coming in on a certain port and using a certain protocol; used by a rule.

- *Probe*: a default or custom URI and timeout schema that will allow the gateway to assess the health of the back-end pool objects. If blank, the gateway assumes it should be able to hit the root of the site on the port specified in the HTTP settings.

- *HTTP settings*: These are defaults used by the gateway to determine things like request timeout, cookie affinity, and whether to use a custom or default probe for health check reasons.

Tip   If you are noticing multiple 502 errors being thrown at the App Gateway layer, be sure to validate the HTTP timeout setting on the gateway. The default value is 30 and can be increased to help eliminate those errors and restore functionality.

In relation to performance, there are a few settings to be mindful of. For starters, when using any SKU, be sure to watch the instance count, found under Configuration. The default when creating a gateway is 2, which ensures a specific amount of throughput for the traffic hitting the gateway. If too much traffic is hitting the site and not completing successfully, you can adjust the instance count to widen the pipe. The HTTP timeout setting is another value that can be changed in the event of high instances of request timeouts or getting a 502 (bad gateway) error.

Adjusting your back-end pool (or splitting the pool into multiple pools) can also help with request processing and performance. For example, if you're using VMs to host a website, adjusting the VM SKU could help with processing speed. Adjusting the number of VMs in the pool could help address availability concerns. If you are using one gateway to handle more than one type of application, you can split the back-end pools up to allow for priority processing, URL-based back-end mapping, or workload-driven routing.

Azure Container Registry

As seen in Chapter 6, there are several options when it comes to deciding how to store published container images. The Andromeda team has several images, all based on the same base image (Alpine Linux). This approach was chosen to keep the file size to a minimum as well as to offset disk I/O in favor of in-memory execution. The file size was a concern due to two reasons:

- Installation and usage in all environments

- Pushing larger files over their network could sometimes be troublesome.

The Andromeda offices will be seeing a speed increase with the addition of the peering networks and enhanced circuits. This will allow for faster publishing and consumption from the registry. However, the team is invested in making the images as small as possible to avoid any potential issues related to image size.

Repository location will also factor into things, as deployments are expected to pull from artifact sources that are within the same region. This is to keep each replica of the platform independent while leveraging the same artifacts for deployment. The primary registry will be in the United States, and when containers are ready for the runway environments, they will be published to a registry in each location where the platform is to be available. This will allow for faster deployments, since the sources will be physically closer to where they need to be stood up and run.

Azure Container Services

The managed Azure Container Service (AKS) is fundamentally different from the unmanaged platform offering in that the managed offering does not let you have line of sight into the machines that make up the cluster. Any configuration of the cluster is to be done through the `kubectl` command, through the Kubernetes dashboard, or through the Azure portal/CLI. You will want these clusters to be stood up in a similar fashion as the container registries, in the same region where the platform is to run.

There are a couple of key areas in which performance can be impacted, whether using the managed or unmanaged container service. First, the size of the virtual machines hosting the cluster is important. If you are deploying a handful of services to the cluster with single node instance for each, the default VM size will likely be just fine. For production-grade work, though, you will want to use larger SKUs to ensure the memory, compute, and IOPS are adequate for what the services and pods within the cluster require.

Another important consideration is that of the scaling of deployments. Unless otherwise specified, the default values used by Kubernetes are to start with one node and scale to a max of two nodes. Again, this is likely fine for lower nonproduction environments. Setting these values upon deploying to the cluster will be more relevant for production workspaces. Starting with two or three nodes and scaling to seven or eight will get you more elasticity and cost savings while still providing a more than acceptable quality of service.

EXERCISE: INITIAL KUBERNETES SCALING LIMITS

Given the number of environments that are required for the platform, along with a general understanding of the relative sizing in comparison to production:

- Set the initial min and max number of nodes for each cluster.

- Set the initial machine sizes, and counts, for each cluster.

Do the machines in the managed service have the capability of being started/stopped? Could they be controlled with the use of automation jobs?

Dealing with Data

Another allure of the cloud is the draw of being able to process large amounts of data with relative ease. While this can be done through the use of such components as Apache Spark, HDInsight, and Data Lake, many pieces of data that are used during application component communication are on a much smaller scale. For example, messages that are sent into an Azure Service Bus queue can only be up to 256kb in size unless you are using the Premium SKU, so anything larger than that would cause an issue. Processing messages that are larger than 256kb in a multithreaded environment could lead to unintended performance bottlenecks if the environment is not sized appropriately, and would require an alternate queuing platform installation to achieve.

Much the same as processing messages, processing inbound data from various sources can be taxing if the data volume is larger than a certain threshold. Understanding what that threshold is, and tuning accordingly, is the best way to ensure that performance is not adversely impacted. Processing outbound data is in a similar problem space, as some operations for creating data responses can be done off-cycle or asynchronously to avoid creating long-running processes when users expect much faster data delivery.

As seen earlier in this chapter, location makes a big difference depending on the type of operation you're attempting to perform, and the volume associated with that operation. Taking location and network bandwidth into consideration is important to ensure a good user experience as well as adherence to any delivery SLAs you may have in place. Tuning the underlying data stores is also important, as an improperly indexed table or collection of documents could make things worse from a processing perspective.

Message Payloads

Generally speaking, messages that are sent using queueing technologies are often meant to be concise—that is, the message size is not anticipated to be large. There are exceptions to this as with any rule, though caution should be taken when designing the payload structure. For example, if you have a component that processes thousands of messages per second, a 256KB payload will be handled faster than a 1024KB payload. Keeping the message concise also helps to ensure that information is being intentionally transmitted. In the case of event publishing, information that is relevant to the model is all that is truly required. Extraneous data in the event could be misconstrued or even ignored.

This has the potential to be less bounded if you are using an Event Grid Topic vs. a Service Bus Topic or Queue. There are no defined message size limitations with Event Grid. The restrictions with Grid are more from a consumption perspective. A primary limit is that of custom topics. Per region, you are allowed up to 20 custom topics. This keeps the number of topics relegated to a smaller, easy to manage size, but does drive a need for further awareness around the size of the event being published to the topic.

Inbound and Outbound API Payloads

The same type of principle that applies to messages also applies to web requests and responses when dealing with Web API (REST). It can be tempting and sometimes far too convenient to include a bunch of loosely related information within one API call and then parse that using conditional logic instead of creating separate APIs for each scenario. A fairly common pattern can be seen in applications that have reached a certain stage of maturity wherein APIs will be exposed for very specific actions, and those APIs will delegate the computation responsibilities to a class or set of classes in an abstraction layer. This reduces the amount of information required for the function or statement to be executed and helps to enforce the idea of singular responsibility.

One type of REST call that can frequently become unruly is that of fetching tabular data for display to an end user. Paging can be achieved by several methods in code or in the query string if OData is being leveraged. This helps to reduce the amount of data being returned but can be less impactful if the query being executed is not tuned to match this. Keeping queries lean and result sets targeted will help tune those potentially cumbersome queries and responses.

Indexing, Storage, and Regionalization

Data access and performance related to that access can come in many different forms. The traditional persistence technologies, most notably relational databases, have certain constructs that help them to optimize the storage and retrieval of data. Indexing is one of the most common constructs for sequencing and identifying records within a persistence store. The foundation of an index is that an index is a copy of specific columns from a database table that has been stored for faster searching. Generally, this copy is also stored with either a low-level disk block or pointer to the actual row containing all of the data. Discussions involving hard disks, block sizes, and low-level input/output operations are well beyond the scope of this text. Knowing how a basic index works, however, will help you determine what values are best added to an index to improve query performance.

From a storage perspective, how hard disks are laid out as well as what type of hard disks are used can contribute to how well (or poorly) a database server performs. Naturally, with managed database instances, hard disk specifications are not relevant as performance is measured by a combination of attributes. There is the notion of database transaction units (DTUs), which are comprised of how many transactions can be executed by a database in a given time frame, what level of I/O throughput is allowed, and even the amount of storage space allowed. A similar construct exists for CosmosDB in request units (RUs). This will reserve compute and memory to perform actions against the database with a certain number of throughputs in mind. Anything that exceeds the reserved throughput will be throttled. It is essential to understand how that can factor into performance in conjunction with traffic pattern studies and baseline/load/max scenarios.

Distributed data can add further complications to an already complicated distributed system. Multiregion deployments can utilize the same schema and general storage mechanisms, so long as the cloud region has the appropriate components available for use. Some data may need to stay within a certain region or geographic zone based on legal necessity, and some data may be required to exist in all locations. Determining what data is required per location and what data is required at all locations will help drive the decision to replicate certain core data across all deployed locations.

EXERCISE: DETERMINING DATA REGIONALITY

Given the type of data that the platform deals with, which of these would be good candidates for regionalization vs. replication?

1. Customer demographics

2. Inventory

3. Private (friend) interactions

4. Trades

5. Customer card collections

For each item, describe why they would or would not be appropriate for regionalization. Perform the same analysis on any items that would be candidates for replication. Are the locations in which the platform is to be deployed in a state that has all of the feature sets that the data tier requires?

Summary

In this chapter, we have reviewed a substantial amount of information related to different factors that can impact how an application or platform performs. You have seen how physical location plays a role in everything from network latency to components that are available for use in Azure. To help set some boundaries, you tested out and observed traffic patterns using a light/medium/heavy approach to ferret out potential issues with configuration. You introduced the notion of chaos engineering into the platform to truly test for fault tolerance and unrecoverable errors. Leaning on work from members of the technology community, such as Jess Frazelle, you were able to create new tools for benchmark testing using Docker and cataloging those benchmark runs. You created specialized stored procedures in CosmosDB to fetch aggregated benchmark data for visualization in Power BI. Equally as important was examining the data you collected on many of the platform-as-a-service offerings for things like container registry, container service, and application gateway. Making adjustments for items like API calls that return too much data as well as performance tiers for the persistence layer round out the considerations you look at with respect to performance. All of the areas you've examined here will help contribute to the overall vision of the target architecture of the platform, which is what you plan to tackle next.

Given what you've learned throughout this chapter, consider the following questions:

1. What factors other than physical distance between components should be taken into consideration when looking at physical locations and latency?

2. In the section about stress testing, are there other tools that could be used to gather more appropriate usage statistics? Can those alternatives potentially be run via a service? A container?

3. Why would using PowerShell or bash scripts be a better way to execute chaos testing than writing a purpose-driven application like the chaos monkey suite?

4. While the Application Gateway is a required component in the design for security reasons, are there other ways to achieve what the gateway can provide? Would any of those methods be more cost-effective?

5. Are there any API calls that seem to be less than optimal with respect to performance? What types of changes did you make to improve them, if any?

6. Could there be a situation where using the managed container registry or managed container service would not be optimal?

CHAPTER 8

The Target

Having weighed out several impact areas, it's time to connect the proverbial dots and start constructing the target architecture. Remember, it is okay if the target vision changes over time, based on requirements that may change or solutions that do not pan out as intended. As is reasonable and customary in many technology disciplines, an iterative approach to putting this target together can be frustrating at times but will lead to a more flexible design and greater credence lent to feedback reception and processing. In many architecture frameworks, iterative design is built into the overall process, highlighting the importance of getting things right and leveraging a tight feedback loop.

It's good to start with a rough cut of the overall big picture for the solution. Understanding some fundamentals about how the solution is meant to interact with its own components, as well as integration points with other systems, helps to paint a picture for technical and non-technical stakeholders. For the initial view, you decide to go with a logical representation of the solution, calling out some key components that you hope will shed light onto how the target state will be different—and improved.

Solution Architecture

The target solution architecture logical view is shown in Figure 8-1. The most architecturally significant components are explicitly called out in the view to show where significant investments of time and effort have been placed in anticipation of current needs and future plans for growth.

The overview itself is composed of three main divisions: the cloud provider (Azure), outside platform components, and on-premises objects. You see a need to separate these to help communicate that there is still going to be a significant amount of ground-based infrastructure. A major change agent in this design is the introduction of the Square point of sale (POS) system, including integrations with the Square APIs that control inventory views, pricing, promotional codes, and customer loyalty data. Since Gamecorp

© Josh Garverick 2018
J. Garverick, *Migrating to Azure*, https://doi.org/10.1007/978-1-4842-3585-0_8

already utilizes Eventbrite for its in-store and offsite events, there is an integration needed between Cardstock and Eventbrite, but no further customized event scheduling and ticketing software are required. Even though the Square integrations are not primarily your responsibility, they do impact how you are going to implement Cardstock and get inventory data.

Another significant change agent is that of authentication and authorization in the form of Azure Active Directory Business to Consumer (B2C) integration. Not only will the onboarding of social media authentication providers be new, but having additional means of integration through other AAD tenants will further complicate the existing authentication scheme. A silver lining exists in migrating the existing ASP.NET membership roles to AAD roles, though.

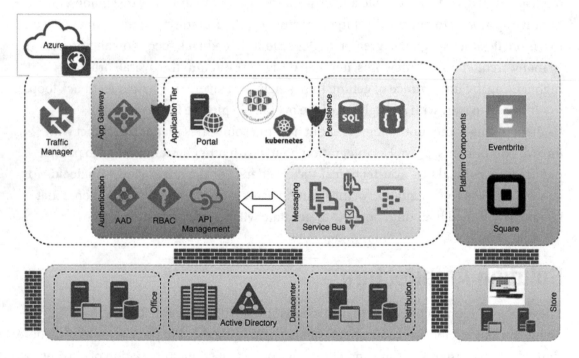

Figure 8-1. *Solution architecture overview*

Building a foundation that is stable and secure is something that is at the heart of the design you want to see. Starting with the network and security layers, you begin laying out several different focal points to make sure your work with capacity planning (Chapter 6) as well as performance considerations (Chapter 7) are fully integrated with your target state.

Infrastructure Architecture

Technology architecture is one of two core component areas that establish the backbone of how all solutions—including your solution—will interact with each other. Taking the existing network structure into consideration and comparing that with the expected network structure gives you some insight into how to sketch out the traffic topology view. You contact one of the senior network architects at Gamecorp for some assistance as well, since you are not a network configuration expert.

Network Configuration and Topology

The network configuration that exists at Gamecorp is fairly standard as far as on-the-ground networks are concerned. Offices, distribution centers, datacenters, and stores are all connected via site-to-site VPN connections and all utilize dedicated circuits for communication. Given the information covered in Chapter 5 concerning the baseline state of Gamecorp's infrastructure, along with capacity information discovered in Chapter 6, you start to piece together how the existing network topology will interact with the various components that make up the means of communicating with cloud-based assets.

To get the most out of the ExpressRoute connections that have been implemented, Gamecorp's corporate infrastructure architects have designed a hub-and-spoke model (https://docs.microsoft.com/en-us/azure/architecture/reference-architectures/hybrid-networking/hub-spoke) to allow individual areas to have peered connections and still have an isolated feel to them. This is helpful in isolating traffic without oversaturating existing connections, as well as isolating network compromises should any resources be hacked by external parties. A reference diagram is shown in Figure 8-2, which is found on the Microsoft documentation site.

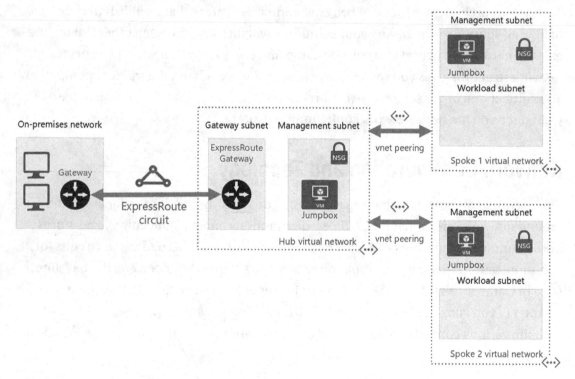

Figure 8-2. *Reference architecture for Hub and Spoke networking*

Additionally, the infrastructure team has designed regional hubs to allow for specific circuit pairings to be separated (primary versus backup networks, for example). To illustrate this, one of the infrastructure architects sends you a diagram showing the proposed layout of virtual networks, as shown in Figure 8-3.

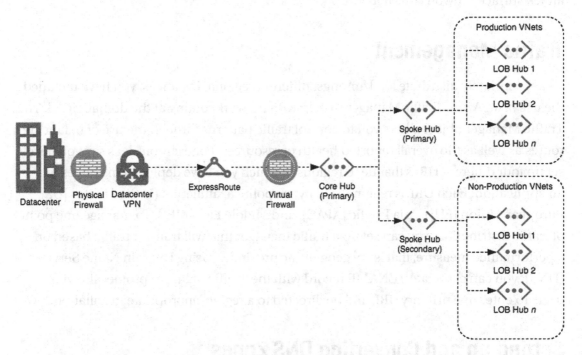

Figure 8-3. *Gamecorp general design for Hub and Spoke*

Network Security Groups

One area that crosses over between network architecture and security architecture is that of network security groups (NSGs). A network security group is a software-defined construct that allows or denies traffic from outside IP addresses or ranges to destination IP addresses or ranges. NSGs can be used at the virtual network level, virtual subnet level, or even at the individual resource level. Using NSGs in a consistent manner greatly reduces the risk footprint for an organization by ensuring that only authorized traffic can flow from point to point. They also contribute to the overall security blueprint seen in the "Security Architecture" section found later in this chapter.

Because the portal uses a more traditional IaaS configuration, you detail the NSGs required to allow traffic to flow from DMZ to application tier to persistence tier. Even when using PaaS components, you can still force traffic to those resources to flow through a specific channel, rather than over the public internet. Doing so offers a smaller attack surface for would-be network snoopers.

Traffic Management

To appropriately distribute load amongst different regional instances, you have included the use of an Azure Traffic Manager to help with network routing at the domain level. The Traffic Manager object allows you to control traffic patterns through the use of balancing routes as well as the overall reported health of resources. For example, let's say you have set up four different URLs that tie to regions in which you have deployed instances of an application. Each URL is regionalized by geopolitical affiliation (United States [US], European Union [EU]), Asia Pacific [APAC], and Middle East [ME]). To manage one point of traffic distribution, you can set up a traffic manager that will transfer traffic based on a performance measure, that is, by geographic proximity. Using Domain Name Services (DNS), you can associate a CNAME record with the Traffic Manager profile, allowing users to enter one primary URL and be directed to a region-appropriate installation.

Setting up and Converting DNS Zones

Part of the overall strategy for operationalizing the cloud includes shifting the maintenance of certain domains to the business units responsible for them. Administering these domains would have meant needing to have IT professionals on staff who would be able to set up and configure Active Directory and DNS services, either as a part of the corporate forest or as a stand-alone entity. Azure has the ability to serve as a DNS server for both public as well as private domains. Establishing these domain areas takes almost no time at all, and options for configuration are bountiful.

Adding New DNS Zones in Azure

Working to ensure the implementation details don't leak into the design work, you try very hard to keep the notation of DNS zone migration to source and destination only. The root domains of Andromeda Games (andromedagames.us), Gamecorp (gamecorp. us), and Cardstock's subdomain are all candidates for moving to Azure DNS. You create new DNS zones for each of the root domains needed, and the network team can take those zones and populate them as necessary with the appropriate zone, resource, and other records.

Allowing for a Private DNS Zone for Nonproduction Workspaces

There is an existing nomenclature in place for associating a local domain to nonproduction workspaces. To help facilitate this when developing in Azure, you put together a proposal to allow the use of Azure DNS zones for these local domains, which point to specific applications within Gamecorp's portfolio. To do this, you create a new DNS zone for each application's local domain, and associate that zone with a specific virtual network that houses the nonproduction resources for an application team. Using the Azure CLI, you can specify the zone type (private) for the zone along with the virtual network to register with the zone. An example would be:

```
az network dns zone create -g <<RESOURCE GROUP NAME>> \
   -n cardstock.gamecorp.local \
  --zone-type Private \
  --registration-vnets <<VNET Name>>
```

More information about using Azure DNS for private DNS lookups can be found at https://docs.microsoft.com/en-us/azure/dns/private-dns-overview, and a tutorial for using Azure CLI can be found at https://docs.microsoft.com/en-us/azure/dns/private-dns-getstarted-cli. Keep in mind that as of the time of this writing, the private Azure DNS zones are in preview.

Business Continuity and Disaster Recovery

One critical aspect to any application, platform, or technology portfolio is the notion of business continuity and disaster recovery. Implementing a business continuity (BC) and subsequent disaster recovery (DR) strategy in the cloud can be different than a traditional datacenter-based strategy. In many cases, a typical DR environment will be a fully built replica of the production infrastructure hosted in a secondary datacenter, lying dormant until the unthinkable happens.

To keep things operating, there are two areas that require a bit of additional attention. One is the queueing mechanism (mentioned in the Application Architecture section) and the other is durable storage—both at the file system level and the database or persistence level. During the planning phase, it was identified that there was a recovery time objective of 24 hours, and a recovery point objective of 4 hours for disaster recovery purposes. To help satisfy this requirement, the continuity plan needs to account for the aforementioned items.

To fold in the persistence and storage requirements, you look into geo-redundant storage accounts for those files, blobs, and other stored items that need to be available at all times. Making sure that storage accounts are geo-redundant ensures availability in the event of temporary outage as well as catastrophic datacenter failure. The infrastructure, given the recovery time objective (RTO), can be reconstituted at any point in any region, giving flexibility to the recovery strategy. Having existing peered network already established means that restoring the infrastructure onto approved virtual networks will not be an issue.

The individual application teams, in conjunction with corporate resources, will have to formulate their own plans to show how they are compliant with the BC and DR needs of their application. You earmark sections within the solution documentation that will allow for details around the plan definition and execution details for Cardstock as well as the portal.

Application Architecture

The selections of application architecture components, as seen in previous chapters, can be involved in and of itself; integrating those components can be laborious as well. Having a good understanding of how everything plays together is essential when laying out the application architecture views.

Adoption of Azure Kubernetes Service

The modular nature of the platform, along with the preexisting use of containers for the trading subapplication, presents an interesting challenge. While each component could be pushed out into separate IaaS-backed machines and implementation-specific machine footprints, you instead decide to focus on how to better leverage some of the platform offerings that Azure has, specifically around the Azure Container Service implementation of the Kubernetes orchestration platform. What is particularly enticing about this model is that the underlying infrastructure is a bit of a black box. There are not any visible virtual machines, network components, or storage arrays to be concerned with.

You prepare some additional material on the benefits of managed platform services to combat any objections you may get from the Gamecorp infrastructure architects. They have a long history of building very staunch and secure on-premises machines and have a great deal of anxiety about managed services they cannot remote into and control. A common illustration of the locus of control as it relates to the cloud can be seen in Figure 8-4.

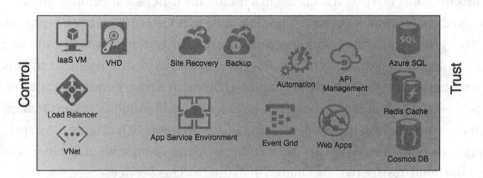

Figure 8-4. The trust vs. control continuum

The idea is that with IaaS components you retain the same level of control you would expect from existing datacenters. On the other side is PaaS, which gives you much less control of the infrastructure and forces you to trust that the service provider is using appropriate backing hardware, security measures, and performance optimizations. Choosing solutions that tip to one side of the spectrum or the other can depend on organization maturity, talent base, system complexity, and willingness to adopt (or avoid) risk.

You see an opportunity to push forward with the managed container service because the platform is fairly isolated, and the development teams have already been preparing the components for individualized builds and deployments. Using Kubernetes as an orchestration engine helps to promote this modularization further. With Kubernetes, you get the concepts of services and pods. Services are logical divisions that enable multiple applications to perform tasks using a consolidated set of functions. Pods are logical application deployments that consist of one or more instances. These instances can be used in scaling and redundancy scenarios, providing a more resilient application.

Using this model as a guide, along with the existing deployment model provided by the Andromeda engineers, you put together a target view of Cardstock where the underlying APIs are deployed as services within the cluster, and the fron-tend components are deployed as pods. You've left a placeholder for an inventory adapter in the event it's needed, but this element may very well be removed in later iterations if the team finds it to be redundant.

Migration of the Gamecorp Portal

The current Gamecorp portal is hosted in a traditional n-tier architecture using a customized installation of Orchard CMS. The version of Orchard has been kept somewhat up to date, giving you a bit of confidence that the data migration may not be too terrible. In order to get the platform up and running, there needs to be a deployment and quality assurance pipeline, as well as a target implementation in Azure. Fortunately, Orchard has a white-box solution in the Azure Marketplace that will install a copy of Orchard CMS into an App Service, with the database being hosted in Azure SQL. Figure 8-5 depicts the migration path of the existing CMS solution to Azure, along with preliminary details around the build/test/deploy mechanics in Azure DevOps Services.

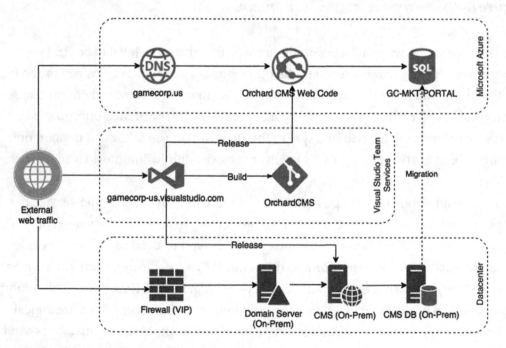

Figure 8-5. *Gamecorp CMS migration path*

The data structures are compatible for the version of Orchard that is being used on the ground versus the marketplace offering in Azure. The implementation plan for converting this data will be outlined in the Data Architecture section found later in this chapter.

Messaging and Integration Points

The application layer of Cardstock is made up primarily of integration services—RESTful API calls that are meant for fast data resolution. In the baseline architecture, the calls to the inventory system were RESTful as well, as the load coming in from the portal and from Cardstock was not high enough to require any other type of solution. With moving the platform onto a regionally and globally scalable stage, you feel that it's time to start looking into different mechanisms for dealing with events related to inventory transactions.

The use of a queueing technology to capture information about events related to the inventory system allows systems to interact with the inventory store without knowing anything more than the need to publish an event and an endpoint to publish to. On the surface it sounds a bit reckless—allowing disparate platforms to have the ability to push data updates about a system it's not intimately concerned about.

The largest integration point that sits on your plate now is the integration of the new inventory management system and the POS upgrade work. While it's not a large portion of your solution, the APIs required by the portal and by Cardstock are dependent on the implementation of the new inventory schemas as well as the POS solution offered by Square. One of the selling points of using Square as a partner in POS integrations is that any inventory updates to store locations can be made in real time, including item holds, site-to-store orders, and store pickups.

Squaring up with Square

Square has a rich set of APIs available to application developers, known as Square Connect. Everything from order management, inventory management, locations, employees, and more can be interfaced with using Connect. The POS devices for the stores will obviously interact with these APIs, as will the Gamecorp Global Inventory System (G2IS).

An interesting point of reference with the Square APIs is that there are different versions of the API depending on the operation being performed. Luckily, the Square Connect SDK handles this for you via abstraction, and having to manage more than one access point is mitigated. There are rate limits in place with the Square APIs, and while the limits are not immediately discoverable, there is a way to determine if the limit has been hit. There is an HTTP code returned in the event of too many connections being received, which is HTTP 429. Building a mechanism into the middleware for handling this return code will be critical to preserving the customer experience.

THOUGHT EXERCISE: SQUARE DATA REVIEW

Take a few moments to review the API definitions as well as the data object definitions associated with the Square Connect SDK (`https://docs.connect.squareup.com/api/connect/v2`). Make note of some common objects that may come into play during the data integration section.

Getting Event Data from Eventbrite

Because Gamecorp uses Eventbrite for all of its in-store ticketed events, integration will be required with their APIs to display information to users of Cardstock. One thing you notice when reading through the specification is that there is a rate limit in place, which could be exceeded depending on how many people hit the APIs every day. They allow 48,000 calls per day, with an hourly limit of 2,000 calls. While this may not immediately be a problem, as the systems grow in use, it could become a problem. Accounting for traffic flows is a topic that was covered in Chapter 7, and this rate limit is a constraint that needs to be called out so that further capacity and performance planning can be done.

One potential solution that a Gamecorp engineer suggests is that of a preformatted JSON feed retrieved from an API call. She explains that as events are updated in the Eventbrite system, a webhook can be triggered, which in turn can feed a generic event into an Event Hub. A serverless function could then grab the updated information, generate the data file, and place it into a content delivery network or storage account where the front-end application (the portal in this case) could consume it and display the information on the home page. You ask for a conceptual diagram to help pull this together, and the resulting diagram can be seen in Figure 8-6.

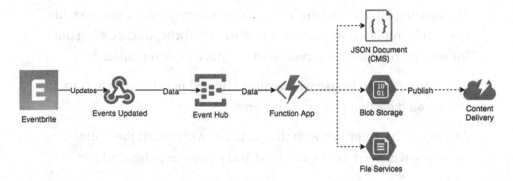

Figure 8-6. *Suggested solution flow for caching Eventbrite data*

THOUGHT EXERCISE: EVENTBRITE DATA REVIEW

Take a few moments to review the API definitions as well as the data object definitions associated with the Eventbrite APIs (`https://www.eventbrite.com/developer/v3/`). Make note of some common objects that may come into play during the data integration section.

Data Architecture

The underpinning of every platform within Gamecorp, and potentially most platforms ever written, is data. How data is ingested, how it is accessed, and how it is persisted can present unique challenges as well as common patterns for solving common problems. With the movement of Cardstock to Azure, and the parallel efforts to move the portal and the inventory system, there is no shortage of snags to push through, problems to solve, and technologies to review. You first focus on the changes to data flows within the systems, hoping to find places where consolidation of information can help bring value while keeping costs in check.

Changes to Data Flows

While migrating Cardstock is a pretty standard lift-shift-enhance scenario, the data flows that correspond with the portal and inventory systems have some significant changes to consider:

- The old integration points for the Andromeda stores to their inventory system will have to be rerouted to start leveraging the new inventory system.

- The existing interface to the in-store event management system will need to be replaced with an interface to Eventbrite, and existing data for which no tickets have been sold will have to be migrated.

- The new data warehouse will require a host of new connections to ensure all ingestion points are covered.

- Any items that interface with the portal, or with which the portal interacts, will need to be examined and potentially changed.

Taking things one flow at a time, you start by looking at the Andromeda side of the business. With the replacement of the inventory system, the integration for the register system and the inventory system will be net new, so no additional analysis is needed there. The integration with Cardstock and the inventory system will be impacted, though. In addition, the inventory data from the existing Andromeda system will have to be migrated to the new Square platform as locations go live with the updated registers. This can be done all at once (preferable) or in stages, based on timed migrations.

Both the Andromeda and Gamecorp portals will have to be consolidated, as customer information stored in Andromeda's portal will naturally transfer over to Gamecorp. The remainder of the content will be assimilated by the Gamecorp portal team, since the in-store specials, sales, and events will be managed outside of the Andromeda team. Flows will need to be designed to allow for the movement of this content into the target system, in this case Gamecorp's CMS back end.

External systems, such as the existing vendor management system, the purchasing system, and human resource management system (HRMS), will need to either be integrated with other platforms or migrated to the Gamecorp equivalent. While not in scope for your project, you take an interest in keeping tabs on these disparate integration points as they could come into play at some point in later phases of the cloud transformation.

Event Structuring

To set the teams up for success with event handling and event sourcing, you look to find something that everyone can use which provides a canonical definition for events being published as well as consumed. You plan to use the CloudEvents (`https://cloudevents.io/`) specification, maintained by the Cloud Native Computing Foundation, to keep event data presented in a consistent format. The underlying data objects that get placed into the individualized events can be of any origin, so long as they can be properly unpacked, interpreted, and acted upon. The burden of interpretation will really be on the event handler as it will need to know and anticipate the data being sent, and what to do with it once received.

A point to remember when forming these events from the data side is that the underlying transport protocol will need to be considered. There are two primary transports that CloudEvents will support: HTTP and Messaging. Within those, there are more specific bindings that can be used given a specific communication scenario. Table 8-1 illustrates the supported protocols along with transport adapter types for each. In all cases the JSON message type is supported, though some proprietary and specialized formats (e.g., AMQP) can also come into play, potentially changing the schema needed. There are also tie-ins to security, as the HTTP adapter requires the use of TLS for securing the channel.

Table 8-1. *CloudEvents-Supported Protocols and Transport Adapters*

Protocol	Adapter	Description	Specification
Any	JSON (JavaScript Object Notation)	Specification for JSON formatted messages (multi-protocol)	https://github.com/ cloudevents/spec/blob/master/ json-format.md (message)
HTTP(S)	Webhook	A pattern of interaction that relays a response after an event occurs	https://github.com/ cloudevents/spec/blob/master/ http-webhook.md (pattern) https://github.com/ cloudevents/spec/blob/master/ http-transport-binding.md (transport) - JSON message format
Messaging/ Queueing	AMQP (Advanced Message Queueing Protocol)	An open internet protocol for transporting business messages between two parties	https://github.com/ cloudevents/spec/blob/master/ amqp-format.md (message) https://github.com/cloudevents/ spec/blob/master/amqp- transport-binding.md (transport) - JSON and AMQP message formats

(continued)

Table 8-1. (*continued*)

Protocol	Adapter	Description	Specification
	MQTT (Message Queueing Telemetry Transport)	Lightweight queueing protocol used in machine-to-machine and IoT devices for reporting information	https://github.com/cloudevents/spec/blob/master/mqtt-transport-binding.md (transport) - JSON message format
	NATS	NATS is a cloud-optimized queueing protocol using queue servers as well as streaming event sources.	https://github.com/cloudevents/spec/blob/master/nats-transport-binding.md (transport) - JSON message format

Problems with Persistence

There are a few immediate persistence needs for the teams as they move toward their cloud-based application migrations. For one, a caching layer will be important to establish, as reducing round-trip calls to databases and external APIs whenever possible will help reduce site latency and improve overall user satisfaction. There are many relational datasets and stores being used by legacy applications, some of which will be migrating and some of which will be consolidated into alternatives based on changes in data flows. The creation of an aggregate inventory data warehouse is a new concept for Gamecorp, and additionally the information security team wants to ensure that there are controls in place for that data store.

To ensure that a proper design is in place for the new warehouse, you work with the data architects to design a modern data warehouse sourced from operational data. They initially sketch up a design that leverages Azure Data Factory to synthesize data coming in from various systems, with a flattened schema for storing inventory order cross-referenced with orders, purchasing, and inventory management records. The schema itself is provided by the National Retail Federation and the Object Management Group, and it leverages the NRF's ARTS model for retail data.

EXERCISE: BUILDING AND STOCKING THE WAREHOUSE

As an experimental exercise, you decide to stand up a new Azure Data Warehouse using the schema that the data architects designed (found in the downloadable content under "DW schema"). You look at the notes you've made around the Square APIs and data model. Using those notes, and the description of the ARTS entities included in the downloadable content, you practice mapping the data entities and relevant fields into the ARTS model. What are some of the commonalities you notice between entities and fields? What are some of the differences and potential challenges you notice?

Security Architecture

A cornerstone of the target architecture will be security, as personal and payment information will need to be under close scrutiny. Encryption standards, enforcement of strict secure transport layers, monitoring, and policies all factor into protecting both the users of the platform as well as the company itself. Before getting into the lower level mechanics around network security and infrastructure security, you begin by laying out the mechanism for accessing platform resources, which is your role-based access control (RBAC) strategy.

Bringing RBAC Back

RBAC is a concept that is overarching and can help to delineate access rights over a wide variety of users, groups, and resources. Authentication and authorization related to the Cardstock platform, as well as the portal, play a key part in the overall strategy. Setting up the role groups for access to each system will be less of a concern, as there are already guidelines for how to construct the groups based on convention.

Gamecorp has established a convention for setting up role and resource groups in Active Directory, and how those groups translate to Azure Active Directory:

- **Role** groups follow a convention of {GroupType}-{Company}-{Unit}-{App}-{Env}-{Access}, where unit refers to business unit, app refers to application or component, env refers to environment, and access refers to the maximum level of access the role has.

- **Resource** groups follow a convention of R-{Company}-{Unit}-
  {Resource}-{Env}-{Access}, where unit refers to business unit,
  resource refers to the resource type (File, Server, Database), env refers
  to environment, and access refers to the maximum level of access the
  role has.

Figure 8-7 illustrates the cloud and ground interaction between the company's on-premises AD services and the synchronization with Azure AD. Further, assignments are given to RBAC roles within target applications in the cloud, such as the Azure portal and Azure DevOps Services. The users and groups are synced from on-premises to Azure AD and are available to assign to any of the groups listed in either the Azure subscription zone or the Azure DevOps Services zone. This includes users and groups from the Andromeda domain, as a business-to-business integration has been established with the Gamecorp domain.

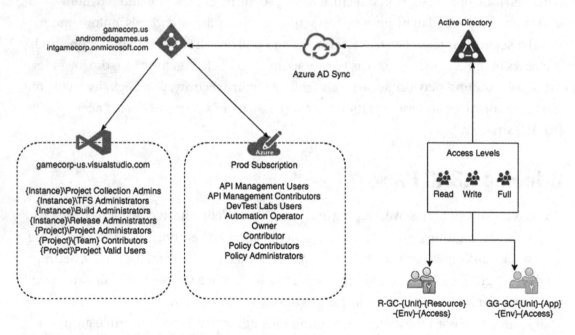

Figure 8-7. *Gamecorp Active Directory and Azure Active Directory overview with RBAC*

HSTS, TLS, and HTTPS

Another area of concern is that of network traffic, specifically in relation to how traffic reaches and is handled by the platform. In order to be fully PCI compliant, as well as embrace best practices, you have added details to the network design that enforce HTTPS Strict Transport Security (HSTS), Transport Layer Security (TLS) 1.2, and certificate-based encryption of traffic via SSL and HTTPS. Using tools such as these allows users to feel secure when using a website or application, and it allows the company to mitigate any risk associated with transporting or displaying protected user information.

It can be easy to confuse these terms in the course of usage with colleagues or peers. Let's take a moment to clarify what each of these acronyms means, and what the primary use cases are for each.

- *HTTP Strict Transport Security (HSTS)*: This is a policy mechanism that allows web servers to demand that browsers or user agents interact with it using HTTPS connections via port 443, and not "naked" HTTP traffic over port 80. It is declared and enforced by an HTTP header value.

- *Transport Layer Security (TLS)*: This is a communications protocol managed by the IETF and is designed to prevent packet sniffing or other transmission eavesdropping though the use of specifics around network packet construction, cipher exchange, compression/decompression, and more. The full specification can be found at `https://tools.ietf.org/html/rfc5246`.

- *Secure Socket Layers (SSL)*: This is the predecessor of TLS and is still used when describing certificates that verify the authenticity of the site that uses them. The certificate will contain information about the certificate authority, the cipher being used to provide secure communication, the issuer of the certificate, and more.

Web Application Firewall

An additional layer of security can be found in the form of a web application firewall (WAF). A WAF provides additional security against certain types of malicious attacks that are typically carried out by denial of service, brute force, SQL injection, or other attack vectors. Settings on the WAF can be implemented to either detect these types of attacks and vulnerabilities, or to prevent them. Setting a WAF to detection mode allows you to audit the traffic to your application but does not explicitly deny all traffic deemed to be potentially harmful. Prevention will restrict all traffic that matches any known attack vectors that sit within the Open Web Application Security Project (OWASP) top ten exploits.

You have accounted for the WAF layer by including the use of an Azure Application Gateway. The gateway allows you to simply switch the SKU in order to utilize the WAF functionality. In the network architecture view, the WAF tier is called out explicitly and is noted to be set to detect until testing is done, to ensure that normal user activity is not mistaken for malicious intent.

Next-Generation Firewall

With the addition of a web application firewall and network security groups, it seems almost redundant to be looking into the use of another firewall appliance for this solution. The Azure Security Center best practices analyzer typically looks for both a WAF appliance as well as what's called a next-generation firewall (NGF). Primary features of an NGF include what would be considered standard firewall functionality bundled with security-minded features such as deep packet inspection (DPI) as well as an intrusion prevention system (IPS). These devices can also offer integration with third-party authentication platforms directly, control quality of service (QoS) for critical platform components, and even antivirus inspection of packets.

SIDEBAR: NEXT-GENERATION ACRONYMS

Several acronyms have been used in a small area dealing with next-generation firewalls. Let's take a closer look at those acronyms and what they really mean.

- *Deep Packet Inspection (DPI)*: a type of data processing that inspects in detail the data being sent over a computer network, and usually takes action by blocking, rerouting, or logging it accordingly (https://en.wikipedia.org/wiki/Deep_packet_inspection).

- *Intrusion Prevention System (IPS)*: a device or software application that monitors a network or systems for malicious activity or policy violations. Any malicious activity or violation is typically reported either to an administrator or collected centrally using a security information and event management (SIEM) system (`https://en.wikipedia.org/wiki/Intrusion_detection_system`).

- *Quality of Service (QoS)*: a bandwidth management process measuring and controlling the communications (traffic, packets) on a network link, to avoid filling the link to capacity or overfilling the link, which would result in network congestion and poor performance of the network (`https://en.wikipedia.org/wiki/Bandwidth_management`).

One topic that has not been covered yet is that of a security information and event management system (SIEM). Take a few moments to search for information on SIEMs and note that while this narrative does not look to factor a SIEM into the security stack, there is certainly a case for a possible integration.

It is not uncommon to see the use of a device like this in scenarios where both cloud and ground-based applications are being built and maintained, and those applications share a common network backbone. The use of peering along with ExpressRoute would qualify as one of those scenarios, mainly because malicious traffic coming into a cloud-based application could traverse the rest of the internal company network if it is not properly filtered, inspected, and neutralized by an appliance that sits on the perimeter. An NGF can provide an extra layer of network isolation in circumstances where many applications are running, and all have the ability to interact with ground-based assets. Based on the design provided by the infrastructure team, you already have an idea about the existence and utilization of NGWs to help control traffic flow around the core network hubs.

Deployment Architecture

As mentioned previously, the Andromeda team is okay with changing certain things in the spirit of efficiency. Having a preexisting library of jobs in Jenkins, it doesn't make much sense to convert all of those assets because you know that Azure DevOps Services contains extension points that integrate with many different platforms, including

Jenkins. There are some changes that need to be made to the agents being used in Azure, however, to ensure compliance with network isolation principles and to promote consistency across development environments.

In theory, each engineering team should be able to have individualized build and release resources to push their independent platform components out to production. As long as there is consistency between each environment, the tools used to build, package, and release those components should be able to be isolated per team. Independence is not as widely encouraged across the teams from management, and politically it is much more difficult to achieve this buy-in and promote DevOps ecosystems. Gamecorp's management, along with the corporate IT staff, is keen to have centrally managed tools for all aspects of the lifecycle. Despite this, they do offer a great amount of support for new toolsets and are open to changes suggested by the team, so long as those changes go through a change review board prior to being accepted into the stack.

Your vision for the target state of the pipelines involves using more transient infrastructure but still retaining the core data needed to keep the tools being used in a persistent state. For example, for those folks using Jenkins as a build engine, persisting the configuration and build definitions will be important because the nature of transient infrastructure is that it could be dropped and recreated at any time. Persisting these settings also makes it easier for other teams to use these same tools and infrastructure if they choose. While this covers the build and deployment of software platforms, building and deploying libraries or packages that other internal teams can use is something that shifts focus a bit from having every environment covered to having targeted tests run at specific stages, and promoting packages to stable after validation has occurred.

Summary

In this chapter, you have taken the information compiled throughout the capacity planning and performance exercises and turned that into a good plan for the target architecture of the platform. You have explored the technical details of each architectural domain and recorded those details in a solution architecture document. Where appropriate, you have gathered information that will be forwarded to development and integrations teams for further use. With a clearer picture of what the target state should look like, you can now look to building out transitional architectures that will help the teams reach their goals of realizing the target state.

Given the examples you have completed in this chapter, along with the narrative, consider the following questions:

1. The hub and spoke reference architecture provided by Microsoft is a good base for more complicated, segmented networks. Is the design supplied by the infrastructure team consistent with best practices? Does it leverage the ExpressRoute circuits to the best of its abilities?

2. The group structure outlined in the role-based access control topic could be achieved in many different ways. Would you be comfortable using the naming scheme and role layout as prescribed by the corporate IT team? What might the structure look like if you did not have any central guidance?

3. Given the structure of the data entities and elements for the Eventbrite and Square models, what did you find was the best approach for determining an API mapping strategy?

4. For the operational data store, the decision was made to utilize SQL Data Warehouse with Data Factory as the primary feeder. Are there other options that would solve this issue? Was the right decision made given the requirements, or lack thereof?

PART III

Bringing it to the Cloud

CHAPTER 9

Transition Architectures

Before getting into the details around component implementation, some work needs to be done to ensure that developers, systems administrators, information security, management, and senior leadership are all equipped with the right mechanisms to safeguard against risk and exposure. Equally important is the notion that development teams should meet as little friction as possible when developing solutions. Items that can cause friction with developers include a lack of tooling or poor tooling, inconsistencies in allowable frameworks, inconsistent deployment mechanisms, and a lack of direction with respect to design patterns. From a management perspective, understanding work intake, progress, and business drivers that push prioritization forward are important. Senior leadership will likely care about all of these items as well as mitigating risk, controlling costs, and (in the case of a publicly-held company), shareholder sentiment. Information security is also concerned with risk mitigation and exposure but will also require compliance with legal requirements depending on location, following best practices for industry standards, and any additional organizational standards that are in place.

This chapter will focus on several core areas that will aid in the design of support services. Without these support services in place, there can be confusion around what is or is not permitted, whether information is secure, whether applications are secure, what actual and anticipated costs can arise from a given implementation, and whether the right people have access to roles and resources to do their jobs appropriately. We will start by looking at roles, resources, administration, and general access.

Focusing on Security and Access

Platform security, authentication (authN), and authorization (authZ) are so wide reaching, they can be covered in almost every chapter in this book. As the roles and resources for internal consumers has been covered in Chapter 8, the primary support structure that

171

© Josh Garverick 2018
J. Garverick, *Migrating to Azure*, https://doi.org/10.1007/978-1-4842-3585-0_9

you will examine here deals more with application level access requirements and providing engineers with a consistent method of interaction with Azure Active Directory to manage that access. Focusing on proactive security, the Security Center offering in Azure helps to keep eyes on potential threats to your application. Finally, the definition and enforcement of subscription-level policies can be brought to life with Policy Management.

Role-Based Access Control

As discussed in earlier chapters, the notion of role-based access control (RBAC) allows for a clear delineation between roles and resources, providing a foundation for a true separation of concern between users and administrators. While Gamecorp has a mature RBAC matrix for its users and administrators, Andromeda does not. In addition, the interest in leveraging B2C for authentication going forward allows you to look into establishing RBAC groups for application authorization.

In the last chapter, we examined the roles needed to allow AD-authenticated users to access specific servers, resources, and data based on the needs of the user and the needs of the organization. Using the principles of just enough administration (JEA), you put together roles that would allow read operations, write operations, and administrative operations. In turn, you then assigned those role groups to specific resource groups per environment. The needs for Cardstock are not identical but do show some similarities to the internal RBAC groups outlined for internal users.

You begin by taking the different areas of the application and mapping those to the list of roles that the Andromeda engineers provided to you during your discovery phase. From that list, you notice that there are really three types of users—members, service accounts, and administrators. This reduces the complexity of the role/resource matrix, but you press on to make sure you capture everything. The available resources to users consist of forums, trades, store inventory, personal inventory, shopping cart, and friends. The inventory roles become interesting as they cross over between the inventory service layer, the IMS, and Cardstock.

You discover that the Microsoft Graph API (`https://developer.microsoft.com/en-us/graph`), a method of interaction with Azure Active Directory and other online services that leverages RESTful API calls, can be incorporated into an identity library and the exposed to engineers for further use. Taking this into consideration, you identify a few API calls that would allow engineers to access grant and revoke methods, giving them the means by which administrative users can add or remove permissions from users in the platform. Figure 9-1 shows an initial sketch of the APIs selected along with role and resource groups the application can use.

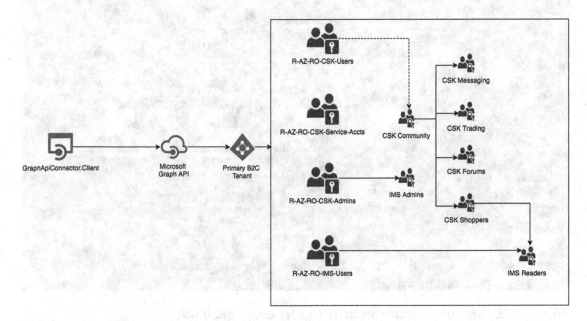

Figure 9-1. *High-level view of Graph API library and role groups*

Microsoft Security Center

As seen in previous chapters, security has played and will continue to play a role in any solution Gamecorp provides, whether internal or external. An advantageous offering can be found within Azure in the form of Microsoft Security Center. This product will provide your subscription with real-time threat monitoring from known attack vectors and suspicious IPs. It also provides you with preventive options for securing your resources, including installing endpoint protection, updating App Services to use web application firewall (WAF) protection, and even suggestions on next-generation firewalls and subnet usage to protect virtual networks. Figure 9-2 shows an example of the Security Center dashboard.

Figure 9-2. *Microsoft Azure Security Center overview blade*

Using this offering in conjunction with Policy Management and Operations Management System, you can reap some fantastic benefits while also finding and fixing security holes in your resources. You notice that you have some prevention items under the Compute category. Clicking into this tile brings up a listing that states some of your VMs are not protected by any endpoint protection. You're certain those machines are test machines, but they should still follow the same standards. From the Azure portal, you can select those VMs, click Install Endpoint Protection, and select between Trend Micro and Microsoft Antimalware. Once complete, click Save to provision the installs and the portal will take care of the rest. Using this method, you can also ensure the safety of other resource types.

Azure Policy Management

One area of increasing popularity and importance is that of policy compliance. Managing access to resources is one thing but managing the types of resources that are available to use, what security scheme they should use, and how resources are tagged is quite another. You could keep track of all of these rules and perform scheduled sweeps to ensure compliance, or you could let Azure do the heavy lifting for you.

Azure Policy Management is an offering that allows you to define custom policies as well as use existing out-of-the-box policies to construct compliance initiatives that apply to any number of resources at the subscription level. A variety of base templates exist and can be used to model custom policies for your compliance needs. You can edit these policies directly in the Azure portal, deploy them using PowerShell, or deploy them using the Azure CLI. A benefit of writing these policies separately is that you can source control your policies, therefore creating a canonical source for all compliance aspects.

To get started with your first policy definition, you will need to create an instance of Policy Management in the Azure portal. To do so, navigate to New ➤ Policy and create a new resource in the subscription using the standard pricing SKU. This will pull in all of the built-in policies that Azure supplies to you and gives you the opportunity to add new policies and assignments as you see fit.

The next step you will need to perform is to create an Initiative. This will define a set of policies that will execute against a given subscription. These initiatives can be grouped in any fashion you prefer, though it is recommended to have an idea of how to organize these to maximize re-use whenever possible. For example, you know that there is a development subscription and a production subscription for the line of business you are working with. Setting an initiative that covers basic reference architecture compliance can be used to enforce high-level constraints, while a separate initiative with much more stringent requirements can be assigned to the production subscription along with the baseline initiative. You decide to create three initiatives to start with, along with some baseline policies (in name only) as shown in Figure 9-3.

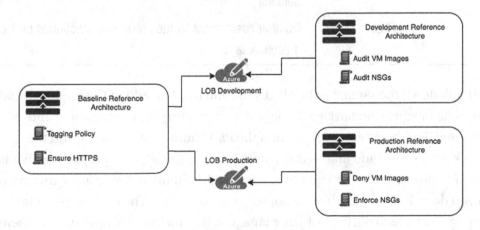

Figure 9-3. Azure Policy Management—iteration 0

You create the preliminary initiatives and assign them to the applicable subscriptions. Now you can start to formulate the policy documents that will be associated with each initiative. A good rule to follow when constructing policies is to leave the action set to audit until you're sure of how it will impact the subscription. Sometimes a policy set to enforce or deny instead of audit will cause other resources to unexpectedly be restrained as well. For example, tagging policies should be set to append in order to add tags non-intrusively. As your first policy, you decide to leverage the example provided by the Microsoft documentation for billing tags and alter it to incorporate Gamecorp's standards for asset tagging. Table 9-1 describes the existing standards for asset tagging currently being used by the datacenter team.

Table 9-1. *Standard Tags for Gamecorp Virtual Assets*

Tag	Sample Value	Description
Region	North America	The physical region (within Gamecorp's purview) in which a resource exists
Cost Center	4410, 3412	Four-digit number associated with the GL cost center for the resource
Client ID	MST3, IRRF	Client identification code used to denote chargebacks for client/partner operations
LOB	RO, SF, FS	Line of business code to assist in denoting ownership and point of contact for support
Environment	Dev, QA, Prod	The logical application environment to which the resource belongs
Project	004, 125, 333	Number assignment by the PMO for a sanctioned project, if applicable

You pull down the sample policy JSON file and begin to add in the required fields based on the tagging standard. Each tag will have an entry for the tag name and the default value. For the project tag, you find the PMO number associated with the Cardstock project and add that as the default value. Ironically, the project number is 404 (project not found?). Another tag that can use a fairly standard value is environment, which you default to Dev for the development subscription. The cost center default is something you have to dig for, but you manage to find the general operations expense account of 5550 and settle on using that for the time being.

Another important area from a policy perspective is that of operating system compliance. In order to ensure consistent experiences on all VM platforms, Gamecorp's architecture team has standardized on both Windows and Linux operating systems. Making sure that these standards are upheld is important for the production subscription. The development subscription, however, is another story. To help developers feel empowered to try new offerings out, the policy for the dev subscription is a bit more relaxed. If someone wants to use a newer OS version to pilot some changes, it's generally acceptable to do so with the understanding that either an approved OS will need to be used or that an exception is filed to allow the new OS into the production space.

A final piece to the base template is that of network security. Gamecorp has a policy for any system that contains or could contain payment card information along with personally identifiable information. It is based on the PCI DSS 3.0 reference architecture supplied by Microsoft and consists of several subnets to allow for network isolation of application components, and additionally secured by using network security groups which police traffic between each subnet. A representative diagram of this reference architecture (found at `https://azure.microsoft.com/en-us/blog/payment-processing-blueprint-for-pci-dss-compliant-environments/`) can be seen in Figure 9-4.

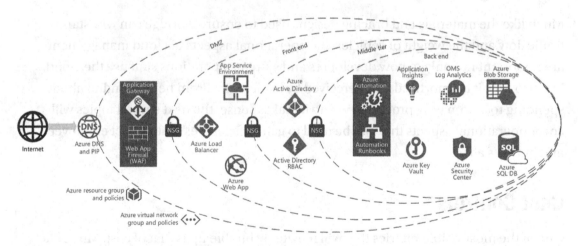

Figure 9-4. *The PCI DSS 3.0 network reference architecture*

For the development subscription, you decide on an audit policy in place to make sure that any subnets within the subscription are using the appropriate Network Security Groups (NSGs), and flag those that aren't. For the production subscription, you decide on the same type of base rule but set the policy enforcement to Deny, so any variance in this requirement will be caught and disallowed.

Tip   Deploying an Azure Resource Manager template with the `-WhatIf` flag via PowerShell will allow you to check your work prior to an actual deployment being performed. This holds true for template syntax / content, dependency checking, or policy compliance.

You upload the new policies to the portal and let them start to run through each subscription. As these jobs can take a fair amount of time to run, you allow them to complete while looking forward to how compliance checks can help operations and stakeholders feel more secure in how the platform's underpinnings are managed.

Building Operational Efficiencies

Much like the materials and bracing designs used to ensure a bridge can withstand traffic flow and the weight of vehicles, the operational aspects of cloud management are important not only to how developers and systems operations staff use the cloud, but also how it is amortized and perceived by leadership. From being mindful about spending to automating processes where it makes sense, the next several topics will cover operational aspects that can be used to gain efficiencies that impact employees and budgets alike.

Cost Controls

One of the most visible metrics that will inevitably bubble up is that of cost. Much like the conservationist idea of turning the lights off when you leave a room in your house, being conscious of resource consumption and its associated cost to the company is a mantra that can help not only the design of cloud solutions, but the company's bottom line. When looking to get information about spend (or "run") rate, there are several options available:

- *Azure Billing APIs*: These REST APIs allow you to build custom queries to pull back billing information for one or more subscriptions, depending on your level of access. This can be combined with a business intelligence tool, such as Power BI, to create reports and dashboards.

- *Azure Portal*: The portal itself can give you a fair amount of information, though it typically will relegate you to information from the current billing cycle and the last full cycle. This can be good for sifting through specific resources or resource groups without having to leave the portal.

- *Azure Cost Management (Cloudyn)*: In late 2017, Microsoft acquired a product called Cloudyn, which provided summary and drill-down interfaces to the Billing APIs. This tool officially became known as Azure Cost Management and is available to customers via a link in the Azure portal.

- *Azure Pricing Calculator*: This online resource gives you a quick way to estimate costs associated with all of Azure's infrastructure and platform offerings.

In some instances where an enterprise agreement is established, access to these tools can be a bit restricted, as enterprise administrators may have those resources locked down to a specific set of users. Information can be displayed in the Azure portal regardless of those restrictions, but the information may be filtered depending on the options selected.

To help set some initial guardrails, you look into some of the existing costs associated with the operation and assess what potential costs could arise given the infrastructure selected. Because much of the equipment for Andromeda is paid for and close to end-of-life, the cost associated with maintenance is fairly low. You decide to also factor in the cost of potentially putting the platform into an on-premises datacenter, as that is the main footprint that Gamecorp uses to host applications. The datacenter operations team uses a headcount-based allocation for general contracting services, and factors in charges based on resource type, required run rate, required uptime, and patching/scheduled maintenance if applicable.

Using the costing chart for Gamecorp's virtual assets as shown in the Asset Pricing spreadsheet found in the supporting documents, you match up asset cost with the results of the capacity planning exercises you went through earlier in Chapter 6.

EXERCISE: UTILIZATION MANAGEMENT STRATEGIES

While accounting for usage and resource types can give you a fair idea of what the overall operational costs might look like, taking it a step further and planning for compute usage can help put additional safeguards in place. Defining a power management strategy for environments within the runway can lead to significant cost savings. In this exercise, you will evaluate the environmental needs of the Andromeda team while also considering the rest of the retail operations engineering teams and what approach would best suit everyone.

After meeting with the engineering managers and the leadership team, you find out that the machines that are used by developers for testing and proof of concept work are generally in use from 8 AM to 7 PM local time, with some limited exceptions by team. The integration environment is needed for testing by domestic resources from 8 AM to 9 PM Eastern. A second integration environment for international testers is also available from 9 AM to 5 PM UTC. Two additional validation environments are available for operations testing on an as-needed basis. Any production environment is considered to be operational using a 99.5% uptime SLA and would not leverage any automatic power down scenario. Given these requirements, construct a power management strategy that would result in the appropriate compute usage for each scenario.

Azure Automation Accounts

Another benefit to using Microsoft Azure is the built-in platform feature of Azure Automation. This offering allows you to automate almost any operational need you could possibly imagine. The three main areas that can apply to operational automation are runbooks, scheduled jobs, and the Azure Automation Desired State Configuration (DSC) service. Runbooks and scheduled jobs fall into the category of enterprise job scheduler features, while DSC services allow you to enforce DSC configurations on virtual machines with a lower barrier of entry than standing up your own DSC administration servers.

Runbooks

Runbooks, in the context of Azure Automation, refer to any runnable script using either PowerShell or Python that can be leveraged to perform a task. This task could be a one-time operation or a scheduled and repeatable operation. There are several types of runbooks available to you, as shown in Figure 9-5.

Figure 9-5. *Listing of Azure Automation Runbook options*

Each type of runbook allows you to construct a runbook that meets specific criteria. Here is a brief outline of the main use cases for each:

- *PowerShell*: This type of runbook is simple. It can contain any valid construct that the language supports. You can draw in modules to further supplement the code.

- *Python 2 (Preview)*: The same concept as the prior item is in play here; the only difference is that you can use Python to author your runbook.

- *Graphical*: This uses PowerShell behind the scenes, but will allow you to drop cmdlets, code, junctions, and more onto a canvas. You can connect these elements together to create a graphical representation of a script's flow. An added benefit of using a graphical runbook is that you can set activity trace levels on or off. This provides additional telemetry around the execution of each part of the runbook when it is run.

- *PowerShell Workflow*: This uses the workflow concept within PowerShell to allow for code-only execution with parallel execution support.

- *Graphical PowerShell Workflow*: A combination of the two previous types, this will allow you to construct a graphical representation of your script and allow for parallel execution support.

You decide to start by creating a runbook that will manage the shutdown and start of virtual machine resources automatically. Any virtual machine that contains a tag of AutoShutdown will be turned off based on the time indicated by the tag value, and any virtual machine that contains a tag of AutoStart will be powered on based on the tag value. In addition, the development teams are geographically disbursed, so someone asking for a power off time of 7 PM in London would be different from someone requesting the same power off time in San Diego. You add another tag called HomeTimeZone that allows the preferred time zone to be set. This way, start and stop times can be managed assuming local time, and a time zone code can be pulled back to verify. A final caveat to this process is that the development teams have requested the ability to override the auto shutdown policy in cases where additional off-hours development or automated testing is required for delivery work. The requirement is that any power off time set between midnight and 5 AM local time will not power the box off before.

Dealing with date and time conversions can be a tricky subject. When dealing with these conversions in runbooks, keep in mind that the local time is assumed to be UTC unless it is explicitly set to something else. You start by experimenting with the date-time conversion steps first, to make sure you get that part correct. Your first draft ends up looking like the following:

```
$vms = Get-AzureRmVM -Status | where { $_.Tags.ContainsKey("AutoShutdown")
      -eq $true }
Foreach ($vm in $vms) {
    $value = $vm.Tags["AutoShutdown"].ToString()
    $TimeZoneID = $vm.Tags["HomeTimeZone"].ToString()
    $date = $value -as [DateTime]
    $baselineDate = [TimeZoneInfo]::ConvertTime([DateTime]::UtcNow,
                    [TimeZoneInfo]::FindSystemTimeZoneById($TimeZoneId))
    if (!$date) {
```

```
        Write-Warning "Warning - The value $($value) is not a valid DateTime."
    }
    else {
        $tempDate = "{0}/{1}/{2} {3}" -f $baselineDate.Month,
                    $baselineDate.Day, $baselineDate.Year, $value
        $start = "{0}/{1}/{2} 12:00:00 AM" -f $baselineDate.Month,
                    $baselineDate.Day,$baselineDate.Year
        $end = "{0}/{1}/{2} 5:00:00 AM" -f $baselineDate.Month,
                    $baselineDate.Day,$baselineDate.Year
        $date = $tempDate -as [DateTime]
        # If shutdown time is in the early morning hours, it is assumed
        that the machine will
        # be powered on overnight.
        if ($date -lt ($end -as [DateTime]) -and $date -gt ($start -as
        [DateTime])) {
            $date = $date.AddDays(1)
        }

        Write-Output "Current time $($TimeZoneId) is $($baselineDate)."
        Write-Output "Shutdown time $($TimeZoneId) is $($date)."

    }
}
```

There are a couple of things going on here that warrant a closer look. First, you pull back the values of the AutoShutdown and HomeTimeZone tags into local variables. Then, you convert the $value variable to a DateTime type for evaluation later. This allows you to see if the value that was entered was a valid time, and if it's not, the opportunity is there to warn or throw an error depending on the need.

To evaluate the time value further, you need to format it after time zone conversion so that it follows a specific pattern. Using the same pattern for the power off time as well as the start and end times for assumed overnight processing, you are able to make a call as to whether or not the machine should indeed be shut down. To test your hypothesis, you insert the following code directly below the last Write-Output statement:

CHAPTER 9   TRANSITION ARCHITECTURES

```
if ($date -lt $baselineDate) {
    Write-Output "Stopping $($vm.Name)..."
    if (!$WhatIf) {
        #Stop-AzureRmVM -Name $vm.Name -ResourceGroupName
        $vm.ResourceGroupName -Force
        Write-Output "What if..."
    }
    else {
        Write-Output "Had this not been a what if scenario, this
        machine would have shut down."
    }

    Write-Output "$($vm.Name) stopped."
}
else {
    Write-Output "Machine $($vm.Name) will not be powered off as
    $($date) is later than $($baselineDate)."
}
```

This code allows you to verify that the machines tagged with certain times will trigger the shutdown but using a "what if" scenario instead of the real shutdown command. A few trial runs prove to be useful, as the machines listed by the job as a result of the query output the messages you would expect based on the tag values you have preemptively supplied. Now you're ready to look into making this runbook repeatable by turning it into a scheduled job.

Scheduled Jobs

One bit of very useful functionality within Automation accounts is the ability to create scheduled jobs. These scheduled jobs consist of two main components: the runbook, and the schedule by which it is executed. As the previous section dealt with runbooks, let's now focus on setting up schedules and attaching them to runbooks to create a scheduled job definition.

Figure 9-6 shows the New Schedule blade in the Automation workspace, which is displayed when adding a new schedule to the account. An important thing to remember is that schedules are not job specific; many jobs could share the same execution schedule. Deleting a schedule from a runbook will remove the schedule completely from the Automation account, not just from the runbook! While this may seem inconvenient, it does allow for object reuse with respect to schedules.

Figure 9-6. The New Schedule blade

Given the varying nature of schedules, this blade allows you to schedule one time or recurring events. You can select a start date and time for the event(s), the time zone to operate under, the level of recurrence, and an optional expiration date and time if the schedule needs to end based on time constraints. The fastest frequency that any one schedule can run in is once an hour.

You create a new schedule called TopOfTheHour, which you plan to use in conjunction with the runbook you just created to test the "what if" scenario around automatic shutdown of virtual machines. Running this job once per hour for a couple of days will allow you to collect run information and make sure the changes you've started to make are actually applied the way you would expect them to be. You set the start date and time to midnight of the following day, with a recurrence of once per hour. You then go back to the runbook and associate the new schedule to it.

With a basis for creating scheduled jobs now taken care of, the next item of focus that comes to mind is that of virtual machine configuration. There are several different options available, from Chef, Puppet, Terraform, and Ansible to plain script files. While the Andromeda team is leaning more toward platform components, the remainder of the engineering teams are still fairly dependent on traditional virtual machine-driven environments. You have done some work with PowerShell DSC, and it just so happens that Azure Automation has a built-in offering that allows you to manage and execute DSC configurations.

Azure Automation Desired State Configuration

As mentioned previously, automation accounts come with a built-in DSC pull server, reducing the amount of work you need to do to get configurations installed on virtual machine resources.

THOUGHT EXERCISE: GROUP POLICY VS. DSC

Many long-time systems administrators in Windows environments are familiar with the practice of developing group policy to help administer widespread rules around access to resources, available programs, and more. In some respects, DSC touches many of the same governance and configuration areas. In a modernized DevOps world, what items would you think would make better candidates for DSC over group policy? Vice versa?

After writing and checking in the remainder of the configuration scripts, you realize that the repo can now be used as a source backing for not only the automation DSC server but for building container images as well.

Microsoft Operations Management Suite

Not to be forgotten, the needs of site reliability and/or IT operations teams also need to be met to ensure compliance with an operating model, and to ensure that applications are always running at their best. To assist in giving ops a cohesive area to monitor and troubleshoot from, Microsoft introduced the Operations Management Suite as an offering within Azure to support monitoring, alerting, log aggregation, patch maintenance, threat detection, and more. Coupled with an automation account, OMS can be a very powerful tool for ops teams to perform change tracking, patching and updates, and virtual machine inventory.

The base product offering for OMS is centered around log aggregation and analysis. From a pricing standpoint, you can aggregate logs and run reports against them for free, with some limitations. The free tier allows you no more than 500MB of transfer/storage per day and does not offer any data retention past seven days. Two other pricing tiers exist for OMS:

- *Standalone*: This allows you to upload an unlimited amount of data but will retain only one month of data by default. Custom retention policies can be established, and data storage is charged per GB.

- *Subscription-based*: Several inclusive and a la carte options exist for subscribing to four different management areas. Details on pricing can be found at `http://download.microsoft.com/download/5/C/4/5C41780B-5821-4EB8-AA23-60404A224568/OMS%20Licensing%20FAQ_FINAL.pdf`. Along with listings of baseline and augmented features for each area (Insights and Analytics, Security Center, Backup and Recovery, Automation and Control).

Investing in the Developer Experience

An important paradigm shift over the past several years has been the notion of moving more and more things—testing, development, quality—to be measured as close to development as possible. The "shift left" movement has allowed for the ability to catch issues and harvest feedback from stakeholders much sooner in the development lifecycle. Making that shift can be difficult depending on several factors, including developer skill set, tooling and testing maturity, cultural maturity, and standards for accountability so everyone is aware of what they should and should not be doing to help enforce quality in the platform. Combining an initiative such as shifting left with another large initiative—pushing to cloud-first development practices—can further complicate things. There is a fundamental difference in approach when looking to leverage the native abilities the cloud can offer. Let's look at some prerequisite things that can help arm developers with the skills they need to be successful amidst the chaos of change.

Preparing to Shift Left

While not completely your responsibility, you know that there will be some difficulties with getting the engineering teams to all embrace this type of change. You start to outline some major areas where you anticipate some pushback or potential skills gaps. Without attempting to sound too buzzword-laden, you come up with three areas that can have significant impact: training, anticipating platform or component failure, and process cohesiveness.

Setting the Stage with Training

A primary stumbling block that many organizations run into is that there is an expectation that shifting left is trivial, and that developers can easily pick up infrastructure as code, configuration as code, policy as code, or even conceptual topics dealing with the world of operations. While there are some engineers out there who are good at both the development as well as the operations side of platform architecture, many are not, and expecting engineers to adopt and embrace additional responsibilities can sometimes come at the expense of more important things, like quality. When beginning a paradigm shift such as this, ensuring your staff is properly trained is one of the very first things to cover.

There is a wealth of websites out there that cater to self-paced online learning, many of which contain courses on cloud-first fundamentals. Examples of such sites include:

- Pluralsight (`https://www.pluralsight.com`)

- OpsGility (`https://opsgility.com`)

- Microsoft Virtual Academy (`https://microsoftvirtualacademy.com`)

- edX (`https://courses.edx.org`)

Similarly, there are in-person instruction options provided either by Microsoft or one of their partners, specifically designed to help shore up gaps in skill sets and push developers into the world of cloud-first development. Meetups, user groups, and localized events such as the Global Azure Bootcamp all give further opportunities to those who wish to sharpen their skills by learning new techniques or honing existing ones. Finding the right balance for the engineers in your organization is not always straightforward, but given the options that exist, planning to get everyone to a common base understanding can be much less painful.

The engineering management staff at Gamecorp begins to ask your opinion regarding the best resources their staff could leverage. You mention Pluralsight and Virtual Academy as two primary self-paced options, which is met with some resistance by management because the fear about cost begins to creep into the conversation. Since all of the engineers have full MSDN Enterprise subscriptions, you politely remind them that a membership to Pluralsight is included with their annual subscription benefits, as well as an Azure subscription with $150 per month to experiment with. You also remind them that Virtual Academy is a free option for online learning.

Concerns start to crop up regarding the pressure to deliver features and whether the engineers will take the initiative to learn this material on their own. You put them in contact with the account representative from Microsoft who manages the Gamecorp subscriptions, telling them that the account rep can work with them to come up with hands-on sessions that can be delivered on site and, if they wanted to manage expectations, mandated. Another option you present is that of tying the completion of certain online courses to larger performance criteria, which could lead to promotion for individuals. For some, the incentivization of this learning could be a more important factor.

One area you suggest as a focal point is that of infrastructure vs. component selections, and how those can impact design decisions or potentially complicate future refactoring or expansion projects. Having just gone through a similar exercise with looking at the Cardstock platform along with the integrating systems it interacts with, one topic of importance is the notion of expecting things to fail.

Embracing Fault Driven Development

One of the biggest changes to design and development falls into the category of anticipating and planning for failures. In most cases, the resources being utilized in the cloud are not always expected to be on, operational, or even in existence in some cases. Not planning for those situations can cause application faults to be frequent and negatively impactful to user experience. With proper fault tolerance built into an application, any issues that arise can be dealt with in a graceful manner, and activities can be retried depending on need and/or platform requirements. The approach of planning for and handling application faults can be referred to as Fault Driven Development (FDD).

This approach does not mean that fault handling and tolerance are the sole responsibility of the developer, though more seasoned engineers will likely have experience that will aide them in making more technically sound decisions related to software and infrastructure needs. Where possible, infrastructure subject matter experts can and should be brought in to discuss complimentary services, such as redundancy or high availability, if required for the application to function. Coupling this guidance with information from the product team around service level agreements and user experience expectations will help set the stage for an adaptive means for handling faults.

There are two primary ideals within FDD that help to mitigate most situations:

- *Fault tolerance*: Tolerance indicates that a platform, application, or component is built to withstand and anticipate failures. There must be a mechanism in place to ensure that necessary data is retained if it cannot be processed, or that transactions can be retried if the platform requires that level of interaction.

- *Fault handling*: More reactive, fault handling is the proper fielding of and responding to faults that may arise during application usage. This may include front-facing error messages and instructions to the end user on what to do (for example, a common message is "Please try your request again later").

Something that spans both topics is telemetry. Properly outputting information so that it can be used to either retry or redirect a transaction is important, and recording that information for later use is critical when troubleshooting or preparing a root cause analysis on a systemic failure. Tying this telemetry into monitoring and alerting technologies gives a second tier of protection, often allowing site reliability, production support, or other technical operations teams to receive notifications and act accordingly.

DevOps Pipelines

As Gamecorp has recently converted to Azure DevOps Services, a nontrivial amount of work has gone into the streamlining of the company's DevOps pipeline. This covers all areas from work intake, triage, and prioritization to building, testing, releasing, and monitoring all software products. Some initial gains have been realized by moving the teams to one common process, as previously each team was given leeway to decide what process they wanted to follow as an individual team. This unfortunately led to a fair amount of drift between the teams, and it made it difficult for management to track and understand exactly where the overall products were at in the process.

Work Pipelines

While not traditionally thought of as a primary component of the continuous integration/continuous delivery (CI/CD) pipeline that many organizations attempt to move toward, the process of work intake, planning, and execution factor into the rate at which teams can deliver software. If the process for managing work is not as disciplined, it can lead to teams overcommitting to work, improper definition of requirements for those work items, even decreases in software quality if the desire to ship features outweighs the desire to ensure those features work as required.

Build Definitions

The build system used by Azure DevOps Services and newer versions of Team Foundation Server (2015 update 3 and newer) leverage a task-based engine similar to systems like Jenkins, Bamboo, and TeamCity. This allows you to construct definitions that are both flexible and powerful. A relatively new feature introduced in late 2017 is the use of YAML (Yet Another Markup Language) to define your build definitions. While it may seem like adding another layer of abstraction onto the existing build definition language, what it allows you to do is source control that definition and use it throughout the lifecycle of your software, including local development.

Using the Andromeda team as a pilot, you introduce them to the mechanics of the Azure DevOps Services build engine, showing them how to create builds from scratch as well as integrate with existing tools. As they are still currently using Jenkins to perform a variety of build tasks, the Jenkins integration task becomes a staple in their definitions. They seem fairly open to changing some of the practices they had been using, acknowledging that the way they have done things may not be the best way.

The team takes to creating definitions quickly, and extracting the YAML for their base definitions is easy because Azure DevOps Services provides a "View YAML" link that is accessible from the process, stage, or task view. Figure 9-7 shows an example of where the link can be found when selecting the process level.

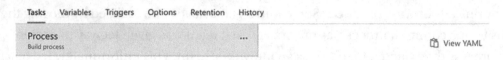

Figure 9-7. *Example of the View YAML link, which displays the YAML interpretation of a build definition*

While the export of the YAML definition is straightforward, the team wonders how they will be able to use this during local development. They find the definition template that allows for using a YAML file in Azure DevOps Services just fine, but the local experience is still a bit of a mystery. After a bit of research, one of the engineers finds the documentation on how to use the YAML definition with a local copy of the Azure DevOps Services build agent.

Release Definitions

The release management feature of Azure DevOps Services uses the same task-based mechanics as the build definitions. It does not, however, allow for the same level of "definition-as-code" that the build definitions do. Despite this, the team looks into how they can start to define the deployment flow for their application given the components they have and the gates that Gamecorp requires for audit and traceability.

DevTest Labs

A final piece to the engineering investment comes by way of providing labs to development teams for various integration testing efforts, proof of concept work, or for internal training initiatives where hands-on exercises are required. Azure's DevTest Labs offer all of these features in a compact interface designed to make administration simple. Automating the creation of a lab using an Azure Resource Manager template makes it a repeatable and reliable option when looking to set up administrative and operational guidelines, as well as leveraging the ability to create custom images for a lab, which gets properly configured machines in the hands of lab users faster.

Setting Operational Parameters

One of the most interesting facets of DevTest Labs is that you can set policies and parameters on a lab-to-lab basis. These can include cost controls, custom formulas and disk images, artifact sources, allowable virtual machine sizes, lab-based power management settings, and more. Having the ability to set these constraints while still offering development teams some autonomy to explore and experiment with new virtual machine technologies works out for engineers and leaders alike.

In conjunction with the DevTest Labs samples hosted on GitHub (`https://github.com/Azure/azure-devtestlab`), you start to build a base Azure Resource Manager template that can be used to quickly stand up a lab for team use with the following policies and settings established:

- A default automatic shutdown time of 7 PM local time

- A maximum of two machines per lab user

- A maximum of n machines per lab, based on the calculation of two machines per user × number of users.

- A cost threshold of $100 per user, resulting in a calculated target of $100 × number of users

- A private artifact repository, using the Gamecorp cloud solutions repository

- A custom formula using a stock image and two artifacts

- A list of approved VM image sizes

To cover the shutdown time, you find the following resource declaration in the GitHub samples, which allows you to modify the time in accordance with a specified time zone:

```
{
        "apiVersion": "2017-04-26-preview",
        "name": "LabVmsShutdown",
        "type": "schedules",
        "dependsOn": [
          "[resourceId('Microsoft.DevTestLab/labs',
            parameters('newLabName'))]"
        ],
```

```
        "properties": {
          "status": "enabled",
          "taskType": "LabVmsShutdownTask",
          "timeZoneId": "[string(parameters('timeZoneId'))]",
          "dailyRecurrence": {
            "time": "[string(parameters('labVmShutDownTime'))]"
          }
        }
      }
    }
```

You focus next on getting some of the calculated fields set up. You create a parameter for the template called `totalLabUsers` and work on the `variables` section to incorporate some calculated values to plug into the `resources` section. You're able to set the maximum number of VMs for the lab:

```
"maxAllowedVmsPerLab": "[mul(2,parameters('totalLabUsers'))]"
```

You're also able to set the cost threshold amount for the cost control policy:

```
"costThreshold": "[mul(variables('maxAllowedVmsPerLab'),100)]"
```

These variables can now be used in conjunction with other resource samples found in the GitHub examples referenced above. The cost policy resource is shown following, and the full template can be found in the example code under the Automation folder. Note the placement of the `costThreshold` variable in the `target` property, just below `status`.

```
{
        "apiVersion": "2017-04-26-preview",
        "name": "targetCost",
        "type": "costs",
        "dependsOn": [
          "[resourceId('Microsoft.DevTestLab/labs',
            parameters('newLabName'))]"
        ],
        "properties": {
          "targetCost": {
            "cycleType": "CalendarMonth",
```

```
        "status": "Enabled",
        "target": "[variables('costThreshold')]",
        "costThresholds": [
            {
                "thresholdId": "96c08eae-885f-4a46-a15d-9dc991a32cbf",
                "thresholdStatus": "Disabled",
                "displayOnChart": "Enabled",
                "sendNotificationWhenExceeded": "Disabled",
                "percentageThreshold": { "thresholdValue": 75 }
            },
            {
                "thresholdId": "5ef03748-2e10-4b3c-afc2-cc766abf2d5d",
                "thresholdStatus": "Disabled",
                "displayOnChart": "Enabled",
                "sendNotificationWhenExceeded": "Enabled",
                "percentageThreshold": { "thresholdValue": 100 }
            },
            {
                "thresholdId": "b0bf180e-2e09-4073-8040-56e8a23dcd84",
                "thresholdStatus": "Disabled",
                "displayOnChart": "Disabled",
                "sendNotificationWhenExceeded": "Disabled",
                "percentageThreshold": { "thresholdValue": 125 }
            }
        ]
    }
  }
}
```

You next set out to wire together a deployment mechanism for this template, along with two additional components:

- Setting up RBAC permission to the lab

- Synchronizing KeyVault values to ensure consistency between labs

The first component is fairly easy to understand, since the users of the lab will need to be assigned to two role groups in Azure: Virtual Machine Contributor and DevTest Labs User. You're able to find an example in PowerShell of how to assign these role groups to an Azure Active Directory object, and the resulting script can be seen as follows:

```
$group = Get-AzureRmADGroup -SearchString "$($TeamADGroup)"
New-AzureRmRoleAssignment -ObjectId $group.Id.Guid -RoleDefinitionName
"DevTest Labs User" -ResourceName $LabName -ResourceGroupName
$ResourceGroupName -ResourceType "Microsoft.DevTestLab/labs"
New-AzureRmRoleAssignment -ObjectId $group.Id.Guid -RoleDefinitionName
"Virtual Machine Contributor" -ResourceName $LabName -ResourceGroupName
$ResourceGroupName -ResourceType "Microsoft.DevTestLab/labs"
```

The second component requires some thought. Traditionally speaking, developers have had access to lower-level account passwords for accessing machines and performing actions. While they typically use their own AD accounts for that, the passwords are available via app configuration files, and can be scraped by anyone with access to the target machine. To help avoid that wherever possible, you try to think of a way where more managed accounts could be used—the name of the account would be well known, but the password would be managed centrally.

In addition, values needed for artifact configuration could be stored and updated using this method. An example of a secret that could be maintained in that manner would be a personal access token (PAT) used to install an Azure DevOps Services agent on a virtual machine and join it to an Azure DevOps Services deployment group. Having a synchronized value for that will allow for reuse between labs without fear of that secret's value leaking anywhere. This gives a greater amount of consistency when configuring machines for deployment scenarios.

After doing some research, you find that the Key Vault created with a DevTest Lab is considered a personal vault—that is, it does not hold common values for the lab itself. For any keys or secrets that are used during the deployment phase, you decide to leverage variables within the Azure DevOps Services definition instead of trying to sync up common values with each individual lab vault. You then finish off the definition as shown in Figure 9-8.

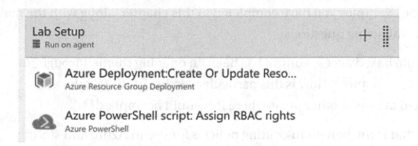

Figure 9-8. *Layout for creating a DevTest Lab using a custom ARM template and Azure PowerShell tasks*

Leveraging Custom Images and Formulas

A bonus of using DevTest Labs is that you can create custom formulas and images to speed up the time to market on configured lab machines. There is a rich ecosystem of artifacts that can be pulled in via the public repository on GitHub, and you can create your own artifacts and pull them in from a private repository as well. Using prebuilt or custom artifacts to keep installations of prerequisites consistent will give developers confidence in the tools they are using, and it will prevent instances of the "it works on my machine" excuse from cropping up.

If you are looking to use custom images or formulas, you can start by including a resource definition for a custom formula in the ARM template you have set up for the deployment of the lab. You can also use Azure DevOps Services to create a new VM in a lab, create an image from that VM, and delete the VM (retaining the image) afterward. To do so, you need only to install the DevTest Labs task extension from the Visual Studio Marketplace (https://marketplace.visualstudio.com) to get started.

Summary

The supporting details for any design are never trivial, and this exercise is no exception. You've covered a lot of ground with these sections, going from security and access to operational concerns to development concerns. Each area has its own host of challenges, problem spaces, and opportunities for innovation. The support work that you have done is much more in-the-trenches than the previous endeavors, resulting in the amassing of a good starter set of administration and configuration scripts. You feel confident in approaching the engineers with some development concepts meant to improve cloud-first deveopment efforts as well as improve engineers' skill sets.

Given the examples you have completed in this chapter, along with the narrative, consider the following questions:

1. Role based access control has been an ongoing theme throughout a few chapters. How is this particular section of RBAC relevant, and are there other areas where this could be applied?

2. What is the benefit to crafting policies for use in Azure and storing them in source control? Is there any way to leverage a deployment pipeline to move those policies to subscriptions?

3. How important is planning for usage in conjunction with overall cost? Are there other ways of retrieving, formatting, and analyzing this information to help make better decisions?

4. OMS has a wealth of options covering logging to alerting to security. What other categories or services would you implement in addition to the examples listed? Are there any services that were missed in the initial implementation?

5. What are some common challenges you can think of that would make the adoption of a shift left strategy more difficult in an organization?

6. Think of some examples from your experience around different teams that you have worked with or worked on. Is it more important to offer more autonomy to distributed teams with respect to build and release technologies, or does a more consistent and consolidated approach make more sense?

7. Does offering DevTest Labs to engineering teams make sense when those teams are primarily developing with platform-as-a-service components? Why or why not?

CHAPTER 10

Development Concepts

After some serious design sessions, concept work, and API building, it's time to get into the details further with the construction of the mechanisms that will get this platform to the cloud in its entirety. Using the target architecture as your guide, along with the cast of supporting services, you are ready to start building out the runways for Cardstock, the inventory management APIs, integrated identity framework, and more.

Taking an incremental approach, each section of this chapter will build on the previous sections. We will be covering the following topics as they relate to all deployable components in the platform:

- Continuous integration

- Continuous delivery

- Continuous testing

- Source and dependency scanning

- Artifact management

- Resource validation

These topics will be further expanded upon in the next chapter, where the concepts become true implementations. To start, however, you piece together the existing deployment architectures in an attempt to see if there are any common threads that can be woven together.

Start with the Big Picture

You revisit the deployment architecture you captured from the Andromeda team and start to look into how the specific pieces of that puzzle fit into the overall plan that Gamecorp has for fully rolling out Azure DevOps Services across the enterprise. As

© Josh Garverick 2018
J. Garverick, *Migrating to Azure*, https://doi.org/10.1007/978-1-4842-3585-0_10

previously stated, the Andromeda engineers have no qualms about switching which Git provider they use, as the underlying source control mechanism is not being changed. They do have a preference to stay with their Jenkins jobs, configurations, and webhooks to reduce the amount of noise around changing build and deploy mechanisms.

Taking this into consideration, you now look to the tangled web of pipelines that the Gamecorp team currently has. While gains have been made to streamline outputs and reduce redundant tools, there are still different release cadences, build requirements, and approval gates between the different teams and components. You decide to sketch out a rough view of what the runways look like, keeping the common thread of environments in mind throughout. The resulting sketch can be seen in Figure 10-1.

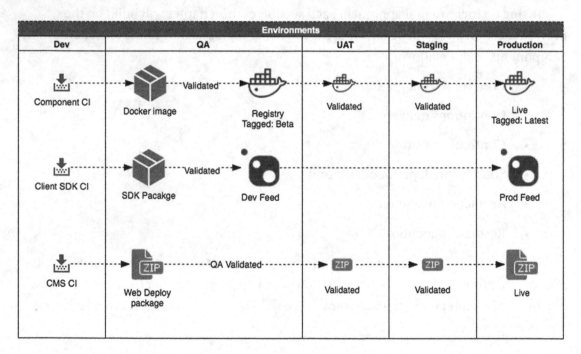

Figure 10-1. *Logical deployment architecture overview*

The deployment landscape of Gamecorp's differing components follows the same linear progression through environments. A brief overview of each environment is listed here:

- *Dev*: This is reserved for local development instances or for special team-based instances that are used as proving grounds before code is allowed to move to QA.

- *QA*: This is reserved for quality assurance and quality engineers to perform a wide swath of manual and automated tests relative to the components' functional requirements.

- *UAT*: This is reserved for user acceptance testing, which is the first round of client-side end user testing. Internal users will validate new functionality is working as expected.

- *Staging*: This is reserved for more intensive load, performance, and security tests as well as a last stop validation before going to production.

- *Production*: This is the environment in which all components are considered live and ready for consumption.

Not all engineering teams use all environments, however. The integrations team, for example, will roll changes out to APIs and have them validated in QA, and if all tests pass, the packages are promoted to production-ready and placed in the primary package feed for use. These packages are then downloaded and distributed as needed throughout the application lifecycle.

Approval gates are leveraged to ensure that no unauthorized changes are pushed to production. In the current state, these approvals are gathered by sending emails, and a responsible party will push the changes to production during an approved window. With the Azure DevOps Services project, the engineers are looking to make use of the automatic approval gate features, which should give them the ability to approve changes in the web interface and release code much quicker.

Building on Continuous Integration

Traditionally, developers will iterate on changes in a rapid fashion, though committing changes and pushing those to the mainline may occur at various times. Things are further complicated by branching strategies being employed. For example, a master-based or trunk-based strategy has much less overhead than a GitFlow-inspired strategy solely by virtue of the number of branches each approach can entail. It is best practice to have an automated build kick off as soon as code is pushed to a remote repository. Can those builds be run more often, though—triggered by the developer or automatically triggered to run locally? In some cases where public agents are not being utilized due to internal, behind-the-firewall builds or deployments, the use of private agents may be capped for budgetary reasons. If many developers are committing at the same time, or close to the same time, it could queue up the builds and delay other CI builds from kicking off. Also, triggering builds locally, with the same mechanism being used in Azure DevOps Services providing consistency. That may not hold true if building the solution using Visual Studio and then committing changes that trigger a build including test steps, static analysis, and so forth.

The short answer to the question of whether they can be run more often is yes, they can. You have a couple of options at your disposal to be able to run the same build definition locally as is run by Azure DevOps Services once code is pushed to the remote. Both involve the installation of an Azure DevOps Services agent on the developers' workstations. One method is more intrusive than the other. You can:

- *Install the agent directly onto the workstation*: This involves having the agent running at all times on the workstation, phoning back to Azure DevOps Services to ensure a proper connection.

- *Stand up an agent via a Docker image*: This involves a less permanent method of creating a container, setting some environment variables, and having the container run on demand.

Thinking through the two options and knowing that the target state is much more container-friendly, you suggest using the Azure DevOps Services agent container as the preferred approach. How does the build definition run locally, though? The build can be triggered by Azure DevOps Services and fed to the agent based on setting criteria for the build and preferred agents. One thing that the Andromeda team has been very keen to do is encapsulate their build and release scripts within the repository itself. Azure DevOps Services has the ability to run YAML-based definitions, drawing the definition from the repository and building it using the agent. What's more, running the agent locally will allow for running that YAML definition directly against the local agent without making the network call to Azure DevOps Services to initiate a build.

EXERCISE: LOCAL BUILDS FTW

Using the approach you have recommended, you work with the Andromeda engineers to set up local build agents in preparation for using the YAML definitions locally and server-side. Use the following task list as a guide for setting up and testing your preferred method of installation:

1. In Azure DevOps Services, hover over the icon in the upper right corner that has your initials/avatar. Click the icon to reveal the context menu. Select "Security" from the menu.

2. In the Security menu, select "Personal Access Tokens" and create a new token. You may allow access to all features or scope the token to just build and release. Set the token timeout to one year.

3. Once created, copy the token and paste it into a file or other secure means of storing the value. The value will not appear again, and navigating away from the page without copying it will force you to have to create a new token.

4. To set up a new Azure DevOps Services agent container, you will require the token value as well as the name of the Azure DevOps Services account. Do not use the full URL of the Azure DevOps Services account—only the account name is required. Once you have both of those items, open a console window and enter the following command, replacing values as marked:

   ```
   Docker run -it --rm --name="vsts-agent" -v <<Path to your
   source>>:/mnt/src -e VSTS_TOKEN="<<your token>>" -e VSTS_
   ACCOUNT="<<your VSTS instance name>>" microsoft/vsts-agent
   ```

5. Change directories to the base folder for your repository, which should be where your YAML build definition is located. Enter the following command in the console window:

   ```
   Docker exec vsts-agent /vsts/agent/run.sh localRun --yml /
   mnt/src/build.yaml
   ```

Watch the output of the local build in the console window. Do you see any differences between the output locally vs. the output captured by Azure DevOps Services when executing a remote build?

With the refinement of the base CI build definition, you are ready to look into layering in more utilities to help identify problems and provide feedback.

Source and Dependency Scanning

There are many examples in the market today of tooling or processes that promote the practice of shifting left—catching as many issues and gathering as much feedback about in-flight feature work as possible. One area that tends to get less press than continuous integration, automated testing, and even continuous deployment is that of security. Security is something that should absolutely shift left with the rest of the application lifecycle. Making security an integral part of development ensures it is thought of from design to delivery.

Two areas that come to mind for shifting security to the left are static code analysis and dependency scanning. While static code analysis can tend to encompass many things, from code smells to cyclomatic complexity to potential poor practices, it can also help to identify areas in which proprietary code could be exploited or be seen as vulnerable to types of intrusion attacks.

Dependency scanning is more common when dealing with third party or open source software components. Not only will scanning a dependency graph help to understand what libraries you're directly referencing, it will also help you to see the full web of components being pulled into your solution. Sometimes a library you really like may have dependencies that you really don't like. For example, many larger organizations could see the use of third-party libraries as risky, and libraries that are distributed under restrictive licenses could be seen as undesirable or even off limits.

The frequency of scans can be important as well. The ideal of shifting left would be to capture any and all potential issues as early in the process as possible. One thing that may cause engineers to dislike these scans might be including them in a continuous integration build definition. It is not uncommon to see static code or dependency analysis scans take many minutes, if not longer. The size of the codebase as well as the depth of the scan can factor into how long the overall measurement will take.

While many tools exist in the marketplace for scanning source code and dependencies, it's equally as important to instill the cultural need to take the results of these tools seriously. A company can pay tens of thousands of dollars to implement solutions such as Black Duck or WhiteSource, but if there is no accountability for fixing security vulnerabilities found by those tools, that money is largely wasted. Establishing the importance of scanning for—and fixing—security vulnerabilities is a very important part of moving an organization's culture forward.

You decide to start with looking into setting up static code analysis via an installation of SonarQube, a mostly free static analysis tool from SonarSource.

It's Not Delivery, It's Deployment

Do all applications, and application components, need to be delivered to a production environment on an automatic basis? While a bit of a rhetorical question, there is some merit to thinking through the need for continuous delivery. Some applications are no-brainers for continuous delivery. For example, delivering updated content for a website can be done at a quicker cadence than updating massive client libraries that are taken as dependencies by dozens of internal applications.

An area of material debate, as well as semantic differences, can be seen in the context of continuous deployment vs. continuous delivery. At first glance, you may find these two terms to be fairly synonymous. After all, deploying code to production is delivering a finished feature, bugfix, or enhancement, right? While that can be true, there are some key differences between continuous delivery and continuous deployment:

- Continuous delivery is the ability to use the output from the CI to build and deploy the new known good build to one or more environments automatically (`bit.ly/28PWsfk`).

- Continuous deployment is the deployment of code to a single environment. A small team might only implement continuous deployment because each change goes directly to production. Continuous delivery is moving code through several environments, ultimately ending up in production, which may include automated UI, load and performance tests, and approvals along the way.

- Conceptually, continuous delivery is composed of the concepts of continuous integration, automated testing, and continuous deployment.

Artifact Management

For Andromeda, artifact management literally involved moving packages to a drop server and using them from that server. For Gamecorp, an independent and private package feed was established to allow framework and API libraries to be published but not be outwardly exposed. As a part of the Azure DevOps Services migration project, one of the areas the project team wants to look into heavily is that of the Package Management offering, which will provide a central and protected repository for libraries produced as a result of continuous integration efforts within each team.

As it stands today, there are two feeds available to engineers: the primary production feed and a development feed. The intent of the development feed is to offer a separate integration point for beta-level packages and a safe place for experimental changes to live and get tested. Through some deep dives and group discussions, the project team, along with several subject matter experts (SMEs) from the delivery teams, have come to a tentative agreement that it makes more sense to use prerelease flags on nonproduction packages and collapse all feeds into one primary feed.

An area of concern using this approach is that there could be conflicts locally with the use of n number of package versions. This is compounded by a handful of developers arguing that packages should be mutable, meaning the package version can stay static and the contents of that package can change. An example posed to you via one of the project SMEs is that one developer states his team makes changes to code, and therefore packages, many times per day. According to the developer, churning that many versions out seems like clutter.

THOUGHT EXERCISE: HIT THE IMMUTABILITY BUTTON

In a circumstance such as the above scenario, how would you approach the engineer in question and properly diffuse the misconception around package mutability? Think of specific scenarios where changes being introduced without corresponding version numbers could be risky or even dangerous.

NuGet packages are just one type of artifact, however. Moving toward the target state, there are also container images, static content, and even schema changes that are versionable and deployable. While the traditional NuGet artifact is going to be stored in Azure DevOps Services Package Management, the other artifacts will need a place to live as well.

As designed and reviewed earlier, Azure Container Registry will be the source of all container images for the platform. A pipeline to move container images through the runway and tag them appropriately will need to be considered. There are ways of building and publishing those container images directly to the registry from Azure DevOps Services. They can also be published from the developers' workstations, though allowing that level of direct publishing is not something you're comfortable with.

The majority of the CMS static content is already handled with the implementation of the CMS subsystem. One area that you did not take into enough consideration, though, was the image store that belongs to the Cardstock area. Throughout the discovery process, it seemed as though the storage on the local servers at Andromeda were enough to handle serving trading card images uploaded by the end users. Looking forward, there will need to be a bigger solution in place to handle this. Once multiple countries come online with the platform, the local storage will not be enough to keep up with the demand, and it is generally best practice to use a content delivery network for static content whenever possible.

For any schema changes that are tied to the CMS database, the Gamecorp engineering staff has landed on using SQL Change Automation, an offering from Redgate that allows them to ship a database package with data definition language updates between SQL Server instances in the stack. There is a core offering available to users of Visual Studio Enterprise, and a paid version available with Redgate's SQL Toolbelt. The specific product that the team is interested in using is called ReadyRoll. Prior to this, scripts were stored in a separate folder and manually run during a release window to get the database up to date.

EXERCISE: ARTIFACT TARGETS

In order to ensure a consistent flow of artifacts into the pipeline, it's essential that you set up the artifact targets for the application. This exercise will lead you through setting up the content delivery network, Azure Container Registry, and ReadyRoll runways for deployment.

To get started, you create a new container registry for test images in the sandbox resource group by running the following Azure CLI command:

```
az acr create --name <<registryName>> --resource-group gc-sandbox
--sku Standard
```

With the registry, you want to ensure you are limiting access to it to only authorized engineers. You decide to revisit the command above and add the flag `--admin-enabled false` to ensure that an independent set of keys cannot be generated or used with the registry. Disabling the admin user allows you to focus on using RBAC to allow access to the registry. You remind the engineers that pushing to the registry is not to be done outside of the Azure DevOps Services service principal, but when pulling images and logging into the registry, Docker must be running for things to work properly.

Next, you switch your attention to building out the content delivery network. Using Azure CDN profiles, static files can be served to many locations across the globe while being stored in a standard Storage Account. Several tiers exist for access to files from various locations, using custom DNS entries to personalize the delivery network, even using custom rules to serve different file types in different ways. If the intent is to create a completely statically hosted website using a CDN profile, only one tier will allow for this (Premium Verizon). Since this use case is not for all web content but rather specific image content, any tier will be sufficient. While simply using a storage account to host static content is possible (https://docs.microsoft.com/en-us/azure/storage/blobs/storage-blob-static-website), you do still have a requirement to use HTTPS, which will be available to you through a CDN profile. Using the Azure CLI, you create a CDN profile using the following command:

```
az cdn profile create --name cardstock-nonprod --resource-group gc-sandbox
```

You decide to create the profile using a "nonprod" naming standard to allow for multiple nonproduction sites to use the same storage account and profile. To serve up content using this new profile, you create a storage account to keep the static image files in:

```
az storage account create --name cardstocknp01 --resource-group gc-sandbox
```

To finish hooking things up, you use the CLI to create a new endpoint that will serve content for the development instance of Cardstock:

```
az cdn endpoint create --resource-group gc-sandbox --profile-name cardstock-nonprod --name cdn-cardstock-dev --origin cdn-cardstock-dev.gamecorp.us
```

A conceptual diagram of the CDN profile, endpoints, and storage account is shown as follows.

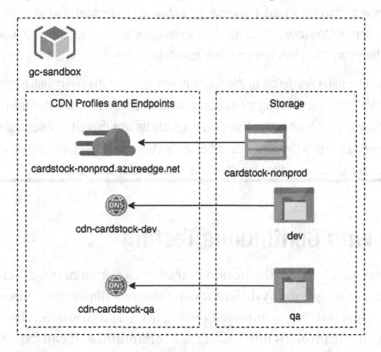

The last piece you look to help with is the use of ReadyRoll to promote a healthy database DevOps pipeline. While this particular case is for the CMS team, there are other engineering teams within Gamecorp watching closely to see if they can also adopt this tooling to help with the painful experiences they have during database deployments.

To get started, you cut a branch from the existing CMS team's repository to ensure you have a clean code base to work with. Next, you add a new project to the solution using the ReadyRoll project type in Visual Studio. To capture the existing state of the database, you use the Redgate tutorial for importing a database into a ReadyRoll project (https://www.red-gate.com/hub/product-learning/sql-change-automation/how-to-import-an-existing-database-to-sqlchangeautomation), after restoring a copy of the CMS database to your local SQL Server instance as per the portal team's instructions.

You notice that after the import, the baseline script is stored in a folder labeled "1.0.0". Moving forward, as new scripts are added, the version number will increment, and all changes will be captured. You commit the new project and find some quick training for the engineers to see how quickly they can adopt this tool into their toolchain.

As a final step in adding ReadyRoll to the solution, you also add the ReadyRoll extension to Azure DevOps Services, allowing for database deployment as well as database unit test execution. Following the information found on the Redgate site (`https://documentation.red-gate.com/rr1/deployment/create-vsts-tfs-release`), you set up initial test tasks and a CI deploy task to allow the database to be quickly tested out.

Working with Continuous Testing

As seen in previous chapters, the notion of testing can span many different technical areas, and have many different connotations depending on your point of view. Most notably, automated testing from a software development perspective typically involves unit testing at a minimum, and can expand in scope to encompass integration, functional, performance, load, stress, and user interface testing. Starting with the fundamentals first, you look for ways you can help the Andromeda and Gamecorp engineers gain more confidence in their code and safeguard against software, infrastructure as code, and configuration as code errors that may arise.

An excellent overview of continuous testing can be seen in the DevOps transformation stories from Microsoft (`https://docs.microsoft.com/en-us/azure/devops/devops-at-microsoft/shift-left-make-testing-fast-reliable`). As discussed previously, the notion of shifting left and pushing quality upstream is a journey unto itself, and getting closer to that goal will help drive agility and quality. Figure 10-2 illustrates a diagrammatic representation of shifting left taken from the article on Microsoft's shift left.

"Shift-Left" == Pushing Quality Upstream

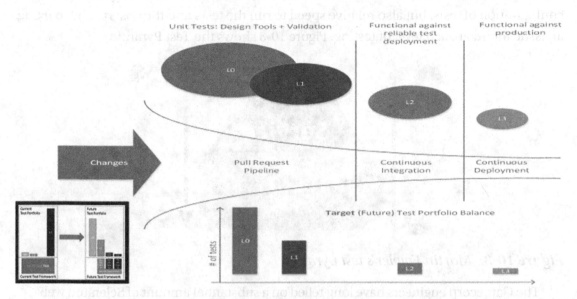

Figure 10-2. *Visual aid relating to shifting left and pushing quality upstream*

Test Classification

As seen previously, there are classifications of tests that help to define markers along the pipeline, constantly looking for validation and striving to keep errors out of production. According to the post, there are four main categories of tests:

- *L0/L1*: Unit tests

  - *L0*: Broad class of fast in-memory unit tests. An L0 test is a unit test to most people. That is a test that depends on code in the assembly under test and nothing else.

  - *L1*: An L1 test might require the assembly plus SQL or the file system.

- *L2/L3*: Functional tests

  - *L2*: Functional tests run against "testable" service deployment. It is a functional test category that requires a service deployment but may have key service dependencies stubbed out in some way.

  - *L3*: This is a restricted class of integration tests that run against production. They require a full product deployment.

Parallels can also be drawn to Martin Fowler's Test Pyramid (`https://martinfowler.com/bliki/TestPyramid.html`), which represents not only the optimal configuration of tests, but also relative speed to run the tests and the cost related to fixing an issue found at each level of testing. Figure 10-3 shows the Test Pyramid.

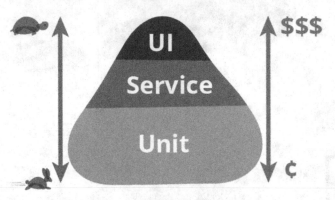

Figure 10-3. *Martin Fowler's test pyramid*

The Gamecorp engineers have long relied on a substantial amount of Selenium web tests to drive quality numbers, with small pockets of unit and integration tests sprinkled throughout their projects. Andromeda's engineers have a modest amount of unit tests, a few functional tests, and no UI tests. Taking what they have established, you work with the engineers to incorporate the tests into their local builds as well as adding them to the continuous integration definitions in Azure DevOps Services. Using the tutorial supplied by Microsoft (`https://docs.microsoft.com/en-us/vsts/pipelines/test/continuous-test-selenium?view=vsts`) you are able to get Selenium test projects added to the pipeline.

Taking continuous testing a bit further, you also make some suggestions about how testing can be incorporated into various stages in the lifecycle.

- *Post-build unit testing*: While in Visual Studio, on the test pane, developers can enable the running of unit test projects after a build completes locally. This will ensure local testing completes after a rebuild.

- *IntelliTest*: For projects or solutions that do not have a base of tests to draw from, the IntelliTest feature in Visual Studio can help generate basic unit tests from existing source code.

- *Live testing*: Another feature of Visual Studio Enterprise is live testing, which will run tests for you automatically when code is changed, and related unit tests can be found (`https://docs.microsoft.com/en-us/visualstudio/test/live-unit-testing`).

Resource Validation

One final area—one that is newer in terms of shifting left and embracing a DevOps culture—is that of testing and validating infrastructure and configuration as they relate to the lifecycle of your application components. Much the same as more traditional software counterparts, these "-as-code" components need to be put into version control, tested, and validated to ensure no unexpected changes are introduced. Having these configurations set up and tested like typical software components also helps to promote repeatability, lending an air of consistency to the underlying application infrastructure regardless of what environment it is deployed to.

EXERCISE: WHAT IF

As mentioned, infrastructure and configuration as code files can be tested as well as validated to ensure they are solid and repeatable. Just as source code is committed to a repository, tested, scanned, and validated, so too should these types of scripts. In this exercise, you will put together a CI/CD pipeline for the infrastructure scripts related to the CMS portal as well as Cardstock.

1. Create a new CI build using the infrastructure subfolder within the Cardstock repo as an entry point. Under Triggers, set the build up for continuous integration and limit the commit path to only the infrastructure folder.

2. For each piece that is independently deployable, create a Resource Group deployment task in the build definition. Ensure that the deployment mode for each task is set to Validation Only.

3. Save the definition and manually trigger a series of builds. Ensure that the builds capture the test creation of the resources in each resource group.

Testing the Developer Experience

You team up with an engineer from each of the two teams you're working with to gain insights into their workflow and into whether the updated developer experience will be positive. To set some baselines, you ask them to go through their daily routine—where the go first, what they do, and how they interact with the systems and other coworkers. The engineer from the portal team uses Visual Studio 2017 as her primary IDE, and the engineer from the Andromeda teams uses Sublime Text as his editor of choice. Each engineer is convinced that they are going to have issues when hooking up to Azure DevOps Services to push code, trigger builds, and run tests.

You explain to them both that the intent is to ensure that no issues are experienced during the course of their day-to-day work. While some things are changing with respect to where the code is stored, and other things are being introduced as new tools, how they edit, build, and debug code should not be impacted. The two main things that could introduce slowdowns or uncertainty are SonarQube and WhiteSource. Both engineers understand the need to monitor code quality and dependencies, and they are cautious to show too much excitement about these tools because outside scans can take time, usually at the expense of being able to move quickly to release.

To help offset the fears that things will slow down when entering the pipeline, you introduce some utilities to the engineers. One is a plugin for Visual Studio, as well as Sublime Text, allowing for code linting to occur based on SonarQube profiles that are in use. The plugin for Sublime does not allow for a direct connection to the specific SonarQube instance but does cover a variety of common C# and web-based language rules. You note that a similar extension also exists for Visual Studio Code, though it is closer in functionality to the generic linter offered in the Sublime plugin.

Note   The term "linting" refers to any action that scans code and highlights errors or suggestions based on an established set of rules.

You explain the need to scan dependencies in the code base from two different angles: the licenses used by dependencies that are known (and not known), as well as vulnerabilities that exist in the libraries themselves. Keeping ahead of any known exploits will keep the platform safe and protect the company as well. An added benefit to using a dependency scanner is that you will end up with a comprehensive list of all packages and libraries that your platform uses, whether you knew about them or not. The licensing aspect of these dependencies is equally as important, as some components may be distributed using software licenses that may require the company to open its code base to the public. In some circumstances, companies developing platforms for end-user consumption do not have an interest in making their intellectual property known outside the bounds of the business. Knowing what licenses and libraries your code base is using can help determine if there is a risk to the viability of the platform or to the company itself.

The engineers install the appropriate extensions for their IDEs and go about the business of testing them in an attempt to validate your previous assumption of non-intrusiveness. The linters do not seem to be troublesome, though some of the front-end development rulesets end up frustrating the Andromeda engineer a bit. You let him know that they can be adjusted, and that back-end scans will really tell the tale since they will pull from the systems directly.

To further quell any uncertainty, you build out two definitions that can be scheduled in Azure DevOps Services—one for initiating a complete SonarQube scan of the code base, and the other for initiating a complete WhiteSource scan. To promote reuse, you export the definitions into YAML and ask that each repository has a copy of it.

Automating the Developer Experience

Equally as important to testing out the IDE and its extensions is the notion of being able to automate the development environment as much as possible. To clarify a bit more, specific user settings, command-line aliases, utilities, and IDE extensions can be bootstrapped in a developer's workstation to ensure consistency within a team and even across teams. This bootstrapping process can then be used by new and existing teammates to get their environment up to speed for working on the code base. The best part about automating these settings is that local workstations and virtual desktop/development interfaces (VDI) can benefit from this type of system preparation. Some examples of items that can be bootstrapped include:

- *System environment variables*: Setting up specific variables kept in memory during a user's session can help drive consistency across workstations. For example, one might use a standard system environment variable to describe the location of all source repositories, or the location of the current version of a framework being leveraged.

- *Local package installation*: Finding programs that assist with development (or writing them in some cases) is one of the activities developers gravitate toward naturally. Bootstrap scripts can be used to install required or desired utilities on any platform. This helps to keep the baseline environment in a consistent state.

215

- *Local container instances*: Much like local package installation, using local container instances to spawn processes or run utilities can keep the baseline environment clean while also allowing for further image customization if desired.

- *User profiles*: Certain programs, such as `PowerShell` and `AutoHotKey`, allow you to set preferences, command aliases, and more in a file related to a user. These shortcuts can help speed up local activities and can be sourced from a central configuration if desired.

- *Dotfiles*: Normally analogous to Linux or Mac, dotfiles are configuration files that help customize the behavior and appearance of programs and utilities like `zsh` or `bash`. They are so named because the file name begins with a period (or dot, if you will). There is some crossover between user profiles and dotfiles depending on operating system and the program being used. For example, `bash` can be used cross-platform, and dotfiles used in a Linux environment for `bash` can potentially be used across operating systems.

You start to gather information from the Cardstock and Portal teams to see what they use by way of configuration settings, editors, and utilities in an attempt to identify commonalities.

EXERCISE: CREATING A DEVELOPER BOOTSTRAP SCRIPT

To help the engineering teams work in a consistent environment, as well as give them some flexibility in what additional commands and tools they can install, you decide to help craft a bootstrap script. This script will serve as a base for other teams, and the vision is to allow for specific overrides or additions to be sourced from a custom location on the file system.

Because engineers have a myriad of different workstation types, either due to preference or equipment that was acquired with the teams themselves, finding a common ground will be a challenge. The first logical step in your mind is to split the core script up into sections based on the elements that engineers normally tend to configure.

As a first pass, you settle on the following sections:

- Identification of the operating system

- IDE / Editor of choice

- Plugins or extensions for IDEs

- Utilities, SDKs, customizations, and other enhancements

Identifying the operating system is possible; however, the potential for having overly complicated logic to determine that is great. Also, because each OS has its own package management system, this increases the odds that complexity will creep in. You decide that the benefit outweighs the risk in this case and start with stub scripts for each major OS shell language, with the intent of having script directories for each customizable area.

There are dueling thoughts around what scripting language to use when interacting with the system. Some prefer PowerShell, others prefer bash. For most cases, the Azure CLI is generally accepted which keeps things a bit easier when dealing with interactive sessions with Azure. Equally as debated is the use of IDE—some are using Visual Studio, some are using Visual Studio Code, and others are using Sublime Text. The engineers using Sublime are far outnumbered by those using the Visual Studio family of products.

At a minimum, you know that Python will be a required installation, as the Azure CLI requires it. The IDE choice will be variable dependent upon the OS and the product family (Visual Studio, Sublime). Extensions for each can be imported and installed from a separate source file. For example, to export extensions installed in your VS Code editor, simply type the following in the console:

```
code --list-extensions >~/extensions.txt
```

This will create a file that can be fed into a separate routine that reads each line and installs the extensions by ID:

```
while read -r extension
do
code --install-extension $extension
done < ~/extensions.txt
```

The preceding sample assumes the use of bash as the scripting language.

For the first iteration of the bootstrap ecosystem, you create two init scripts in the root of the directory (init.sh and init.ps1). You then create three directories under the root directory: ide, util, and custom. The custom directory is where additional custom scripts can be placed for local or team-based customizations.

In the `util` directory, you place a shell script and a PowerShell script to take care of initializing the package manager (pacmgr). For the PowerShell script, you perform a quick check to verify that things are running on Windows. If they're not, you redirect to using shell scripting:

```
<#
Package management setup
1. Install chocolatey, if windows
2. Install package(s), if windows
#>
if($env:OS -eq "Windows_NT") {
  Set-ExecutionPolicy Bypass -Scope Process -Force
  iex ((New-Object System.Net.WebClient).DownloadString('https://chocolatey.
  org/install.ps1'))
} else {
    .$PWD/util/pacmgr.sh
}
```

On the shell side, this is where you put together the logic that helps to decide what the package manager should be, along with what OS is being used (Mac or Linux):

```
#!/bin/bash

# Figure out what OS is being used and either update or install
OSVer=$(uname)
if [ "$OSVer" = "Darwin" ]; then
    BREW=true
    brew -v >/dev/null 2>&1 || BREW=false
    if [ "$BREW" = "true" ];then
        echo "Homebrew installed. Updating."
        brew update && brew upgrade
        brew cleanup
    else
        echo 'Homebrew not found! Installing.'
        /usr/bin/ruby -e "$(curl -fsSL https://raw.githubusercontent.com/
        Homebrew/install/master/install)"
    fi
    PKGMGR=brew
    PKGINSTALL=install
```

```
fi
if [ "$OSVer" = "Linux" ]; then
    YUM=true;APTGET=true;RPM=true;APK=true
    PKGINSTALL="install -y"
    which yum >/dev/null 2>&1 || YUM=false
    which apt-get >/dev/null 2>&1 || APTGET=false
    which rpm >/dev/null 2>&1 || RPM=false
    which apk >/dev/null 2>&1 || APK=false
    if [ "$YUM" = "true" ]; then
    PKGMGR="yum"
    elif [ "$APTGET" = "true" ]; then
    PKGMGR="apt-get"
    elif [ "$RPM" = "true" ]; then
    PKGMGR="rpm"
    elif [ "$APK" = "true" ];then
    PKGMGR="apk"
    PKGINSTALL="add -y --no-cache"
    fi

    $PKGMGR update
fi

# Call in the packages
. $PWD/util/packages.sh $PKGMGR $PKGINSTALL
```

The last line references a new file, packages.sh, that will install some basic requirements based on Mac or Linux needs. Because there are slight differences in how Homebrew installs packages vs. most other Linux-based package managers, you put in some logic to help identify those differences:

```
#!/bin/bash
if [ "$1" = "brew" ]; then
    $1 cask $2 dotnet dotnet-sdk powershell
    $1 $2 git
else
    $1 $2 git dotnet dotnet-sdk powershell
fi
```

The idea is that the first argument is the command for the package manager, and the second is the installation verb (in most cases, install). To set up the IDE install script, you use a similar structure to determine the package manager as well as some additional logic to get the actual package name for the IDE, as it will vary by OS.

Using the bootstrap directory under the Automation folder in the supplied codebase, update the scripts to include additional packages, and perform some test runs to ensure each option works as expected. Are there any conventions that could be used to simplify this further? Would switching to one common script language make things more portable?

With the bootstrap scripts committed and available to engineers, you recommend that each team maintains its own branch from the baseline with any customizations that team may need. In addition, you note that these scripts can come in handy if the need arises for building virtual developer desktops, as having preconfigured workstations will help reduce the cost of onboarding new engineers.

Having looked across many different fundamentals for the developer experience, you set out to further refine the delivery mechanisms for the platform.

Summary

Throughout this chapter, we have looked at ways shifting left can help bring clarity and attention to feedback about feature work as well as help catch and diagnose areas of concern within the codebase. Your planning of the CI/CD pipelines for all artifacts has given you insight into the different deployable pieces and has also given you a solid foundation on which to continue moving changes through the pipeline to production. You have seen how testing comes in many forms, and validation of functionality as well as infrastructure is critical to making the end-to-end lifecycle run smoothly. You have also helped drive some of the cultural and technological changes on the engineering teams, working with developers to explain the different components of the pipelines and introducing ways to make adopting the changes to come much easier. Having put some thought into the mechanisms for deploying these solutions to the cloud, you're ready to move on to building and putting the pipeline through the paces.

Given the examples you have completed in this chapter, along with the narrative, consider the following questions:

1. Are there alternatives to the content delivery network chosen in the example? What other potential component services exist currently that could also be dropped in? Is there a compelling reason not to consider an IaaS approach?

2. Can you think of other methodologies that would enhance the developer experience while still keeping the build and deployment logic with the code?

3. Are there other utilities that can be used early in the build process to determine code metrics, code health, or code security?

4. What types of situations would potentially benefit from having a continuous deployment setup but not a continuous delivery setup?

5. Given the teams' differing schools of thought on branching, deployment, and gating, is it better to work the teams toward one common method for approaching these things, or can the teams continue to work in a truly autonomous fashion without impacting others?

CHAPTER 11

Deployment Pipelines

After a good amount of time spent on designing and laying out the pipelines to deliver the Cardstock platform, it's now time to kick the tires and see how the design and preexecution phases have managed to pan out. Your intention is to walk through the developer experience from code commit to release, as the pipeline for this platform is just as important as the value it brings when deployed. Following the process, you will be able to validate the remainder of your design decisions from a platform and an application lifecycle management perspective, leveraging Azure DevOps Services. The results of these tests will give you opportunities to make adjustments to the pipeline to increase efficiency and tighten the feedback loop.

Before embarking on the journey to see the world through the engineers' eyes, you take a moment to review the deployment architecture and ensure that all service hooks, build pipelines, definitions, and extensions are appropriately installed. At a minimum, you have to make sure that the following are accounted for:

- Service hooks into Azure for both development and production subscriptions

- Service hook for SonarQube

- Service hook for WhiteSource

- Scalable Azure DevOps Services agent resources to handle variances in build and release traffic

- Key Vaults (in each subscription) for storing deployment secrets

- Tasks and extensions are installed

- Role groups are appropriately assigned to prevent unauthorized access to resources

© Josh Garverick 2018
J. Garverick, *Migrating to Azure*, https://doi.org/10.1007/978-1-4842-3585-0_11

For the technical and hosted aspects, you feel that Kubernetes may be an interesting choice for putting together such a reusable pipeline. Noting this as a potential design, you set out to perform the Azure DevOps Services maintenance once the baseline cluster is established, as the team's projects will need to be configured to publish appropriately with the right services and tasks.

Building Flexible Pipelines

You realize that you need to stand up a SonarQube instance if you are to create a service endpoint for the team project to send results to. In order to do this, you can do one of several things: create a new standalone Sonar instance using Azure VMs, create an instance using a Docker container, or use SonarQube as a hosted service with SonarCloud (`https://about.sonarcloud.io`). Given the pricing structure of SonarCloud (charge per lines of code per organization, or free for open source), you look to the first two options as more viable. Given your idea of possibly using Kubernetes to help host these pipeline elements, you settle on using the Docker image for Sonar. Before you can get too invested in the Sonar piece, you recognize that creating the basics for the cluster is likely a better place to head to next.

In thinking about how to best construct the cluster so it is able to handle the operations that will be thrown at it, you focus on two areas that seem to be needed:

- A persistent storage area for holding configuration files and plugins that will be used across teams

- A central datastore for Sonar to connect to

Kubernetes has a facility for attaching a persistent storage claim, so the file system issues should be less of a concern. The database, however, can go in a couple of different directions. There's the possibility of having it run in another container within the cluster, while utilizing a storage account or claim for the database file system. There's also the possibility of leveraging Azure SQL to allow for a managed database experience. To allow for potential expansion to other teams at Gamecorp, you decide to leverage Azure SQL and give all teams a single managed SQL Server to report information back to. Each team would require its own database, however, since Sonar's licensing would not allow for you to connect multiple instances to one singular database without paying for a higher platform tier.

For a test run, you decide to model out the essentials using Docker Compose. Once the appropriate model has been constructed, you will be able to convert the Compose environment into separate deployable Kubernetes artifacts using kompose. Kompose is a utility that will traverse through a Compose file and generate YAML files for each of the services called out in the Compose file. Starting with the basics, you decide to set up the Sonar instance first. Before hooking up the volume using a storage account, you first look into creating the new database that Sonar will use.

EXERCISE: SET UP AZURE SQL AND SONARQUBE

To get started using a fresh Azure SQL instance, you will first need to create a new SQL Server in Azure. Creating a new Azure SQL Server in PowerShell is fairly straightforward:

```
Param (
    [SecureString]
    [parameter(Mandatory=$true)]
    $SqlPassword
)
$SqlUser = "<<your-username>>"
New-AzureRmSqlServer -ServerName <<ServerName>> `
-ResourceGroupName <<ResourceGroupName>> -Location "eastus" `
-SqlAdministratorCredentials $(New-Object -TypeName System.Management.
Automation.PSCredential -ArgumentList $SqlUser,$SqlPassword)
```

You will want to ensure the password is being passed in as a mandatory parameter so that it prompts you to enter a value and returns it as a SecureString. You can enter a clear text password and convert it to a SecureString if you wish, though using the param notation will enforce a SecureString variable value without advertising the password's true value. Next, create the SQL database using the new SQL Server you've created as its home. Be sure to name the database something meaningful (e.g., sonar-<<teamorappname>>).

```
New-AzureRmSqlDatabase -ServerName <<ServerName>> `
-DatabaseName sonar-cardstock -ResourceGroupName <<ResourceGroupName>>
```

You will also want to create a firewall rule on the server to allow you to be able to see and work with the database you've just created. The following PowerShell will create a new firewall rule using your new server, given a supplied WAN IP. To obtain your WAN IP, you may visit a site such as `https://www.whatismyip.com` and `capture the public IPv4 address displayed.`

```
New-AzureRmSqlServerFirewallRule -ResourceGroupName <<ResourceGroupName>> `
    -ServerName <<ServerName>> `
    -FirewallRuleName "MyClientWanIP" -StartIpAddress <<YourWanIP>>
```

Azure services will be able to reach the SQL Server by adding in service endpoints. To enable both the SQL Server and the Storage endpoints, you will need to find the resource group that was created when you first created the managed Container Services instance. Typically, that resource group is prefixed with "MC_".

Now you can move on to setting up the Docker Compose file that has the initial services you're after. In this case, you're only working with the Sonar instance to start with. Start with an empty YAML file and fill in the following details:

```
version: "3"
services:
  sonar:
    image: sonarqube
    ports:
      - 9000:9000
    environment:
      SONARQUBE_JDBC_USERNAME: "#{SqlUser}#"
      SONARQUBE_JDBC_PASSWORD: "#{SqlPassword}#"
      SONARQUBE_JDBC_URL: "jdbc:sqlserver://#{ServerName}#.database.windows.
      net;databaseName=sonar-cardstock"
```

You will replace the tokenized values just shown with the actual values of the SQL Server user, password, and server Uri of the SQL Server you created earlier. The token formats in this YAML file are different than those listed in the PowerShell examples—this is because the token formatting will be used as a part of an automated publishing pipeline for the Docker images you will use for subsequent Kubernetes clusters. These values will go directly into the Dockerfile for SonarQube, which will change the previously listed YAML file. However, for local testing, starting off using these environment variables in the Compose file will be a quick way to validate your setup.

To get things rolling, enter the following command at the command line, assuming you are in the directory where your YAML file is located.

```
Docker-compose build && docker-compose up
```

This chained command will build out the sonarqube image for you and stand up a new container using the variable values you specified for the SQL connection. You should now be able to navigate to http://127.0.0.1:9000 and see the SonarQube splash page. Once this main page is available, the required back-end table structures will have been created in the database for you. This means that any time you wish to stand up a new instance of SonarQube within the target Kubernetes cluster, you will be connected to the same database, thus keeping any settings and user accounts you create in between container lifecycles. To access the site for the first time, log in using the default Admin credentials.

To get utility files that will allow you to replicate your Docker Compose setup in a Kubernetes cluster, install the kompose utility and, from the command line, navigate to the folder that contains your docker-compose.yaml file. From there, enter kompose convert, which will create deployment and service files that match up to the services you've defined in your compose file. Using this utility will help you to detect differences in the compose file versus the manifests that Kubernetes expects.

After getting a successful initial run of your SonarQube container, you decide that you will need to create a separate administrator account and disable the built-in Admin account to ensure that no unauthorized changes can be made. You navigate to Administration ➤ Security ➤ Users and create a new account that will be used to perform application maintenance. Adding the user to the sonar-administrators group finalizes the settings. You save your work, log out, and log back in using the new account. You then navigate back to the Users page and delete the default Admin account.

With the transfer of administrative rights complete, you can now look at the storage aspect of your SonarQube instance. Using Compose will be different than using Kubernetes to manage the file storage options. You can use a local instance of Kubernetes (MiniKube or Docker for Windows/Mac), or you can use a test instance of the managed Azure Container Service (AKS) to work out the kinks. You choose to go with the latter option only because getting the components sorted in Azure will give you a working area to build on.

EXERCISE: SETTING UP STORAGE

Using the Persistent Volume tutorial found at `https://docs.microsoft.com/en-us/azure/aks/azure-files-dynamic-pv` as a guide, you set out to create a new storage account that will serve as the backing for persistent volumes in the cluster. You take special care to ensure the storage account is created in the same resource group as the managed Container Service instance, as per the tutorial. Once complete, use the names of the sample YAML files to store the volume information and deploy to the cluster:

```
kubectl create -f azure-file-sc.yaml
kubectl create -f azure-file-pvc.yaml
```

Next, update the container specification to include a volume that will point to the storage account. In the spec, add the following:

```
Volumes:
  - name: azure
    azureFile:
      secretName: azure-secret
      readOnly: false
      shareName: sonarqube
```

Specifying the share name will create a new folder in your storage account. To persist extension information, for example, add the following to the container section of the spec:

```
volumeMounts:
  - name: azure
    mountPath: /opt/sonarqube/extensions
```

Creating this volume mount point will tell the container to use the storage account instead of local disk for that particular folder.

Make the changes in either the pod configuration or the deployment configuration, then monitor the log output for the SonarQube pod as it starts back up. Do you notice anything different? Can files be seen in the storage account now?

After thorough testing, you feel good about the progress you've made with the SonarQube bits. It's time to move on to configuring Azure DevOps Services more in-depth.

Team Project Prework

Using the list provided at the beginning of the chapter as a guide, you start to lay out the work you need to do to prep the team projects for the engineering teams. The existing Gamecorp portal team uses a team project that was set up for that team. As Andromeda's developers were using GitLab, the source control import is not a large undertaking, and helping them import their work items from the spreadsheets they were using is not terribly difficult either. The two teams work in different ways, however, and setting up a new team project for Cardstock development assets and work items appeared to be the best way to maintain each team's work structure. Since there are two different team projects in play (one for Cardstock, one for the portal project), you will need to set up certain things per project; others can be set up once, at the project collection level. You move to install Azure DevOps Services account-level extensions first, as those will be needed to configure build and release definitions later on.

Before getting too far into configuration, you will want to create a personal access token (PAT) for use with setting up build agents, release agents, and deployment groups (if applicable). To do this, mouse over your avatar and select Security. The first section will display PATs for you, with the ability to click Add. Create a new one and save it locally for the time being. Set the expiration to 90 days and scope the permissions as you see fit. You will need to establish a more long-term solution for this, however, as using a PAT associated with an individual user account is generally not a best practice.

SIDEBAR: THE PRINCIPLE OF SERVICE PRINCIPALS

In many organizations, it is common practice to create accounts in Active Directory that are considered privileged. Whether those are service accounts, administrative accounts, or other special-use accounts, the practice of designating specialized AD objects to limit exposure and access is something that keeps an organization insulated from potential service outages due to someone using their own account as the "admin" for a website or service, and then leaving the company.

Within Azure AD, there is a notion of service accounts as well. They are known as service principals and can also be referred to as App Registrations in the Azure AD blade in the portal. It is possible to create a service principal in several ways:

- From the Azure Portal, by creating a new App Registration

- Using the Azure PowerShell cmdlets for administering Azure AD

- Using the Azure Python CLI for administering Azure AD

- Directly from an application tied to an Azure subscription (e.g., Azure DevOps Services)

Let's focus on the last option for a moment. When using Azure DevOps Services, it is very easy to create a service principal that authorizes deployments into one or more subscriptions that you, as a user, have access to. The UI is intelligent enough to show existing Azure Resource Manager endpoints within Azure DevOps Services as well as subscriptions you have access to that are not yet authorized in Azure DevOps Services. If you choose to authorize a subscription that does not yet have a service endpoint in Azure DevOps Services, you will be creating a new service principal connected to that subscription, usually involving an almost indecipherable naming convention.

Why is this a potentially onerous option? While the naming within Azure DevOps Services may look fine, the naming in Azure can be confusing, especially if an administrator is attempting to update role-based access controls for that account. For example, if an administrator wanted to limit the resource groups available to a specific account, and there are five similarly named accounts in Azure AD, it may not be easy to identify which account should be scoped down.

One approach that helps simplify the service principal names for administrators and users alike is to create service principals that are purpose-built and created using friendly names. In a traditional setup, you may have one subscription for nonproduction resources and another for production resources. Using names such as "Azure DevOps Services [AppName] Non-Prod" and "Azure DevOps Services [AppName] Prod" can help bring clarity to the scope and intent of each principal. They can also be added to various RBAC groups within Azure to allow or restrict access to resources.

Another approach is to create a traditional AD service account and have that account synchronized with Azure AD. This would be applicable only for those organizations that have an on-premises AD presence and directory synchronization between on-premises and Azure AD. This approach will also allow you to assign a basic license to that service account and generate a PAT, which can then be used in automating things like build and release agents for Azure DevOps Services.

EXERCISE: NEW SERVICE PRINCIPALS

Create two new service principals that will control nonproduction and production access to Azure by leveraging the Azure CLI. The following commands will set up the service principals:

```
az ad sp create-for-rbac -n "VSTS Cardstock Non-Prod"
az ad sp create-for-rbac -n "VSTS Cardstock Prod"
```

Be sure to record the output of each command—it will contain the Azure AD tenant ID, the client (application) ID, and the account's initial password, which will be needed for setting up Azure service endpoints in Azure DevOps Services.

Installing the Right Extensions

There are a few extensions that will be useful right out of the gate. To install Azure DevOps Services extensions, you can either click the Marketplace icon in the upper right corner of any page (near your profile), or simply navigate to https://marketplace. visualstudio.com and start searching. First off, you will want to install the Sonar extension as well as the WhiteSource extension (not the WhiteSource Bolt extension). The WhiteSource Bolt extension is for a specific add-on related to WhiteSource, and you are more interested in the general scanning and coverage that the flagship WhiteSource product offers. Next, there are several utility extensions that will come in handy when constructing and testing the pipelines later in this chapter:

- Code Search
  (https://marketplace.visualstudio.com/items?itemName=ms.
  vss-code-search)

- Package Management
  (https://marketplace.visualstudio.com/items?itemName=ms.feed)

- Delivery Plans
  (https://marketplace.visualstudio.com/items?
  itemName=ms.vss-plans)

- Docker integration
  (`https://marketplace.visualstudio.com/items?itemName=ms-vscs-rm.docker`)

- Replace Tokens
  (`https://marketplace.visualstudio.com/items?itemName=qetza.replacetokens`)

- Jenkins integration
  (`https://marketplace.visualstudio.com/items?itemName=ms-vsts.services-jenkins`)

- Team Project Health
  (`https://marketplace.visualstudio.com/items?itemName=ms-devlabs.TeamProjectHealth`)

- Azure DevOps Services Analytics
  (`https://marketplace.visualstudio.com/items?itemName=ms.vss-analytics`)

After installing the basics, you're now ready to start setting up service endpoints for interaction with Azure, Sonar, and more.

Setting up Service Endpoints

The first task to ensure the team project can connect to everything it needs is to establish service endpoints. To set up endpoints for the Azure subscriptions, SonarQube endpoint, and WhiteSource endpoint, let's review where to go within Azure DevOps Services:

1. Click the cog for Administration of the team project.

2. Click the Services link.

3. Select the "New Service Endpoint" and choose the appropriate endpoint type from the list displayed to you. In this case, you will want to select "Azure Resource Manager" to create a new Azure service endpoint.

Figure 11-1 illustrates the preceding steps in the context of the Cardstock team project in Azure DevOps Services.

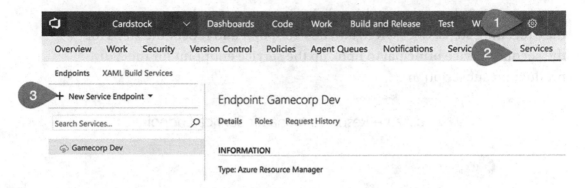

Figure 11-1. *Steps to add a new service endpoint in Azure DevOps Services*

Once you have clicked on Azure Resource Manager, a dialog box will pop up requesting some basic information from you. As you will be creating these endpoints using the service principals you created earlier, you will need to use the full version of the Add Endpoint dialog. Click the link labeled "use the full version of the endpoint dialog" to enable the advanced view.

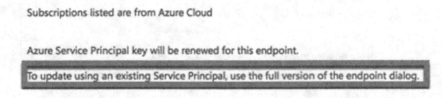

1. Enter a friendly (human-readable) name for the endpoint. This will come in handy when associating the endpoint to tasks in both build and release definitions. As the first endpoint will be for nonproduction deployments, name this "Gamecorp Dev."

2. Enter the subscription ID from the output of the first service principal command.

3. Enter the name of the subscription associated with the ID.

4. Enter the client ID from the output of the first service principal command.

5. Enter the password from the output of the first service principal command.

6. Enter the Azure AD tenant ID from the output of the first service principal command.

233

Figure 11-2 shows the resulting dialog box and areas that correspond to the preceding steps. Click OK to add this endpoint and repeat the steps for the second service principal to hook up the service endpoint for the Azure production subscription.

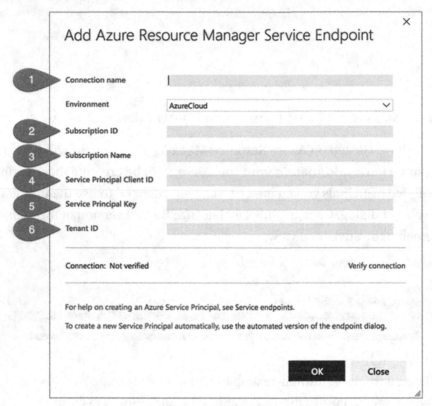

Figure 11-2. *Steps for configuring an Azure Resource Manager endpoint*

Following the example for setting up a new service endpoint, you now add a new service for the SonarQube endpoint that will be used by the team for code quality. Once the dialog is displayed for adding a new Sonar endpoint, you notice it's slightly different.

1. Enter a name for the connection.

2. Enter the server URL that will be used for the Sonar instance. This URL needs to be reachable by the agent and does not have to be available externally.

3. Enter the token for interacting with the Sonar instance.

Figure 11-3 illustrates the dialog for the SonarQube service creation. To generate a token for Sonar, follow the instructions at `https://docs.sonarqube.org/display/SONAR/User+Token` as applied to the instance you have stood up.

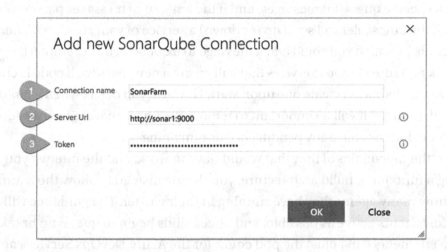

Figure 11-3. *Adding a new SonarQube endpoint connection*

EXERCISE: WHITESOURCE SERVICE ENDPOINT

Using the previous examples as reference points, set up a new WhiteSource service for the team project. If you do not already have a WhiteSource account, you can register for a free 14-day trial at `https://www.whitesourcesoftware.com`. Having this account set up is required for the service endpoint configuration to be set up properly.

Follow the instructions for creating an API key found on the WhiteSource website. Enter the details required in the dialog box that is displayed when you add a new endpoint. To test the connection, you may add a WhiteSource task to a new or existing build definition and run the build to see if the task can connect successfully using the new endpoint.

Now that the endpoints are established, you move on to setting up the build agent farm within the Kubernetes cluster. In some cases, you may not need to have agents stood up all the time. In fact, it may make more sense to set the minimum instance count to zero and scale as needed. This raises an interesting thought—could these agents be auto-scaled, and how would that occur? Default metrics such as CPU utilization and RAM utilization may not fully encompass the conditions under which you would need to scale out build agents. You begin to look into ways of interrogating the Azure DevOps Services APIs for builds that are queued to see if that may be a viable metric.

After some searching, you find a project on GitHub that deals with using Azure Service Bus as a way to gauge how many agents to use. The project, found at `https://github.com/torosent/kube-azure-servicebus-autoscaler`, gives you the ability to monitor a specific queue for messages, and if the amount of messages passes a certain threshold, the autoscaler will scale up (or down) a service of your choosing. There are two methods by which you could add a message to a queue in this example: by creating a webhook in Azure DevOps Services that will create a new message if code is checked in, or have the definition create one upon start. How will you detect when a build has completed, though? It will be important to remove messages that are not needed if the agent queue does not have any pending builds remaining.

Given the mechanics of how that would have to work, and the interest you have in having a functional build architecture, you decide instead to allow the teams to control how many agents they have running in their cluster. The guidance will be to have as few agents active as possible, and once builds begin to queue up or take too long, the engineers can adjust the pod count for the Azure DevOps Services agent deployment to help level out the requests.

EXERCISE: ESTABLISHING THE BUILD SERVICE

Creating the service and deployment artifacts for the build agent farm will be the next step to get things rolling with your on-demand pipeline. Given that the teams will need some general frameworks along with specifics, you poll the engineers to see what the requirements are. You end up with the following items:

- ASP.NET MVC and .NET Framework 4.6.2

- .NET Core

- Node.js

- Azure PowerShell / Azure Command Line Interface (CLI)

Through some initial experimentation, you find that you're not quite able to get the Azure PowerShell commands working when using Linux build agents in the cluster, or even with the hosted Linux agents provided by Azure DevOps Services. There is, however, another option to use the CLI instead. There is a supported task handler for the Azure CLI within the Azure DevOps Services build agent, which allows you to not have an additional dependency added to your image. It does mean that some of the code written will need to be altered to allow for the CLI equivalent (if available) to be executed.

To account for these dependencies, you decide to build out your own agent image using a Dockerfile. In order to capture everything you feel you will need, you will want to make sure that the package manager being used within the image is updated, that the appropriate libraries are installed, and that the references to .NET Core are also picked up. You put together your Dockerfile as illustrated here:

```
FROM microsoft/vsts-agent

RUN apt-get update

RUN curl https://packages.microsoft.com/keys/microsoft.asc | gpg --dearmor >
microsoft.gpg
RUN mv microsoft.gpg /etc/apt/trusted.gpg.d/microsoft.gpg
RUN sh -c 'echo "deb [arch=amd64] https://packages.microsoft.com/repos/
microsoft-ubuntu-xenial-prod xenial main" > /etc/apt/sources.list.d/
dotnetdev.list'
RUN apt-get install apt-transport-https -y
RUN apt-get update
RUN apt-get install mono-complete nodejs npm dotnet-sdk-2.1.104 -y
```

Any other NodeJS-specific dependencies can be installed using npm. The Mono runtime, aside from giving you the .NET Framework, will also give you MSBuild. This will come in handy when building C# project files, as MSBuild or a compatible build engine is required.

Once you have built the custom Docker image, you will want to publish this to your registry. As Gamecorp is using its own Azure Container Registry, you can utilize that registry to store your new image. To begin, you will need to log into the registry using Docker.

```
docker login gamecorp.azurecr.io
```

Next, tag the agent image you have built with the repository. To do this, you can use the `docker tag` command to append another tag onto the image. Alternatively, you could also tag the image when using the `docker build` command to specify the repository.

```
docker tag vsts-agent gamecorp.azurecr.io/vsts-agent
```

Now you will be able to push the custom image up to ACR. Using the docker push command, send the new image up.

```
docker push gamecorp.azurecr.io/vsts-agent
```

Before you will be able to use this image in the Kubernetes cluster, you will need to create a secret that contains the appropriate credentials to access the ACR instance. You can create a secret by creating a new object in the Kubernetes dashboard by clicking on Create, or you can use `kubectl` to create a new secret. For this example, you use the kubectl utility to create the secret.

```
kubectl create secret docker-registry gamecorp --docker-server=DOCKER_
REGISTRY_SERVER --docker-username=DOCKER_USER --docker-password=DOCKER_
PASSWORD --docker-email=DOCKER_EMAIL
```

You replace the values in all caps with the appropriate values from the ACR instance. Once complete, you see the gamecorp secret object in the Kubernetes cluster's Secrets section. To use this when creating a deployment or pod from a private registry, you will need to specify the imagePullSecret field, using gamecorp as the value for that field. This will tell Kubernetes that the registry you're using will need the credentials in that secret to allow for creating containers from an image stored there. Through the dashboard UI, you create a new application and expand the "Show Advanced Options." This exposes the imagePullSecret field, where you can enter the appropriate value. Figure 11-4 shows an example of where that information would be entered.

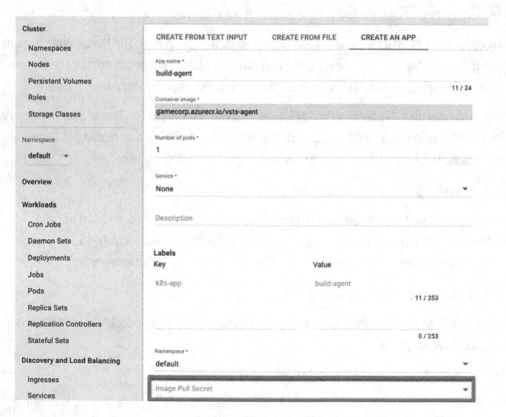

Figure 11-4. *Creating an App in Kubernetes, using an image pull secret*

Before creating the application, be sure to enter in two environment variables. One will be the name of your Azure DevOps Services instance (using VSTS_ACCOUNT as the environment variable name) and the PAT you created earlier (using VSTS_TOKEN as the environment variable name). For the Azure DevOps Services account, only enter in the name of the instance you created, not the entire visualstudio.com URL value. Once you create the application, you can go to the Administration section of your Azure DevOps Services instance and view the Agent Queues area. When your new application starts up, you should see a new agent being added to the Default queue. Figure 11-5 shows a high-level overview of all components in the Kubernetes solution, along with relationships.

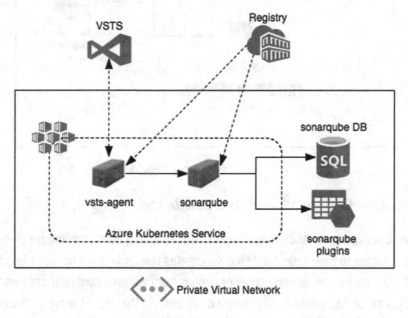

Figure 11-5. *Development Kubernetes cluster*

Now that you have created one copy of this cluster, it can be replicated for many other teams. One thing you realize is that you have not accounted for the use of Jenkins by the Andromeda team. Fortunately, Jenkins does have a standard Docker image and it can be wired into one of the development clusters with no problem. To utilize an external data store as well as a file system for storing common plugins, you decide to reuse the layout you constructed for SonarQube.

You create a new persistent volume pointed at a new share within the same storage account as the SonarQube share. When creating the application in Kubernetes, you specify the jenkins_home variable to pass into the container, telling it where to map the plugins directory to. Figure 11-6 shows an updated architectural view of the cluster setup.

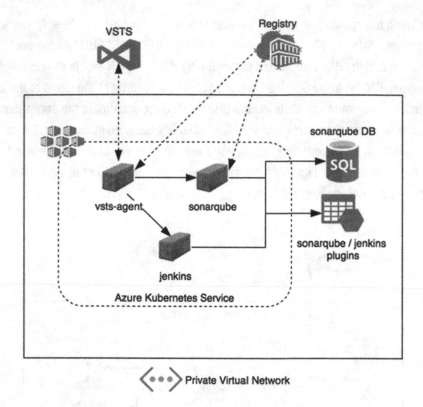

Figure 11-6. *Development cluster, Andromeda style*

Another issue surfaces: the Andromeda engineers are building container images when they make changes to their code. While the Kubernetes cluster is great for executing the actual build mechanics, producing container images from within a container appears to be problematic. One option would be to create a dedicated VM that would serve as the image creation point. After some research, however, you find that there is something out there that may fit the bill and avoid having to stand up more infrastructure.

You find the utility img from genuinetools on GitHub (https://github.com/genuinetools/img). It is a utility that can be installed during the creation of a Docker image and run while the container is running to build a new container image. To use this utility in the context of your build agents, you add the following snippet to your Dockerfile for the vsts-agent image (slightly modified from the binary install directions found in the GitHub project's README file):

```
# Export the sha256sum for verification.
ENV IMG_SHA256="dad4cec955803d3e8f42b9348c3ae25ee5fca73369364cd4419f77ec
1e713040"
```

```
# Download and check the sha256sum.
RUN curl -fSL "https://github.com/genuinetools/img/releases/download/v0.4.7/
img-linux-amd64" -o "/usr/local/bin/img" \
    && echo "${IMG_SHA256}  /usr/local/bin/img" | sha256sum -c - \
    && chmod a+x "/usr/local/bin/img"
RUN echo "img installed!"
```

Now, as a part of the build process, any calls to docker build or docker push can be replaced with img build and img push. This will allow images to be built within the cluster in an isolated fashion.

Moving the Built Bits

Making sure the pipeline for new features or bug fixes is as smooth as possible is a task that can be daunting. As described previously, the intent for the platform is to have independently releasable and testable containers wherever possible. This allows for independent deployments to occur and finite feature management to flourish. The environment structure of the platform is not terribly complex. As stated in prior chapters, it consists of an integration environment, a user acceptance environment, a staging environment, and production. The idea is that once integration testing is complete, a container will be tagged as ready to move into the pipeline. The updated container(s) will be deployed to the appropriate environments, and as testing continues and approvals are granted, the changes move seamlessly out to their eventual resting place.

Choosing Continuous Delivery

In Chapter 10, you explored the differences between continuous delivery and continuous deployment. Each has its merits and can be used to deliver functionality to customers while still enabling a rapid cadence. The engineering management team at Gamecorp is keen to have some controls in place, and is more concerned with having successful releases, as opposed to multiple potentially unstable releases per day. You describe some key features of Azure DevOps Services Release Management to them, including the use of pre- and postdeployment approvals, along with release gates that can be applied before or after a deployment to an environment.

Using Release Gates

A somewhat recent addition to Azure DevOps Services, release gates allow for the programmatic evaluation at the pre- or postdeployment level, per environment. There are four types of release gates:

- *Azure Functions*: This option allows you to directly invoke an Azure Function.

- *REST API call*: This option allows you to directly invoke a REST APT.

- *Azure Monitor*: This option allows you to monitor App Services, Virtual Machines, Storage Accounts, or Application Insights.

- *Work item query*: This option allows you to use a work item query to determine if there are any open issues related to the deployment.

With each release gate, you define the determinant for success. The gate can be set to run on specific intervals and time out after a certain period if no success is achieved. In addition, approvals can be garnered before, after, or despite a result being returned. The general strategy you aim for is to require approvals after successfully clearing a gate, which will keep the leadership team happy and allow for a more quality-focused pipeline.

Leveraging Approvals

Deployment approvals can also be plugged into release definitions, either before a deployment occurs or after. The use case for a predeployment approval may be that a team or individual wants to know that a release is in the queue, and this predeployment approval allows them to let it through to the environment in question. For postdeployment, the approval chain could be a group or individual, and the approval itself can serve as an audit record stating the changes are as planned, and the release can move to the next environment. A postdeployment approval after a production release gives an additional audit record showing that live site operations are in good shape.

To facilitate the use of groups over individuals, you create four groups within the team project:

- Cardstock Integration Approvers

- Cardstock UAT Approvers

- Cardstock Staging Approvers

- Cardstock Production Approvers

Cross-functional team members can then be added into those groups and be assigned approval slots at every environment in the release definition.

Keeping Definitions Lean

Azure DevOps Services gives you the ability to have as little, or as much, configuration within its UI as you wish. Given the myriad of tasks available to you in the Visual Studio Marketplace, you can easily overload a definition with tasks dealing with the potentially infinite granularity of deployment steps. In some cases, having that ability to go granular can be helpful. In others, it can cause anxiety and frustration, especially for people who inherit said definitions with an improper amount of explanation behind them. Given the nature of the deployments for the platform (containers), it makes more sense in your mind to use generic tasks for variable replacement and for Kubernetes deployments, having those tasks driven by artifacts and variables.

EXERCISE: CHOOSE YOUR OWN RELEASE ADVENTURE

After laying out the basics around the release pipeline mechanics, you set out to create the initial revision of the pipeline definition. For any release definition, you will need at least one artifact type to allow the definition to be triggered. From there, you can create one or more environments that will use those artifacts. Figure 11-7 displays the artifact types that are available.

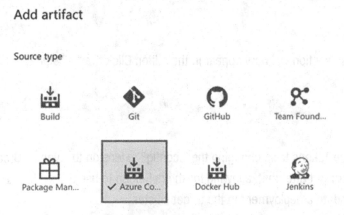

Figure 11-7. The artifact selection pane in Azure DevOps Services

Select Azure Container Registry as the artifact type, as the intent will be for containers to move through the pipeline once pushed and tagged as ready. For each section of the application, add an artifact source pointing at the `gamecorp` ACR instance, looking for any changes in the named container repositories. You should end up with five artifact sources: the Cardstock repository (Git), Trading, Messaging, Inventory, and front end (UI).

Next, use the "+ Add" option in the Environments section to add a new environment. A pane will appear on the right side of the screen, allowing you to change the name of the environment and adjust some properties. Name the first environment "Integration" and click the "x" to close the pane.

Now it's time to define the tasks you will need for applying these changes to the cluster. Click the link directly below the name of the environment to open the environment editor. You will be taken to a new page that looks very similar to the build definition editor. Here you can specify any number of tasks to be run at the agent level, deployment group level, or even agentless. Since deployment groups tend to be geared more toward virtual machine deployments, the agent phase is a logical choice.

Create a new agent phase by clicking on the ellipsis located on the environment's grouping bar.

Next, select "Add agent phase" from the dropdown that displays.

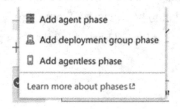

The Agent Phase section will now appear in the editor. Click the "+" sign to add tasks.

Create a Replace Tokens task, changing the ".config" extension to ".yaml". Create a Kubernetes task right after that, allowing for the definition to use the `kubectl apply` command to update a deployment in the target cluster.

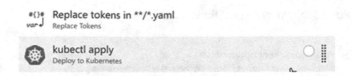

Fill in the details for the target cluster as well as the details for the configuration files. Check the "Use configuration files" box and browse the artifact source for the Cardstock repository for one of the deployment configuration files. Select the directory where the file resides as the source of the configuration files.

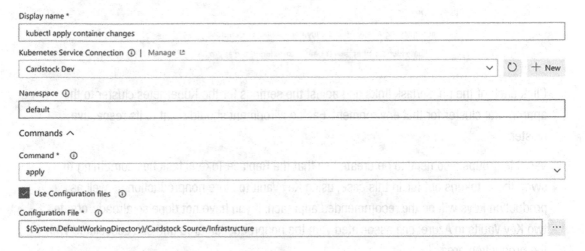

Click "Pipeline" in the command bar. Mouse over the Integration environment and click "Clone" when it appears. This will create a copy of the Integration environment that is linked to the existing environment. Click the "Copy of Integration" environment and change the name to "UAT." Follow the same process by cloning the newly created environment after changing its name. Your pipeline should now have four environments listed: Integration, UAT, Staging, and Production.

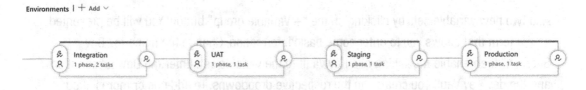

To set up approvals, click the person icon shown on the right side of the Integration environment. This will allow you to add one or more approvers. For this environment, select the Cardstock Integration Approvers group after enabling Post-Deployment Approvers. Close the pane by clicking the "x" in the upper right corner.

Click each of the phase/task links and adjust the settings for the Kubernetes cluster to the appropriate cluster for that environment. Each environment should point to its respective cluster.

Variable groups also need to be created so that the Replace Tokens task has something to swap those tokens out for. In this case, using Key Vault to store nonproduction as well as production keys will be the recommended approach. If you have not done so already, create two Key Vaults in Azure: one associated with the nonproduction area and one associated with the production area.

Click the "Variables" link in the command bar and select "Variable Groups" from the list on the left. There will be an option to link existing variable groups or manage all of the groups you have. Click the manage link and a new tab will open, allowing you to add or edit variable sets stored in the team project's Library.

Add two new variable sets by clicking on the "+ Variable group" button. You will be presented with a form that allows you to enter some basic information. Change the name to "Dev Secrets," then enable the linking of a Key Vault to the variable set. Enter the Dev subscription and the dev Key Vault you created in the respective dropdowns. To add one or more linked secrets, click the "+ Add" link toward the bottom of the screen. Then, click Save. Perform the same actions to create the Prod Secrets variable set.

Library > Dev Secrets

Properties

Variable group name

Dev Secrets

Description

Non-production keys

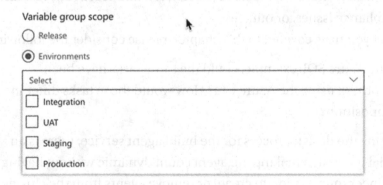

🔵 Link secrets from an Azure key vault as variables ⓘ

Azure subscription * | Manage ↗

Gamecorp Dev   ⌄   ↻

ⓘ Scope: /subscriptions/bef0cc89-4657-431c-8d6b-aa033e662dfe/resourcegroups/gc-sandbox

Key vault name *   Manage ↗

gc-dev-keyvault   ⌄   ↻

Variables

Delete	Secret name	Content type	Status	Expiration date

＋ Add

Return to the tab containing your release definition. Click "Link variable group" to attach the
newly created groups to your definition. Unlinked groups will appear in a list on the right
side of the screen. You can scope the linked group to the entire release, or one (or more)
environments. For the Dev linked group, select Environment, then select Integration from the
dropdown list. For the Prod linked group, select Environment, then select all options except for
Integration from the dropdown list.

Variable group scope

○ Release

⦿ Environments

Select   ⌄

☐ Integration

☐ UAT

☐ Staging

☐ Production

You finalize the settings and ensure that the components are all valid. You save the definition
and alert the teams that it is ready for their review and testing.

Having put together the pipeline for the teams, and with their testing getting underway, you look now to the last stop in the lifecycle—production, and more specifically, operations and site reliability. You grab your notes about operating models and begin to help define roles and responsibilities that will benefit the teams, and hopefully the company as well.

Summary

In this chapter, the overall pipeline for the Cardstock platform, as well as the Gamecorp portal, has been established. You have looked into creating reusable Kubernetes clusters that can be run locally as well as in the cloud, providing a single method of building and scanning source code. You have seen how SonarQube can be stood up easily as a Docker container, and how the persistence of scan data can be held in an Azure SQL database. Even settings and extensions that are in use by SonarQube can be stored in Azure Storage accounts, promoting reuse and nontransient configurations. You have put together a custom Docker image for Azure DevOps Services build agents, giving your engineering teams a repeatable and reliable way to spawn build agents when needed. When components are ready to enter the release pipeline, you have given the teams a solid way to view changes, approve changes, and promote artifacts from one environment to another.

You now have one more stop to make on this journey—ensuring that the initial work you carried out on the operating model and platform monitoring gets properly disbursed to the teams that will need to use them most. Going through these items with engineers responsible for site reliability and operations will help transfer the knowledge to other parties and empower those engineers to proactively, and reactively, respond to platform changes, compliance issues, or outages.

Given what you have covered in this chapter, please consider the following questions:

1. In the Azure SQL example, could the same tasks have been performed using the Azure CLI? How would those tasks differ in composition?

2. During the design process for the build agent service, there is an initial interest in making the agent count dynamic without having engineer intervention to create or remove agents from the cluster. How would you approach that potential need for true autoscaling? Are there methods to track or poll queued builds in the Azure DevOps Services agent pool? Is there even a need to do that?

3. Does the approach to include the YAML definitions for the SonarQube and WhiteSource scans make sense? Is there another way a central YAML definition could be kept and made available as needed?

4. Is there any benefit to using task groups instead of listing out all deployment related tasks per environment? Why or why not?

5. Where would/could feature flag strategies play into the pipeline definition and creation?

CHAPTER 12

Operations and Site Reliability

Now that your designs have been tested and proven out, albeit with some adjustments, you can look toward the transition plan to move responsibilities into the appropriate groups. Gamecorp has a team of site reliability engineers (SREs) who are responsible for the traditional production support role along with optimizing the platform when possible. Not all of the SREs are at the same skill level, and some are fairly green with respect to infrastructure in general, let alone cloud-based infrastructure. Before handing over the reins to the engineers and site reliability staff, it's important to make sure a defined operating model is in place. You've made a good deal of progress on outlining the target state and how operational staff should be involved in the maintenance and operation of the target. Further defining roles and escalation paths will help to ensure everyone has a good handle on what they should do in the event of a platform problem.

Through interviews with the SRE staff as well as some of the engineers on both the Gamecorp portal team and the Andromeda team, you glean some common themes with respect to gaps that need to be filled. In most cases the engineers have identified that the decision trees they use to troubleshoot areas of the platform are really rudimentary and poorly documented, and unless they have a subject matter expert on the phone, the chances of them solving the issue are fairly slim. Escalation typically involves calling a handful of engineers who have experience with the system, followed by a smaller group of architects, followed by someone on the leadership team who presumably has the ability to summon either an engineer or architect to assist. Putting some structure around this loosely held telephone chain will help drive specific accountability and clear up any confusion around where to go when things start to break.

© Josh Garverick 2018
J. Garverick, *Migrating to Azure*, https://doi.org/10.1007/978-1-4842-3585-0_12

Operating Model Revised

You dust off the initial revision of the operating model you devised earlier. In reviewing your first pass, you notice some significant gaps that need to be plugged. Roles and responsibilities need to be well defined for processes to work smoothly. Identifying and mapping capabilities of the new cloud platform to these roles will help further scope down the spheres of influence needed. After defining the roles and responsibilities needed, you can work to get operational processes in place and automated. The same will hold true for the site reliability team, though their areas of concern will be somewhat different than the true operations folks. Before you get started with anything, however, you finish the review of your operating model's first draft and prepare to expand it to meet the needs of the teams impacted.

Roles and Responsibilities

When defining roles across the engineering teams as well as across the business, you notice there are quite a few job titles but only a handful of distinct roles that actually apply. Centers of knowledge in those roles may differ based on technical or nontechnical concentrations. In some cases, one person may have several different roles, depending on the team makeup and the needs at hand. You outline the core roles that you see within the organization along with some high-level attributes for each. The focus of this operating model, and the roles and responsibilities within, are centered on the adoption of a cloud-first mentality. While each role may have many more attributes, you focus on those that are relevant to the adoption and operational aspects of the cloud. The results are shown in Table 12-1.

Table 12-1. *Core Technical and Security Roles Within the Organization*

Role	Attributes

Engineer	- Usage of automated build and release mechanisms
	- Usage of APM/telemetry capture in code
	- Understanding of networking
	  - Basic: software engineer
	  - Intermediate: DevOps/Site Reliability Engineer
	  - Advanced: network/infrastructure engineer
	- Understanding of fault tolerance vs. fault handling and related design patterns
	- Basic understanding of security requirements via Information Security and regional legal teams

Architect	- Understanding of different cloud technologies and how they can impact application performance - Knowledge of different data persistence technologies and use cases - Knowledge of different messaging patterns and use cases - Knowledge of general cloud design patterns and use cases - Intermediate to advanced knowledge of security requirements
Manager	- Understanding of different cloud technologies and how they can impact delivery timelines - Knowledge of product/platform business, technical, and security requirements
Compliance Officer	- Knowledge of regulatory and compliance requirements and now to implement controls for them in a cloud environment - Knowledge of certifications in cloud environments and associated controls (ISO-27001, HIPAA, HITRUST, etc.)
Analyst	- Knowledge of business, technical, or security requirements and applicability to implemented platform design
Operator	- Knowledge of business, technical, or security procedures and related processes for implementation

You plan on adding some more details around responsibilities when you begin mapping out the overall capabilities, roles, and responsibilities matrices for each architectural domain. One item you add into the operating model is that the expectation for all parties is to not only embrace the key roles and functions related to each capability, but also to shoulder the responsibility of support and remediation related to any issues that may arise from the execution of a capability. Thinking through some of the capabilities you've been taking notes on, one that comes to mind is that of establishing and maintaining backups. In this case, the responsible parties are the engineers working with those components and not a centralized IT resource. If the backup mechanism fails for any reason, those engineers are also responsible for fixing the mechanism for backups and ensuring it continues to run smoothly. After composing that note regarding responsibilities, you look toward the seemingly insurmountable job of updating the target operating model.

Assess Capabilities and Role Mappings

You begin the laborious task of detailing out as many of the capabilities as you can that relate to the organization in the context of cloud-first engineering. Split up by domain, you begin with the business aspects of the operating model, making sure to keep the context to the needs of the teams implementing the model.

Business Domain

The business domain centers on the nontechnical management aspects of interacting with a cloud-first world. Important capabilities include risk management, procurement, licensing, vendor management, and more. Table 12-2 contains the capabilities, key roles, and key functions related to the business domain.

Table 12-2. *Business Domain Capabilities, Key Roles, and Key Functions*

Capability	Key Roles	Key Functions
Risk Management and Remediation: *The identification and remediation of any risks to the business, either for the line of business or the company*	- Engineering Management - Business Operations Management - IT Operations Management - Site Reliability Engineers - DevOps Engineers - Database Administrators	- Solution construction using best practices and standards for compliance - Monitoring all operations within the platform - Ensuring internal users adhere to the highest integrity and compliance standards
Procurement: *The financial transactions associated with purchasing software, technology, or platform services from a preferred cloud or technology vendor.*	- Accounts Payable - Corporate Procurement - Finance - Cloud Program Management	- Execute contracts or purchase orders to secure preferred pricing for technology and services - Ensure the use of approved vendors as established by vendor management
Platform Licensing and Governance: *The establishment of business agreements with technology vendors and the governance of those processes*	- Cloud Program Management - Corporate Procurement - Corporate IT Operations	- Negotiate preferred discounts and service rates - Ensure license compliance with all technology, software, and services
Vendor Management: *The management of the relationship between WTW and various cloud platform vendors*	- Cloud Program Management - Corporate IT Operations	- Establish relationships with preferred service vendors - Maintain contacts and negotiations to ensure optimal usage - Ensure vendor offerings continue to bear significant benefit to the firm

Application Domain

The application domain is comprised of items that deal with the lifecycle and design of the entire application, inclusive of any components within that application. Table 12-3 contains the capabilities, key roles, and key functions related to the application domain.

Table 12-3. *Application Domain Capabilities, Key Roles, and Key Functions*

Capability	Key Roles	Key Functions
Lifecycle Management: *The management of the application's lifecycle, from design to delivery*	- Software Developers - Engineering Management - Release Engineers - Site Reliability Engineers - Quality Engineers - DevOps Engineers - Software Architects	- Defining steps within the lifecycle - Mapping roles and responsibilities to each step - Work item tracking/work planning - Establishing metrics, definition of ready, definition of done - Quality gates - Testing (unit, integration, functional, smoke, load, performance) - Application component build and release processes - Application monitoring/telemetry - Incident management (intake, triage, resolution)
Application Design: *The collaborative act of designing technical and functional behaviors in an application, resulting in one or more product features*	- Software Engineers - Software Architects - Product Managers - Business Operations Stakeholders	- Analysis of requirements and/or specification documentation (functional and technical) - Application component integration - Service level agreements for component processing and transaction completion - Creating an overview of the technical design that will allow the requested functionality to successfully deliver value

(continued)

Table 12-3. *(continued)*

Capability	Key Roles	Key Functions
Application Platform Management: *The management of an application, suite of applications, or suite of components that comprise a greater functional platform*	- Site Reliability Engineers - Software Engineers	- Telemetry capture per component - Performance capture per component - Telemetry capture per value transaction (mission critical)
Product Capacity Management: *The management of a software application's (product's) ability to handle user traffic and computational load*	- Software Engineers - Product Managers - Software Architects - Site Reliability Engineers	- Analyzing customer user census - Analyzing feature requests - Analyzing and mitigating performance bottlenecks
Capacity Planning: *The proactive planning for and anticipating of changes in application usage*	- Site Reliability Engineers - DevOps Engineers - Software Engineers - Software Architects	- Forecasting capacity based on usage trend and performance monitoring data - Analyzing new and existing customer base for changes in user census

Infrastructure Domain

The infrastructure domain touches on the underpinnings of each application as well as the overall platform experience. This covers everything from design to implementation. Table 12-4 contains the capabilities, key roles, and key functions related to the infrastructure domain.

Table 12-4. *Infrastructure Domain Capabilities, Key Roles, and Key Functions*

Capability	Key Roles	Key Functions
Application Infrastructure Design: *The design of any application underpinnings that enable functionality, including PaaS and/or IaaS components*	- DevOps Lead - Software Architecture - Site Reliability Engineers - Cloud Architecture	- Component selection in relation to application requirements; - Observance of core factors for component usage (time, cost, effort, reliability, maintainability, operability)
Application Infrastructure Management: *The monitoring, provisioning, maintaining, and updating of any application-related infrastructure*	Development Leads Site Reliability Engineers DevOps Engineers	Component patching (IaaS, if using OMS) Monitoring for components Creation of workflows or policies for provisioning resources
Platform Level Patching: *The patching of core platform components, such as operating systems. Applicable to IaaS components*	- IT Operations - Cloud Operations - Site Reliability Engineers - DevOps Engineers	- Scheduling of patch acquisition and rollout - Application of (or rollback of) patches during appropriate maintenance windows - Selection of patching provider (Corporate IT or OMS)
Platform Capacity Management and Optimization: *The management, monitoring, and planning associated with ensuring the firm's cloud estate is able to handle the needs of the business*	- Cloud Operations - Cloud Architecture - Enterprise Architecture - Cloud Program Management - Site Reliability Engineers - DevOps Engineers	- Establish subscription and resource needs for each LOB - Plan for and forecast estate growth per LOB and the enterprise - Where appropriate, analyze and consolidate resource pools - Ensure applicable CIDR blocks are available for peering - Requisition new CIDR blocks if necessary

Technology Domain

The technology domain deals with technical items that reach across applications, infrastructure, and teams. Items such as platform tooling, frameworks, platform selection, capacity management, and more are covered within these bounds. Table 12-5 contains the capabilities, key roles, and key functions related to the technology domain.

Table 12-5. *Technology Domain Capabilities, Key Roles, and Key Functions*

Capability	Key Roles	Key Functions
Platform Tooling: *The curation or procurement of any technical products that offer toolsets to colleagues for the purposes of interacting with a cloud platform*	- Cloud Architecture - Cloud Operations - Enterprise Architecture	- Platform Evangelism - Creation of custom products or evaluation of 3rd party products meant to streamline cloud operations
Platform Selection: *The selection of a preferred cloud platform provider.*	- Cloud Architecture - Enterprise Architecture	- Choice of platform offering that best fits the needs of the firm - Document deviations from the preferred platform if applicable - Evangelism of preferred platform to stakeholders
Subscription Allocation: *The act of fulfilling a request to create one or more Azure subscriptions under the Corporate enterprise enrollment*	- Cloud Operations	- Provisioning of new subscription(s) under the enterprise enrollment - Provisioning of baseline requirements (policy, network, etc.)

(continued)

Table 12-5. (*continued*)

Capability	Key Roles	Key Functions
First Line Platform Support: *The act of providing support to consumers of the cloud platform in the event of technical roadblocks, platform errors, or platform shortcomings*	- Cloud Operations - Microsoft Premier Support	- Troubleshooting network functionality - Troubleshooting ExpressRoute - Integrations with vendor-of-choice products (e.g., Azure and Azure DevOps Services) - Platform component malfunctions
Major Incident Response: *Any response to an event that compromises stakeholder or shareholder interests and involves regulatory or legal guidance*	- Corp Communications - Legal - Compliance	- Exposure and Risk Mitigation - Notification of proper authorities
Platform Design: *Any design work related to the platform's operation or maintenance, of which others will be the consumers*	- Enterprise Architecture - Cloud Operations	- Platform component use cases - IaaS use cases - Networking guidance and standards
DR Planning and Execution: *The act of planning for, and successfully testing, an application's disaster recovery plan.*	- DevOps Lead - Application SMEs	- Plan construction for DR (runbooks, procedures) - Provisioning of target resources - Simulation of cutover from existing to backup resources

(*continued*)

Table 12-5. (*continued*)

Capability	Key Roles	Key Functions
Upgrades and Patches: *The acquisition of and application of component upgrades or security patches relevant to the LOB application*	- Site Reliability Engineers - Software Engineers - Release Engineers - DevOps Engineers	- Upgrade of existing JavaScript framework - Patching of existing 3rd party C# library
Role and Resource Maintenance: *The management of personnel who will support the needs of the business from a technology perspective*	- Engineering Management	- Team organization - Requisition management
Second / Third Line Platform Support: *The act of providing support to business operations, stakeholders, or end users in the event of an error related to application code, misconfiguration, or misuse*	- Site Reliability Engineers - Software Engineers - Software Architects	- Troubleshooting of web, service, middleware, or database malfunction - Troubleshooting of improper configuration at the application component level - Troubleshooting code-related errors - Incident intake, triage, and resolution
OS Provisioning: *The creation of virtual machine operating systems in accordance with standards set forth by Corporate IT*	- Site Reliability Engineers - DevOps Engineers - Software Engineers - Software Architects	- Provisioning of versioned operating system - Application of required patches, settings, policies, and software - Placement of computer object into appropriate organizational unit (if using Active Directory) - Establishment of OS patching responsibility

(*continued*)

Table 12-5. (*continued*)

Capability	Key Roles	Key Functions
Environment Support: *The maintenance of logical deployment environments, based on the requirements of the application and line of business*	- Site Reliability Engineers - DevOps Engineers - Release Engineers - Quality Assurance / Engineers - Software Engineers	- Provisioning of new environments - Troubleshooting build or release errors - Troubleshooting environment performance issues - Utilization management (power on/off cycles)
Platform Engineering and Delivery: *The act of working with the cloud platform to build and deliver a solution using the components available*	- Software Engineers - Site Reliability Engineers - Software Architects - DevOps Engineers	- Assessing components to determine the best functional option - Orchestration of software build and deployment to selected components
Network and DNS Management: *The provisioning, usage, and maintenance of required network components within the platform*	- Cloud Operations - Site Reliability Engineers - DevOps Engineers	- Provisioning of virtual networks - Provisioning of network security groups - Provisioning of DNS records for internal or external objects - Provisioning ExpressRoute circuits - Establishing virtual network private and public peering

(*continued*)

Table 12-5. (*continued*)

Capability	Key Roles	Key Functions
Configuration Management: The management of application, software, or cloud platform configuration settings	- Cloud Operations - Site Reliability Engineers - DevOps Engineers - Software Engineers	- Adding components to approved virtual networks - Peering private IP ranges to ExpressRoute circuits - Establishing database connection strings - Installation of OS-level features needed for application functionality (e.g., Internet Information Services) - Use of configuration as code (e.g., Desired State Configuration)
First Line Production Support: *The shared responsibility of fielding production problems that can be related to either cloud platform or application platform faults*	- Cloud Operations - Site Reliability Engineers - DevOps Engineers - Software Engineers - IT Operations - Database Administrators	- Intake and triage of outage or error report - Incident routing to appropriate first line team - Stakeholder communication as appropriate - Incident resolution or escalation

Data Domain

The data domain accounts for any creation, maintenance, design, or tuning related to application or platform data and its associated persistence stores. Table 12-6 contains the capabilities, key roles, and key functions related to the data domain.

Table 12-6. *Data Domain Capabilities, Key Roles, and Key Functions*

Capability	Key Roles	Key Functions
Database Backups: *The act of initiating a backup of an application database or leveraging a platform component that performs the same operation*	- Site Reliability Engineers - Release Engineers - Database Administrators	- Triggering a backup operation at the database server level - Storage of backup assets - Definition of and adherence to retention policies
Database Restores: *The restoration of an application database to a specific point in time*	- Site Reliability Engineers - Release Engineers - Database Administrators	- Restoration of a database backup to production - Restoration of a database backup to nonproduction server
Application Database Provisioning: *The creation of new application database instances*	- Site Reliability Engineers - DevOps Engineers - Database Administrators	- Database creation - Database naming - Allocation of resources (Cores, CPUs, DTUs)
Application Database Builds / Changes / Releases: *The management of changes to an application's data or schema, and the advancement of those changes from development to production*	- Site Reliability Engineers - DevOps Engineers - Release Engineers - Database Administrators	- Migration script creation, maintenance, and release - Change management - Change testing and validation
Application Database Design: *The act of performing schema and data object design that correlates to application functionality*	- Software Engineers - Software Architects - Site Reliability Engineers - Database Administrators	- Design of data objects or entities - Designation of relationships between entities - Authentication, authorization, and scope - Schema design

(*continued*)

Table 12-6. (*continued*)

Capability	Key Roles	Key Functions
Database Maintenance and Tuning: *The execution of maintenance jobs, manual or automatic, that keep database operations in line with expected performance metrics*	- Software Engineers - Software Architects - Site Reliability Engineers - Database Administrators	- Table Indexing - Stored Procedure Tuning - View Tuning - Execution Plan Review and Tuning - Data file shrinking
Application Database Monitoring: *The observation of database performance and usage through manual or automatic means.*	- Site Reliability Engineers - Software Engineers - Database Administrators	- Setting alerts on threshold values for performance (high CPU, high I/O) - Gathering telemetry on execution times for queries, stored procedures, functions - Ensuring uptime through the use of agent reporting

Security Domain

The security domain contains capabilities that are intended to safeguard the interests of consumers as well as the company. These capabilities range from security control implementation to policy administration to setting standards at the platform level. Table 12-7 contains the capabilities, key roles, and key functions related to the security domain.

Table 12-7. *Security Domain Capabilities, Key Roles, and Key Functions*

Capability	Key Roles	Key Functions
Security Control Implementation and Validation: *The understanding and implementation of security controls as prescribed by the larger corporate governing body, with the intent to secure end-user data as well as mitigate risk to the firm*	- DevOps Engineers - Site Reliability Engineers - Software Engineers - Engineering Management	- Use of encryption at rest, in transit - Providing scoped application level authorization to administrative users - Requesting and implementing service accounts - Requesting and implementing administrative accounts - Adherence to security reference architecture
Security Operations: *The review and adjudication of any violations of enterprise-level security policies or controls*	- InfoSec Analysts - InfoSec Management - Enterprise Architecture - Audit and Compliance	- Determine decision trees and escalation policies in the event of a violation - Routinely review security requirements of the firm in conjunction with all domestic and international legal obligations
Policy Administration and Monitoring: *The enforcement and auditing of enterprise cloud platform policies and standards*	- Cloud Architecture - Cloud Operations - InfoSec Analysts	
Platform Policy and Standards: *The establishment of policies and standards that govern the usage and configuration of cloud platform components within the firm's cloud estate*	- Enterprise Architecture - Cloud Architecture - Audit and Compliance	- Draft, collaborate on, and release cloud platform policies - Ensure policies meet all legal and compliance requirements on behalf of the firm - Ensure standards conform to best practices as determined by the industry as well as the platform provider

Having gone through the painstaking exercise of cataloging all of the capabilities, roles, and responsibilities you could think of—with as much enterprise coverage as possible—you turn your attention to automating as much of the operational and security concerns as possible.

Operational Automation

From the perspective of IT operations, making sure that things are running smoothly and within appropriate cost controls can be challenging. While not all teams are equipped with the same skill sets or tools to help, having some key foundational aspects in place will help empower operations teams to perform their jobs to the best of their abilities. From compliance monitoring and enforcement to platform component and utility monitoring, many possibilities exist to make things more consistent for operations.

Compliance Monitoring and Enforcement

Due to the extensive predesign sessions you held with the security team, you are very aware that monitoring and enforcing security controls is of paramount importance. Despite the very wide array of categories these controls fall into, there is a way to help wrangle and make sense of these controls in a centralized way. There are tools on the market that will provide this functionality for you, and generally speaking the cost to acquire and implement them may be more than procurement or management is willing to pay. Fortunately, there are utilities within Azure that allow you to be as loose or restrictive as you want:

- *Management Groups*: These are groups set up at the tenant level that can cascade policies and settings down to child groups, which can contain one or more Azure subscriptions. There is a nesting level cap at six levels of hierarchy.

- *Azure Policy*: Through the use of JSON-based definition objects, Policy allows you to define individual policies as well as policy sets (also known as Initiatives), which can be applied to management groups or to subscriptions. They are flexible enough to monitor behavior (audit) or outright prevent it (deny).

These offerings, used in conjunction with EventGrid subscriptions, Activity Log alerts, and Azure Automation runbooks, can be very powerful tools in your compliance toolbelt. When examining how to logically organize different management groups, parallels can be drawn between management groups and organizational units in Active Directory. A specific nested group under the main tenant can be used to scope permissions and enforce standards. Conversely, that same nested group could have a need to override an existing tenant-wide restriction, and separating this out at the nested group level allows this flexibility to be possible.

Structuring your management groups and policies in a way that allows for reuse and easy administration is essential. To get started, you use the Azure CLI to create a new primary group for the company. The group ID as well as the display name for the group are required. The group ID should be a unique but meaningful identifier for the group, and the display name is the human-readable name associated with the group. The group ID cannot be changed after creation, but the display name can be. Using the command window, you enter the following:

```
az account management-group create -n gc-main --display-name Gamecorp
```

To create subgroups for the main application teams, you enter the next series of commands:

```
az account management-group create -n gc-cardstock --display-name Cardstock
--parent-id /providers/Microsoft.Management/managementGroups/gc-main
az account management-group create -n gc-portal --display-name Portal
--parent-id /providers/Microsoft.Management/managementGroups/gc-main
az account management-group create -n gc-gims --display-name GIMS --parent-
id /providers/Microsoft.Management/managementGroups/gc-main
```

This will take care of the primary groups you're interested in for this particular conversion. Next, you move on to looking at Azure Policy for establishing baseline rules.

EXERCISE: CONFIGURING BASELINE AZURE POLICIES

To get started with Azure Policy in conjunction with Management Groups, you decide to start by exploring the Policy area in the Azure portal. By clicking the Gamecorp management group, you see there is a menu item for Policy in the management group blade:

1. Click Policies to open the Azure Policy blade in the context of your management group.

2. Click "Definitions" to start browsing available (built-in) policies and initiatives. The following blade opens up.

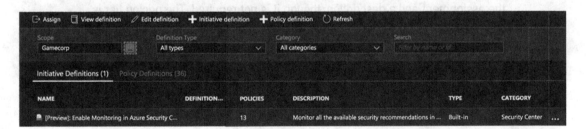

3. Click the initiative and click "View definition" to see the contents of the initiative. Clicking any policy will allow you to view its definition.

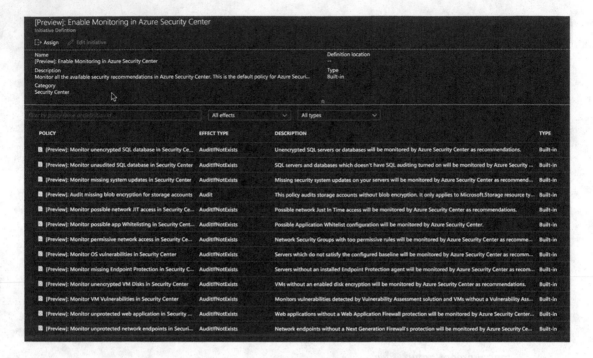

4. Click "Assign" to assign the initiative to the Gamecorp management group. Anything managed by this master group will have these policies in effect. A new dialog appears, allowing you to set some values. You may enter a new name for the assignment and a description, though it is not required. The pricing tier is selected for you automatically, which ensures you will be getting the ability to compare results and action them. One item you must set is the Scope.

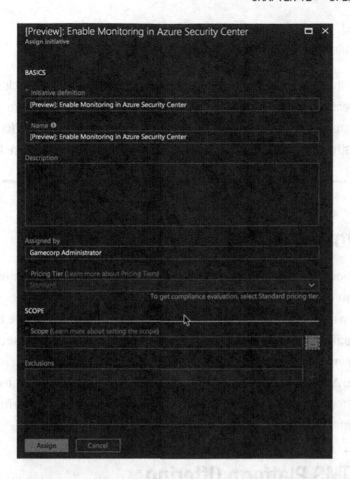

5. Click the blue ellipsis to select the scope of this policy. As mentioned earlier, this assignment will be put into place for the Gamecorp management group. Select that management group and ensure the subscription and resource group dropdowns are left blank. Press the Select button at the bottom of the dialog to continue.

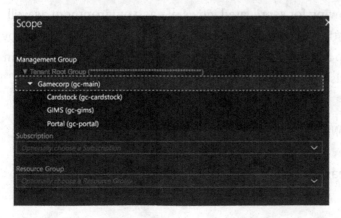

6. With the scope set, you are now ready to assign the initiative to the management group. Click the Assign button to complete this action.

Explore the Policy area of the Azure protal further and put together some additional policies for monitoring network connections and for restricting certain resource types from being created. Start with restricting the creation of public IPs and ExpressRoute circuits to get the feel for how the rulesets are constructed. What are some other controls that you can put in place to provide better guardrails?

Platform Monitoring

Gathering information about the expanse of an application's estate and aggregating that information can be an overwhelming task. It is important, however, to have something that serves as a one-stop shop for the team's monitoring needs. There are several different commercial and open-source aggregation stacks that can be used to streamline the collection and analysis of systems data. In addition, you can plug into the native functionality of the Azure platform by using offerings such as Azure Monitor, Log Analytics, Network Watcher, Security Center, and others. Collectively these offerings are referred to as the Microsoft Operations Management Suite (OMS).

Leveraging the OMS Platform Offering

The first item to set up and configure is the OMS workspace. While there is no direct OMS item in the Azure portal, you begin by navigating to All Services > Log Analytics and creating a new Log Analytics workspace. Your thought is to set up one for each runway environment, allowing for segregated views of each environment as well as the ability to scale the pricing tier up or down, depending on need. You use the following PowerShell script to set up a log analytics workspace for the integration environment, as the equivalent command is not available in the Azure CLI:

```
param (
[string]$ResourceGroupName,
[string]$WorkspaceName,
[string]$Location = "eastus"
)
```

```
# Check that the resource group is valid
Get-AzureRmResourceGroup -Name $ResourceGroupName | Out-Null
# Create a new Log Analytics workspace if needed
Write-Output "Creating new workspace named $WorkspaceName in region $Location..."
# Create the new workspace for the given name, region, and resource group
$Workspace = New-AzureRmOperationalInsightsWorkspace -Location $Location
-Name $WorkspaceName -Sku Free -ResourceGroupName $ResourceGroupName
```

While making some assumptions about the validity of the resource group, the script itself can be used to create all of the workspaces needed. You save the file as `Create-LogAnalyticsWorkspace.ps1` and run the following commands to set up each of the workspaces you need.

```
./Create-LogAnalyticsWorkspace.ps1 -ResourceGroupName "gc-operations"
-WorkspaceName "gamecorp-int"
./Create-LogAnalyticsWorkspace.ps1 -ResourceGroupName "gc-operations"
-WorkspaceName "gamecorp-uat"
./Create-LogAnalyticsWorkspace.ps1 -ResourceGroupName "gc-operations"
-WorkspaceName "gamecorp-staging"
./Create-LogAnalyticsWorkspace.ps1 -ResourceGroupName "gc-operations"
-WorkspaceName "gamecorp-prod"
```

Now that the workspaces are established, you move on to looking at the monitoring components that are available in OMS, and how they align to the resources for Cardstock and the portal.

Component Monitoring

Azure infrastructure and platform offerings are all able to be monitored in a slew of different ways. Usually you are able to set up monitoring directly from the resource itself, by clicking the "Monitor" menu item or by exploring the "Monitoring" subsection in the resource's blade. Another way to make great use of consolidated functionality and aggregated platform telemetry is by configuring OMS to monitor, track, and notify based on situations and component settings. Figure 12-1 shows the main page of the Solutions Gallery, which offers four purpose-built solutions along with many different individual offerings.

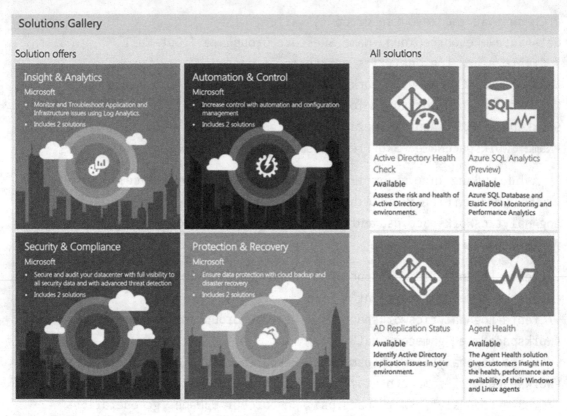

Figure 12-1. *The OMS Solutions Gallery*

These bundled offerings can incur additional charges, especially if the pricing SKU for OMS is not the Free tier. Some offerings are not available unless the OMS (per-node) pricing SKU is selected, which can be costlier than the standalone (usage-based) SKU. See `https://azure.microsoft.com/en-us/pricing/details/log-analytics/` for more details regarding the different SKUs and price points.

The four solution offerings shown on the left are explained in a bit more detail as follows:

- *Insight & Analytics*: This offering allows for the bundling of Network Performance Monitor and Service Map. The Network Performance Monitor requires configuration to capture traffic on applicable virtual networks. The Service Map offering requires additional agents to be installed on the resources to be mapped out, and typically these are IaaS resources. This bundle does not include any Application Insights aggregation.

- *Automation & Control*: The two offerings bundled into this solution are Change Tracking and Update Management. Change Tracking will look at any resources being monitored and determine what, if anything, has changed over time. This could be related to file systems, structures, system registry changes, even individual file changes. Update Management allows for monitoring of patch compliance and allows for the scheduling of one-time or recurring patch windows for Windows and Linux machines.

- *Security & Compliance*: This offering bundles the Security and Audit module with the Antimalware Assessment module. These work in tandem with Azure Security Center to help identify threats or potential security holes due to insufficient security patches, as well as to find any infrastructure components that are not running antimalware endpoint protection.

- *Protection & Recovery*: This bundle offers up two components: Backup and Azure Site Recovery. The tie-in to business continuity and disaster recovery are set up to allow for infrastructure components to be backed up and restored to a failover replica set in another Azure region.

In addition to the bundled offerings, there are several different modules offered in the Solutions Gallery.

Application Gateways

For the monitoring of Application Gateways, you find and enable the Azure Application Gateway Analytics module in OMS. This allows you to see access logs, failed requests, requests per hour, host health, and more. Having this integration also allows for displaying stats on the OMS dashboard, which will become the command center for the site reliability and operations folks.

App Services

With most app services—web apps, function apps—you can integrate Application Insights with the service directly, either at the time of creation or after. To make use of this information, you can integrate Application Insights with your OMS workspace to capture all data. This can come in handy during application component errors and troubleshooting outages.

Kubernetes

To set up OMS integration for Azure Container Service with Kubernetes (AKS), you will need to deploy a daemon set to the cluster that reports back to a specific OMS instance using the workspace ID and key. This should be done prior to enabling the Container Monitoring Solution module in the Solutions Gallery.

Using the tutorial found at `https://docs.microsoft.com/en-us/azure/container-service/kubernetes/container-service-kubernetes-oms` as a guide, you pull down the YAML configuration files needed to deploy to each cluster. Instead of using the generic configuration file, you decide to leverage the scripts that generate and store the secrets for the OMS connection to avoid any issues.

Virtual Machines

In order to capture information for virtual machines, you will need to install the OMS agent on each machine. This involves downloading the Microsoft Monitoring Agent from the OMS workspace administrative area and enabling it on each machine. The virtual machines backing the Kubernetes clusters will be taken care of by the OMS daemon set you created. You focus on getting the Windows agents installed on all of the virtual machines that need it. To do this, you plan on creating an Azure Automation runbook. After searching the Runbook Gallery in your automation account, you find an "Install OMS Agent" runbook that will do the trick. You import the runbook and notice that it is intended to run on hybrid (on-premises) workers. Instead, you take the code inside the runbook and save it to a PowerShell file. You then create an Azure PowerShell script that will gather the virtual machines you want and install the Custom Script Extension on each one, running the code that was in the runbook you imported.

Once you complete the initial setup, the end of the listings in the Solutions Gallery will show all of the "owned" modules. Figure 12-2 shows you a representation of all the modules you have enabled in your OMS workspace.

Figure 12-2. Solutions Gallery in OMS with listing of owned components

Network Monitoring

Two distinct areas exist in Azure where you can get information about the health of your networks. One is through Network Performance Monitor, found in OMS, and the other is by using Network Watcher, a component offering in the Azure portal.

In the last section, you chose to enable the Insight and Analytics solution, which contains the Network Performance Monitor piece. To use this module, you need to configure the specific items you wish to monitor. When pulling up the configuration page, you are able to hook up common settings by installing OMS agents on the IaaS resources you wish to monitor. For now, you skip this section and go on to the next area, which is the Performance Monitor. Select "Use TCP for synthetic transactions" and click "Continue ➤." You skip past the Service Endpoint monitoring section, as PaaS components are not yet supported. Finally, you notice that in order to configure ExpressRoute diagnostics you have to install an OMS agent on at least one VM in Azure and one VM on premises and perform additional installations to allow for bidirectional communication to occur. You use two utility boxes that fit those criteria and follow the instructions on the screen for allowing that traffic flow to occur.

The Network Monitor component can be created directly in the Azure portal, and will give you a set of functionalities that, when enabled, will provide you with a wealth of information and troubleshooting capabilities for network connections between IaaS components. Figure 12-3 provides a view into the various tools at your disposal with Network Watcher, once it is enabled for the Azure regions you have.

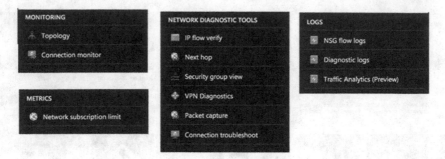

Figure 12-3. *A side-by-side view of the Network Watcher blade menu*

From the Overview menu item, you open up the list of regions associated with each of your Azure subscriptions. You enable East US, East US 2, and Central US in each subscription to turn on the Network Watcher. This creates specific deployments for each enabled region, all tied back to a central "NetworkWatcherRG" resource group in the portal. For the portal team's VMs, you follow the instructions found at `https://docs.microsoft.com/en-us/azure/network-watcher/network-watcher-packet-capture-manage-portal` to enable the VM extension on the portal team's IaaS components.

Security Monitoring

The networking components offer a great deal of flexibility and diagnostic capabilities, but they do not give you any particular sense about active attack vectors, potential malicious traffic, or attempts to breach the perimeter of your network. Azure Security Center will give you insight into those areas as well as providing you with best practices for securing your networks, virtual machines, storage accounts, and more.

You look through the Overview dashboard to see if any areas stand out as immediate risks. You notice that disk encryption stands out on the Linux nodes associated with the Kubernetes clusters. This is additional OS-level encryption of the disk itself, above and beyond the encryption offered by managed disks. You make a note to come back to this and move on to the Networking menu item.

The layout of the virtual networks and related network interface cards comes back with no glaring omissions. It does point out that not all of the clusters have network security groups (NSGs) associated with them. You take down another note to ensure that NSGs are incorporated into the overall implementation as you move to the Security Solutions menu item.

The Security Solutions pane allows you to see a few stock solutions that Microsoft offers, most of which pertain to IaaS components. In addition, you notice that the Application Gateways created for each runway environment are listed above those stock solutions with an "Add" button on them. You click the "Add" button for each gateway to onboard it into Security Center. Once complete for all gateways, they appear in the Connected Solutions area with health indicators on each. You mark down this area as complete for the time being and sort out action items for the encryption and NSG items you noted earlier.

Finalizing the monitoring settings, you start to think about the next step. Monitoring is great, but what happens when alerts are triggered based on the information collected during monitoring? You set out to learn more about incident management with respect to the Azure platform as well as the applications themselves.

Incident Management

A critical piece of the application lifecycle is how issues are raised and ultimately remediated. Incident management refers to the intake, triage, and resolution of platform or application level errors that impact one or more users. In some cases, the incident may be raised through a simple alert—something that an end user would not see, but an operations team would. In other cases, a user or group of users may call a customer service representative to inform them that the company's website is not functioning properly. This may cause the representative to open a ticket in the company's IT service management (ITSM) system, if one exists.

Earlier in this chapter, you looked into roles, responsibilities, and capabilities. One section of those capabilities dealt with incident and error management. Defining what the expectations are for the teams responsible for handling incidents is just as important as defining the overall process of incident management. All teams must agree on the intake method, triage and prioritization method(s), and what constitutes a resolved incident. Much like the concept of Definition of Done in the Agile software methodology, defining what each state in the process is and what ensures an incident is truly resolved will go a long way to helping teams understand and trust the ITSM process.

Another aspect of incident management is the notification tree, sometimes seen as the escalation path. Making sure reliable colleagues are available to handle incidents as they come in is one way to guarantee that issues are being responded to in a timely fashion. If something comes up, though, and that colleague is not available for whatever reason, having a second and third line of defense becomes an added way to ensure incidents are handled. Escalation paths and decision trees are typically components of a runbook for a specific operational component, but can also be extended to incident management due to the need for concise instructions when dealing with application errors or platform outages.

There are plenty of options to set up, monitor, aggregate, and send notifications about alerts. There are commercial solutions available that will aggregate alerts from a variety of platforms and allow administrators to create simple or complex escalation policies for notifications. Aggregation and notification platforms such as Big Panda, SumoLogic, and PagerDuty are considered strong 3rd party contenders for this type of integration. In addition, there are ways to configure Azure subscriptions and resources to also act in a similar fashion:

- *Azure Alerts*: Azure has a platform offering that allows an administrator to create simple or complex alert conditions and assign one or more handlers (action groups) to the alert. This can include email/SMS notifications, Logic App triggers, Function app triggers, and more. While this requires more setup, it is a robust option.

- *Azure Log Analytics*: Any queries or log searches that can be performed in Log Analytics can also be used to drive alerts. A query that looks for certain CPU or memory thresholds can be used to trigger an alert via Azure Alerts. The advantage with this method (as well as subsequent methods listed) is that the configuration and parameterization is done for you in more of a step-by-step or "wizard" fashion.

- *Azure EventGrid*: Resource or subscription events that occur can be captured in EventGrid and acted upon in a similar "wizard" fashion. One note of caution with this approach is that whatever target you run (Logic or Function Apps, for example) will be triggered every time an event is published. Metered resources will incur charges for each execution, which may or may not be a sticking point with management or with cost-effective resource consumption.

- *Application Insights*: Using the Application Insights blade for a particular resource in Azure will also allow you to set an alert rule based on specific data points available. This allows you to create an alert that is based on information you gather in real-time from the application itself, as opposed to infrastructure or platform components.

- *ITSM Connector*: There is a bridge between a select few ITSM systems and Azure OMS, which will allow you to not only monitor issues in the OMS portal but also create tickets directly in those ITSM incident databases. Currently only four providers are supported: ServiceNow, System Center Service Manager, Provance, and Cherwell.

To help capture these alertable events, you decide to take a slightly less conventional approach and look into using Logic Apps to handle creating incidents in Gamecorp's ServiceNow instance based on key data from Activity Log. Since you have installed the Activity Log module in OMS, you will be able to leverage queries against that data specifically targeting any platform or component failures.

EXERCISE: ACTIVITY LOG ALERTS AND NOTIFICATIONS

To help keep operations informed of potential exceptions and outages, you decide to assist in developing a mechanism for integrating native Activity Log alerts in Azure with Gamecorp's ServiceNow implementation. Having this integration will be valuable to the ops team, as they will receive immediate (and trackable) work items as a result of a critical error being thrown. The integration will be done in two parts:

- A Logic App that will create a ServiceNow ticket when a critical error is thrown

- An Activity Log Alert that will use the address of the Logic App to invoke it and create the ticket.

You first start by creating a new Azure Resource Group project in Visual Studio and selecting Logic App as the component type. You notice right away that you can only see the JSON configuration of the app. To use the designer instead of the code view, you need to install the Logic App Tools for Visual Studio, which gives you the ability to visualize the JSON definition.

1. Select the HTTP request trigger type for the initiation of the Logic App flow. You must enter a valid JSON schema for the request, as the app will not function properly if it receives a notification and cannot parse it.

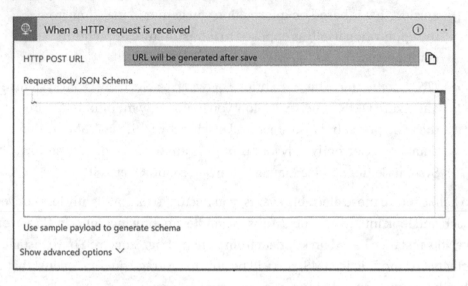

2. Click "Use sample payload to generate schema." A dialog box will appear, requesting a sample JSON request. In this case, you are after the schema for an Activity Log event.

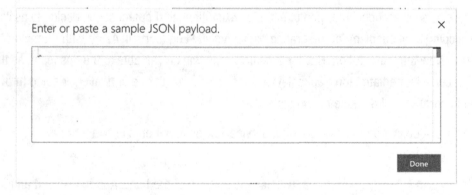

3. Go to any resource in the Azure portal and click "Activity Log." In the list of events that appear on the right, click one. A pane appears below the list, showing the Summary view. Click the JSON tab and copy all of the JSON found in that tab view. Paste it into the dialog box and click "Done." The schema will now appear in the "Request Body JSON Schema" window.

Request Body JSON Schema

```
{
    "type": "object",
    "properties": {
        "authorization": {
            "type": "object",
            "properties": {
                "action": {
                    "type": "string"
                },
```

4. Add a new item to the workflow. In the search box, type in "servicenow" and allow the search to complete. Select "ServiceNow - Create Record" from the list of Actions.

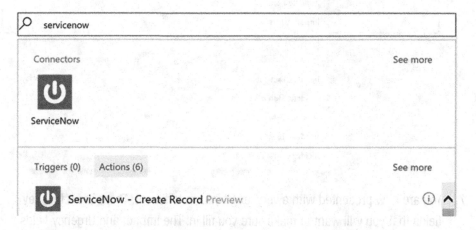

5. As you have not yet created a connection to ServiceNow, start by using Gamecorp's staging instance, so as not to impact the production instance and subsequently anger the operations team. The action will now display a dialog allowing you to create a new connection. Enter the connection name, the URL (Instance Name), the user name needed to connect, and the user's password. Click "Create."

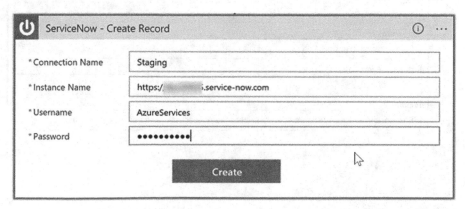

6. Now it is time to search for a record type. In this case, you're interested in creating a new Incident ticket any time a critical error comes up. Using the dropdown, search for "Incident." Select the record type.

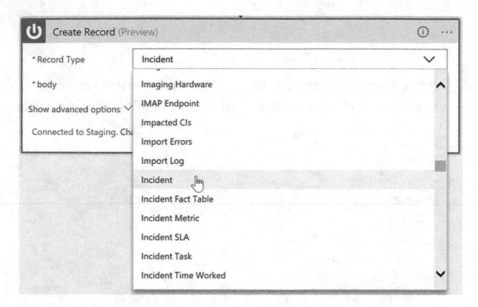

7. You are now presented with a very lengthy form to fill out. There are a few key fields that you will want to make sure you fill in. The Impact and Urgency fields are two of the most important to set, as these determine the overall Severity of the incident. To set the incident as a Sev2 (severity level 2, just below a full platform outage), set Imapct and Urgency to 2.

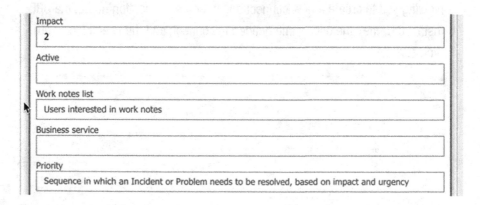

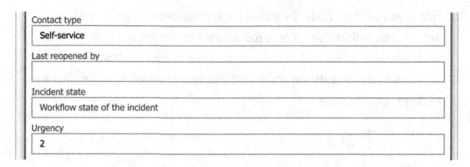

8. You will also want to ensure that the correlation ID from the Activity Log event is captured, which will allow support team members to look up the event in the Activity Log, and reference related log messages in the portal. Gamecorp has already created a location in ServiceNow called "Azure," which allows for generic issues to be assigned to the cloud location. To properly categorize the alert, you use the Cloud Management category.

9. You also set the subcategory as Outage, as a critical failure coming through this workflow will be considered a component or software outage. To help narrow things down, you also include the name of the resource provider (e.g., Microsoft/Compute for compute resources) as well as the status being returned.

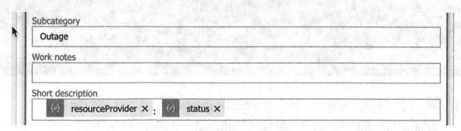

10. Finally, you want to ensure the Incident is appropriately assigned to a team to avoid issues with delayed triage. You set the Assignment group to "Service Desk" to allow for the first-line operations team to field the ticket. For further information, you include the action that was being performed at the time the alert was thrown.

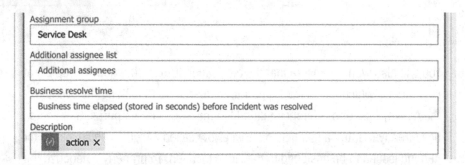

Once you save the Logic App, a URL will be generated in the Trigger step. Copy this URL, as you will need it for the next section.

You plan to use OMS as the source of any alert data, since it will be a bit easier to pick out areas of concern without having to catch all information being logged. To set up an alert, first go to Log Searc. This will bring up a list of applicable alert rules that have already been created. To create a new alert rule, click New Alert Rule. You will be presented with a new form requesting information about what to monitor, what to capture, and how to handle it.

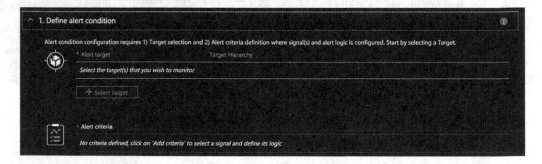

1. To begin, click "Select target." You will be given a dialog that will display information like your available subscription(s) and allow you to browse by resource type and name. The target resource to monitor in this case will be the log analytics (OMS) workspace that was set up previously. Filter by resource type (Log Analytics) and by the name of the OMS workspace (gamecorp). Click the resource shown and click "Done."

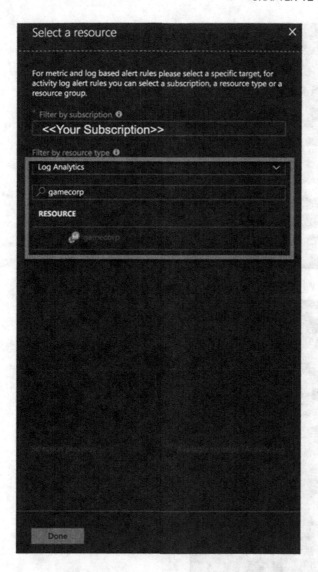

2. You will also need to fill in alert criteria. Click "Add criteria" to display a new dialog asking you to choose the alert's signal logic. For this alert, the Custom log search will be used. Click the first signal name you see.

This will display a new area where the signal criteria can be entered.

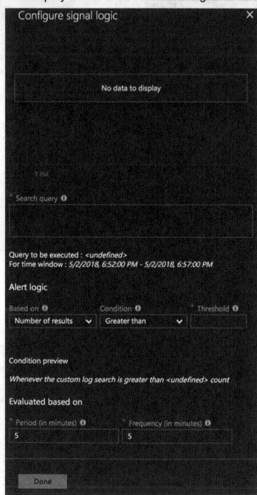

For the search query, you will need to write a query using the Log Analytics query language. This is similar in nature to many SQL-like querying languages used with big data tools—-see `https://docs.loganalytics.io/index` for more details. Certain tables are available to you by hooking up OMS. Also, since you established the OMS agents in the Kubernetes clusters earlier, you will also have data related to container execution and underlying VM execution. To get activity information about the resources as well as performance data related to the CPU usage per cluster node, enter the following text into the Search Query textbox:

```
Perf
| project Computer, TimeGenerated, CounterName, CounterValue, CounterPath
| join (
AzureActivity
| project Computer=tostring(split(ResourceId,'/',8)[0]),
    ResourceGroup=tostring(split(ResourceId,'/',4)[0])
) on Computer
| where TimeGenerated > ago(10m)
| where Computer startswith "aks"
| where CounterName == @"% Processor Time"
| summarize avg(CounterValue) by Computer, bin(TimeGenerated, 10m),
    ResourceGroup
| where avg_CounterValue >= 0.75
```

3. To start off with, you want to make sure you're getting data in order to validate the creation of the ServiceNow tickets. In the Threshold textbox, enter in 0. This will ensure that an alert will fire off whenever any machine has a processor time value above 75%. For the Period and Frequency, set each of these to 5. The minimum for alert frequency is five minutes. Click "Done" to save your changes.

4. Next, you will need to fill in some baseline information about the alert. At a minimum, you will need to give the alert rule a friendly name, a description, and a severity. Click the section labeled "2. Define alert details" to display the form where this information will be filled in. Use the text entered into the following form fields to fill in the alert details.

5. The last step for setting up the alert rule is to set up one or more action groups.
    An action group is a series of steps that will be initiated when the alert fires. The
    group will normally have a full name, short name, resource group (for creation of
    the action group), and one or more steps. The steps can trigger email/SMS alerts,
    Azure Logic Apps, Azure Function Apps, a webhook to an external system, an
    Azure Automation Runbook, or an ITSM system. As you were not able to get the
    ITSM integration installed, you will use the Webhook action.

Once you select the webhook action type, a new dialog will appear asking you
to enter the URL of the webhook. Enter in the URL that was generated when you
saved the Logic App. Click "OK" to save this information.

6. Once all of the required fields are filled in, the "Create alert rule" button will
    become activated. Click this button to create the rule and enable the new alert.

Using these steps, create a few different types of alerts based on analytics or other events
captured by Azure. What differences do you see with the alerts you've created?

Summary

Throughout this final chapter, you have laid the groundwork that will enable the
operations teams and site reliability engineers to successfully monitor, predict, react
to, and remediate anything the new platform can throw at them. Defining the roles and
responsibilities helped to clarify things for both teams, and the updated operating model
will serve as a blueprint for any net-new cloud projects as well as application migrations.
Setting up a new Operations Management Suite workspace allowed you to capture many
different facets of the resources in Azure, including utilities for security and network
monitoring. Through the use of Logic Apps, you were able to create integrations into
Gamecorp's ServiceNow instances, leveraging data from alerts to create incident tickets
for any alerts that get triggered.

The journey to this point has been long, sometimes complex, but ultimately
rewarding. Despite this being the first iteration, you feel comfortable with the guardrails
you've established, the designs you've helped create, and the knowledge you've
imparted on the teams who will need it most. The final implementations of the updated
portal application and the integrated Cardstock platform may not roll out within a week,
but they will be well poised to deploy to production with confidence. The Andromeda
team is still apprehensive about the ongoing acquisition and new management
structures. Their excitement around the new technological landscape in front of them is,
at least for now, overshadowing any trepidation they may have.

Given the exercises and content within this chapter, please reflect on and answer the
following questions:

- In the roles and responsibilities section, could there have been more
  clarification around additional roles needed? Responsibilities?

- The identification of and explanation of the various domain capabilities for the operating model contained a lot of information. Were there any areas you felt were lacking in definition? Were there any domains that had an unbalanced amount of capabilities? Could any of the capabilities have been condensed to better represent the overall activities?

- Was using a Logic App as the basis for processing an alert's data the right solution? Could there be other solutions that would have achieved the same goal with less effort?

- In the security monitoring section, mention was made of Security Center. What other tie-ins could Security Center have with monitoring and alerting?

- As a stretch goal, think of a couple of security policies that are not covered by the built-in definitions in Azure Policy. Referring to Microsoft's GitHub account and the `azure-policy` repository, do some research into whether the custom policies you've thought of could be implemented in a custom policy definition. What barriers, if any, would be prohibitive to your efforts?

Index

A

B

C

© Josh Garverick 2018
J. Garverick, *Migrating to Azure*, https://doi.org/10.1007/978-1-4842-3585-0

Disaster recovery (DR), 151
Domain architectures, 25
    application collaboration, 27–29
    application component matrix, 26
    application interaction diagram, 36
    application maturity matrix, 30
    build process, 41
    components, 29
    data flow, 38
        eventual consistency, 40
        immediate consistency, 38
    deployment runway, 41–42
    event storming, 29
    information, 36
    Infrastructure
        baseline, 31–32
        networking, 34
        physical devices, 33
    interactions, 35
    portal and Cardstock applications, 29
    primary components, 26
    secondary component, 26
    tertiary component, 26

E

E-commerce, 47
Event-driven architecture, 114
Eventual consistency, 40
Eventual consistency *vs.* immediate
    consistency, 36

F

Fault driven development (FDD), 190
Federal enterprise architecture framework
    (FEA/FEAF), 6
Functional/integration testing, 133

G

Gamecorp global inventory system
    (G2IS), 155
General data protection regulation
    (GDPR), 93
    data privacy laws, 51
    EU parliament, 51
    EU-US privacy, 52
    general data protection regulation, 52
    ISO27k, 53
    safe harbour, 51
Geo-redundant storage (GRS), 112
Group policy *vs.* DSC, 186

H

HTTP strict transport security (HSTS), 163
Human resource management system
    (HRMS), 158

I, J

Identity and access management, 55
Immediate consistency, 37–38
Incident management, 279
    activity log alerts and notifications,
        281–291
    application insights, 281
    Azure subscriptions and resources, 280
    EventGrid, 280
    intake, triage and resolution, 279
    ITSM connector, 281
    log analytics, 280
    notification tree, 279
Infrastructure (technology) architecture, 5
Intrusion prevention system (IPS), 165
IT service management (ITSM)
    system, 279